In
YOU
POCK

Fishing
Forays

Editors David Birley and Tom Lawrence

KENSINGTON WEST PRODUCTIONS LTD

HEXHAM ENGLAND

Fishing
Forays

Acknowledgements

Kensington West Productions Ltd
5 Cattle Market, Hexham, Northumberland NE46 1NJ Tel: (0434) 609933
Fax: (0434) 600066

Front Cover : Frank Wright The Fisherman *Courtesy of Rosenstiel's*
Back Cover : Philip Dunn *Courtesy of Rosenstiel's*

Print Catalogue available Tel: 0434 609933 Fax: 0434 600066

Design Kensington West Productions Ltd

Cartography Camilla Charnock, Craig Semple

Typesetting Tradespools Ltd, Frome

OriginationTrinity Graphics Hong Kong

Printing Emrierre

Introduction

Fishing Forays In Your Pocket is a condensed version of the celebrated colour guide book Fishing Forays. Its publication has come about for two major reasons. Firstly, to enable the fisherman to carry essential information more easily in his car, pocket, case or with his fishing tackle and secondly, to provide a vast amount of useful information at a competitive price. Let's face it, in this day and age every penny counts!

In essence, the book endeavours to select, price and pinpoint in detail a variety of waters from the mighty Tay to a humble loch in the wilds of Scotland. All manner of forays are suggested to suit both the nomadic, seasoned campaigner and the beginner equally well.

We are grateful to the many who have kindly assisted us in producing this, our first edition. However, it is not a complete edition and we would be delighted to receive recommendations of waters or hotels to include in future editions. Fishing Forays In Your Pocket is, in short, a glorious summary of an abundance of waters fit for the desk, car or library for all lovers of this fascinating sport.

Contents

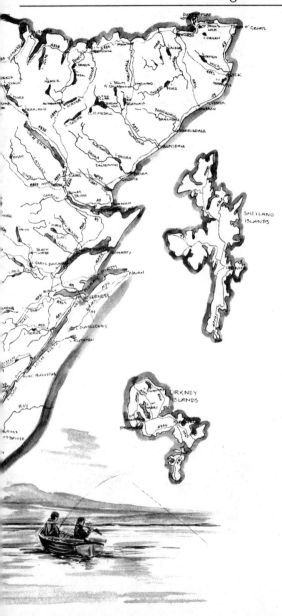

Caithness is the most northerly county in Britain. These days, the much-improved A9 makes getting there much less of a tortuous route march than it once was. Further time can be saved by using the new bridge over Dornoch Firth, where previously one had to journey via Bonar Bridge. It should be pointed out that the longer route allowed the opportunity of making a small detour to the Shin Falls, a sight which cannot fail to gladden an angler's heart, and for those of you with time on your hands this route should still be considered. Travelling on main roads is undoubtedly quicker but turning off at Helmsdale on to the Melvich road will afford a fisherman's treat, for the road follows the Helmsdale, and, after Forsinard into Strath Halladale. Already the office seems a distant memory and the heart pounds—not from pressure of work, but from sheer exhilaration.

The Halladale

For those who aspire to discover the undiscovered, the Halladale falls into the 'hidden gem' category. The water is now under the auspices of the the Bulmer family—they of cider fame—who are keen fishermen, and run the river through the Halladale Partnership. Although some twenty miles in length, there are no lochs in the system and it is very much a spate river. As a result, Halladale rods look for rain and the sport which almost inevitably follows. At Forsinard it is a tumbling stream but for much of its journey it can appear unpromising and sluggish. This, however, is the deceptive face of the river and there is fishing of the finest quality to be found for a persevering angler. It is a fly-only river and the season runs from January 12th to September 30th. The best time has traditionally been from June to September, although a good spring run has been had of late. Weekly rates vary from £132 to £660 plus VAT, and day permits are restricted to locals (to discourage poaching!). The river is let through an agent, Mrs J. Atkinson, 8 Sinclair Street, Thurso (0847) 63291. The Forsinard Hotel (0641) 7221 has one of the upper beats and a popular fishing lodge which sleeps fourteen.

As the Halladale flows through peat country it is heavily stained when in spate and virtually unfishable. But rest assured, for the very next day it will as often as not fall and begin to clear. In such conditions patterns such as the Garry Dog and Yellow and Orange are as good a bet as any. The pools are of a size that can be easily covered and favourites include Bridge, Macbeth, Munroes, Run Out and Ashill. Being generally slow-moving and a fly-only river it is sometimes necessary to gently handline to give your fly a touch of life. The average size is about 7lb, though fish of 14lb and 15lb are caught, the best fish in the 1990 season being 16lb. Assuming the rain gods are kind, the numbers can be excellent. Sea-trout may be caught in the estuary but there is not much of a run up into the river. Apart from the all-important hip flask, insect repellent is a must to combat the midges! The Melvich Hotel (06413) 206 is a good place to stay and has delightful views out onto the estuary. The proprietors can arrange salmon fishing for you, if given enough advance warning, and also provide trout fishing on their three lochs, with arrangements possible on several others.

The Forss

The Forss takes its name from an old Norse word meaning waterfall, but despite its fairly extensive headwaters and tributaries, the area of the Forss of greatest interest to the serious fishermen is the fairly short section flowing out of Loch Shurrery. Favoured flies include the Munro Killer and fish average at around the 8lb mark. The river is fly-only and it fishes best in the spring and from July to September. This is a time share river but it is sometimes possible to get on it through Salar Management Services Ltd (0667) 55355. The cost varies between £150 and £350 per week and £20 to £50 a day depending on the time of season. If you do get a day's fishing, Falls Pool is likely to be the most productive even in low water, or so I am reliably informed by local luminaries!

The Thurso

Arguably the most prolific river in the area, the Thurso used to be regarded as one of the best spring rivers producing bright silver ingots of fresh-run fish. In common with many other rivers, however, (with not even the mighty Spey excluded), spring runs are nothing like they used to be and the best sport is often autumnal. Although netting still takes place, the nets and estuary are owned by Thurso Fisheries. The boats are manned by ghillies, with the result that the rod fisherman's sport is born very much in mind. The dam and sluice gates at Loch More allow reasonable water levels to further the fisherman's enjoyment.

Although there may be salmon in the Thurso in January and February the season doesn't really get under way until March when, surprisingly, the upper beats near Loch More can prove most productive. At this time of the year two-inch tubes in patterns such as the Munro Killer or Yellow and Black can prove effective; worthwhile alternatives include long-winged flies such as the Tadpole or Collie Dog. June can be a difficult month on the river if the weather is hot, but you can always try your luck on Loch More which fishes surprisingly well in such conditions. Late July, August and September are the best time (assuming a decent rainfall!) and old favourites like the Stoats Tail, Hairy Mary and Garry can all work well. In all its twenty-five mile journey from Loch More to the sea the river only falls some three hundred feet, and consequently there are quite a few slow- moving pools. In such conditions it is worth trying *backing-up*. This involves starting at the bottom of a pool, rather than the top, and casting a long line straight out. Allow a few seconds for the fly to sink to the required depth then draw in a few yards of line to set the fly on its way. Taking a few paces upstream will keep the fly on the move and you can work your way up the pool like this. It sounds illogical and is against all tradition, I know. But it works. The locals promised it would and our experience did little to disprove the theory!

The whole river is owned by Thurso Fisheries Ltd, which belongs to Lord Thurso, and prices vary between £560 and £860 a week, including accommodation, according to the time of the season. Bookings are taken through the company secretary's office (0847) 63134. The fish average about 9lb but there is a chance of a 20lb fish. This is a most agreeable river to fish and is divided into fourteen rotating beats. As the whole river is under the control of one riparian owner, it is probably the only river in the British Isles that can be fished in its entirety within the space of a fortnight! This, moreover, is an area where the wild brown trout are truly wild. A dam on the river is used to catch the native fish which are then transferred to the lochs. The Ulbster Arms (0847) 83206 is the place to stay here. This comfortable, well appointed hotel offers excellent trout fishing. It has ten hill lochs (seven with boats) and can also arrange fishing on Lochs Watten, St John's and Calder. It is particularly suitable for a family holiday—their lochs have difficult fishing for the experienced rod and easier water for novices and children.

The Wick

Fishing on the River Wick, lying to the east of the Thurso, is managed by the Wick Angling Association. This river offers reasonably priced salmon fishing at either £50 a week or £12 a day. Permits can be obtained from the Hugo Ross tackle shop in Wick (0955) 4200 which can also offer boat fishing on Loch Watten and Loch Hempriggs if required. The average catch on the river is 250-300 salmon a season with the average being 9lb, though a fish of over 22lb was caught in 1979. It is a spate river and somewhat sluggish in character. Some nine miles long, it can all but disappear in times of drought.

The Wester System

There is little sea-trout fishing in the rivers we have discussed thus far but a few miles north of Wick there is the classic water of the Wester Sysytem (a loch and a river). The river is only half a mile long so sea-trout have easy access to the loch and can provide tremendous sport in the autumn. As we know, these wonderfully shy, hard-fighting fish give a very good account of themselves, especially here where the average is 1lb 8oz and most seasons produce at least one memorable fish of over 5lb. One chap in 1991 had eleven sea-trout to his name at the end of the day, all over a pound—due no doubt to the salmon and sea-trout restocking programme. Daily permits are available from Auchorn Farm, Lyth (0955) 83208, for £5 per day (boats available).

Caithness is renowned for its lochs and the genuinely wild brown trout they produce. The angler who is accustomed to fishing the stillwater stocked lakes in the south, where anglers moan if the stocking size is under one and a half pounds and fish of five to ten pounds are regularly caught, may wonder why people rave about loch fishing for wild brownies when a fish of one pound is often considered a good fish. Try it, I would simply say to such critics, in the confidence that they will quickly be converted! These trout come greedily to the fly and having taken it, set off at a furious pace giving the fisherman a memorable tussle.

Loch Watten

Scotland is blessed with some fine brown trout fisheries but few are as bounteous as Loch Watten, where £7 buys you a day ticket with a boat and there is no bag limit. The fish average a pound but run to over two. Some three miles long by up to three quarters of a mile wide, the loch can often be windy, so an outboard motor is essential unless you are either a fitness freak or a rowing blue. The fish are of excellent quality, a challenge to catch and a delight to hook. Both boat and bank permits are available, and for further information contact Mrs Wilson on (095582) 370. The best fishing is in May, June and September.

Loch St John's

Another renowned Caithness loch is St John's near Dunnet Head. Much work has recently been done to improve the quality of fishing here. A full day with a boat will cost £10 (£5 for an evening) and there are significant mayfly and cranefly hatches. Please contact the Northern Sands Hotel (0847) 85270 if you require more details.

The Dunnet Head Lochs

These are the most northerly lochs in Britain. In fact Dunnet Head is the most northerly point of Britain and not John O'Groats as popularly thought—look at a map before dissenting. You can win many a pint at a bar armed with this little known fact! The lochs are stocked on a regular basis and the fish average around the 2lb mark. These lochs are also an ornothologist's delight, for there are several pairs of red-throated divers and fishermen are expressly asked not to disturb them. Permits are available from The Dunnet Head Tearoom between 12.00 noon and 9.00pm (0847) 85774. Packed lunches (including vegetarian) are also available.

Loch Heilen

The most fickle loch in the area. On these 170 acres of windswept, shallow water one may never see a fish all day, but of course they are there and run up to 8lb. Anything less than 2lb should be returned. It is the type of water that can either reduce one to tears or provide a real red letter day. Please contact H. Pottinger Esq. (0847) 82210 for further details.

Loch Calder

Unusual for two reasons. Firstly Calder is the only loch in the area which is fishable on a Sunday. Secondly it is the only Caithness loch not restricted to fly-only. However, one or two of the riparian owners are looking to make changes so check with Harpers Fly Fishing Services (0847) 63179 before arriving with spinners on a Sunday! Other lochs in the area worth noting are Stemster, Airig, Lethaigd, Garbh, Caol and Ruathair and of course there are the hundreds of hill lochs which can often provide a memorable day.

Living off the land has never been easy in the Highlands, and a crofter's life is notoriously tough. But existing here is certainly easier than it used to be. If you fish Loch Naver spare a thought for the two thousand crofters exiled in the nineteenth century—evicted by the Duchess of Sutherland to make way for sheep-farming. The statue local people erected to her husband overlooks the sea, not his estates. The countryside is still sparsely populated and roads are few and far between. It is an area of great natural beauty and of course there is fishing—some of the finest in the kingdom!

The Naver

Probably the best salmon stream in the far north, and privately owned by four estates making up the River Naver District Salmon Fishery Board. Only as a guest of one of the owners can one cast a fly on this fine water. Those lucky enough to do so will find the six beats have fifty named pools divided between them. However, all is far from lost as the Bettyhill Angling Club has the right to fish for salmon and sea-trout for a mile or so above Naver bridge. There are three main pools and three permits a day are available at a cost of £14 each from the Tourist Information Centre at Bettyhill (06416) 342. Below the bridge the fishing is free. June to August is a good time for the grilse run.

The Borgie

Journey west of the Naver and you will quickly reach the River Borgie. This beautiful and well-managed river covers some seven miles in its journey from Loch Slaim to the sea. A hatchery means that each year the river is stocked with salmon fry and this augurs well for future anglers. Like so many in the area it is essentially a spate river, but the sluice gates at the loch help to maintain reasonable water levels. Four beats with two rods per beat are available from Mather Jamie (0509) 233433 at a cost of between £200 and £400 per rod a week. There are also one and a half miles of permit water on which tickets are obtainable from David Crichton (0641) 2231, the Water Bailiff. Good management has improved the fishing over the past few years and the salmon are in great condition in May, when Waddingtons are particularly effective. For the grilse run in June and August it is on to doubles and in September it's the faithful Waddingtons again.

The Dionard

Travelling further west we come to Strath Dionard and Cape Wrath, or the Parth as it is known locally. A quick glance at the road atlas will show you why this area is so special. The A838 is the only road in the area—you are alone! Those prepared to explore the remote hill lochs will be particularly well rewarded and are liable to return with a heavy basket of breakfast-sized trout. Fishing may well also have been accompanied by the piping of greenshanks. This is an area for the true fisherman but ghillies are available to help the newcomer.

A distance of twelve miles separates the Dionard from its source in the loch of the same name, to the sea at the Kyle of Durness. Fishing on the lower water is held jointly by E.G. Fishings (0387) 54424 and The Cape Wrath Hotel (0971) 511212, while the fishing above Rhigolter Bridge is owned by the Gaulin Estate (0971) 521282.. E.G. Fishings allow four rods on their water and a week will cost £285. Cape Wrath Hotel has four beats with two rods per beat at £345 a week. Gaulin Estate can offer five beats and fishing on the loch on a rotation basis at a cost of £60 a day for two rods. Recent years have seen several improvements including a stocking programme. Like many rivers, fishing on the Dionard has been variable with 280 fish caught in 1989 and 80 in 1990, though 7 fish have been caught in a day. The average weight is around 7lb, but each season produces a fair amount of heavier fish with the odd one over 20lb. Falls Pool is probably the best and also one of the prettiest pools in the North.

The Durness Lochs

If conditions on the river are against you, do try the limestone lochs at Durness. These waters are famous for their land-locked sea-trout. The fish feed off freshwater shrimp, are pink-fleshed and make superb eating. They can also be rather large! Loch Larlish which is the smallest, produced a whopper of fourteen and a half pounds in 1990. Local opinion is divided on whether the fish are brownies or sea-trout but if you are lucky enough to catch a fish like that, terminology matters little! Loch Borralie, which is the deepest, also holds Arctic char. The fish in these lochs average just under three pounds and anything under a pound should be returned. It is important to remember that being limestone, the waters are crystal clear and so casting errors must be avoided. The Cape Wrath Hotel will be able to assist you in fishing these lochs.

Loch Hope

Loch Hope is probably the best sea-trout fishery in the far North. It lies close to the Borgie and its six miles are divided into five beats. The Altnaharra Hotel (0549) 81222, a renowned fishing hotel, is the place to stay here. It can also offer fishing on eight other lochs and the River Mudale. Permits for this loch are available from Mr I. MacDonald at the Keeper's House (0847) 56272. Outboard motors are not allowed on Loch Hope which has a reputation for being windy, so it is advisable to have a ghillie, both for his expert advice and to avoid having aching shoulders at the end of the day! The sea-trout run to 7lb and there are some huge brownies, one of 7lb 13oz being recorded recently.

A favourite and very successful method on this loch is *dapping* Some people frown at dapping, but it is not as easy as it may appear, especially if the wind is up. For the uninitiated, dapping is a method which entails eliciting the help of the wind to blow your fly around. For this method you will require a floss-silk dapping line. Experts have it that the more blustery and dull the day, the more the fish are likely to take. If they spot the fly above them they will race towards it and come leaping out of the water often to three or more feet and will perhaps take it while the fly floats in the air or when it touches the surface. To see the fish rocketing from the depths is a memorable sight which will cheer many a fireside memory. One further point. If having tempted your prey you lift the dap at the last moment there's a good chance he may take the traditional wet flies being used by your fellow rod.

Lochs Stack, Loyal & More

'The Laxford,' Francis Francis wrote in 1874, 'is by no means a large or heavy river and Loch Stack is quite a small sheet of water compared with many of its neighbours and the stream is a short one, but the crowds of sea-trout and salmon that constantly swarm up it are prodigious.' Fishing is not what it was, but that applies to every water and Loch Stack is the best in the area. As recently as the 1970s two rods accounted for 50lb of fish in a day. It is well stocked every year and the best fish in 1990 was a six-pounder. Five boats are available and there is no bag limit though fish under a pound should be returned. Most fish are taken close to the shore for the loch has many bays and corners where the fish lie. You might care to try Wilson's Bay, North Bay or the bays where the feeder streams enter. July and August are the best times for sea-trout and because of the fame of this loch, advance booking is a must. The cost for two rods including a boat at this time of year is £40, falling to £30 in September. A ghillie will charge you £30 for the day.

Just the other side of Ben Screavie is the more modest water of Loch More. Here a boat for two rods will cost you £30 if you fish at the Kinloch end or £20 for the Smiddy end. After mid-August prices fall to £25 and £15 respectively. Like Stack this is a fly only water and is stocked every year. Similarly there is no bag limit and fish under a pound should be returned. Sea-trout average 1¾lb and August is the best time for them.

Both Loch Stack and More are owned by Reay Forest Estates and permits are available from the Scourie Hotel (0971) 502396. This comfortable and well appointed hotel was originally built as a coaching inn by the second Duke of Sutherland. Guests can enjoy fishing in the many hill lochs, 250 of which abound in the hotel's 25,000 acres. The hotel can also offer salmon and sea-trout fishing on waters such as the Lower and Upper Duart and Badna Bay. Travellers of the turf may be interested to note that here you can see the peaks of the original Foinaven and Arkle! The legendary chaser was owned by the Duchess of Westminster. As you look around you do remember that Arkle as a racehorse was never bettered. Name and place are singularly appropriate.

Helmsdale Country

This is yet another Scottish example of unspoiled moorland, mountain and shoreline. All manner of rivers thread their way through this remote area and the fishing, needless to say, is wild and wonderful. It is also fairly tricky to get on to the region's principal water, the Helmsdale. However, there are possibilities and there are also numerous hill lochs which produce some excellent game fishing, with brown trout that fight with a vigour that belies their size.

The Helmsdale

There are fewer more famous or productive salmon rivers in Scotland than the Helmsdale. The reasons are largely self evident, for here is some of the best fishing in Sutherland and, for that matter, the whole of the north of Scotland. Furthermore, there can be few more idyllic settings than the Strath of Kildonan. Although we all know of its reputation, facts are more difficult to ascertain. This is primarily due to the secrecy of those who fish this river and it has been said that your best chances of a spot on this river are through divine relationship (or intervention!). The question begs itself—what is all the fuss about? Although catch figures are seldom reported, a few years ago Beat 4 produced 31 fish in a day with a best week of 94 and a season's total of 599.

The river is owned by six estates which jointly make up the Helmsdale River Board. It is divided into twelve beats, the dividing point being the Kildonan Falls. The beats rotate on a daily basis and there are two rods per beat. The season runs from January 11th to September 30th but fish are unlikely to mount the falls until the water rises to an acceptable level, usually around the end of March. However, the overall quality of the Helmsdale is outstanding and there is a good chance of landing a salmon on the opening day. At the start of the season the pools may be frozen over and you and your ghillie may have to break the ice to clear a pool. This may well stir up the fish which could mean using a big tube fly such as a Willie Gunn, Garry Dog or Black and Yellow on a sinking line. April and May are traditionally the best months and a Stoats Tail may prove effective during this period.

The grilse run is from June to August. A popular technique for fishing the broken headstreams of pools in low water conditions is *dibbling*. This involves fishing with a dropper which should be longer than normal—say about seven inches and tied about six feet above the point fly. The dropper dibbles across the surface cutting a wake in its path. Favoured flies for dibbling are such patterns as the Garry, Shrimp Fly and Elver Fly.

Those lucky enough to fish this first class river will always want to return, but because it is so good it is among the most difficult river to get on. However, do not despair, for the Garvault Hotel (0431) 3224 can sometimes get you a rod on one of the private beats and the Roxton Sporting Agency Ltd (0488) 683222 in Hungerford lets beats. Much more generally accessible is the Association water which comprises the lower mile of the Helmsdale. Prices range from £14.10 to £17.63 a day according to the time of year. Day tickets are from 9.00am to 9.00am the following day—so you can fish all night for sea-trout—and these can be obtained from A. Sangster Esq. (0431) 2343. It is worth mentioning that in the summer time there is almost constant daylight while in the winter months the evenings come correspondingly early.

The Berriedale

Travelling north from Helmsdale we come to the Berriedale Water. Owned by the Langwell Estate, this wild, natural river produces over fifty fish a year with an average weight around the 8lb mark. The Berriedale is divided into three beats which rotate on a daily basis and whose two rods can fish thirty-eight named pools. Access to some parts, particularly the middle beat, can be awkward—so elderly gentlemen (not to mention your exhausted editors!) should tread carefully. In fact there is one somewhat gruelling story that tells of a sprightly octogenarian breaking a somewhat spindly leg whilst endeavouring to fish the water. He was not rescued for twenty-four hours but the resourceful chap managed to land a 6lb fish shortly before dawn and his eventual rescue. There may be an element of exaggeration here but the moral (or one of them at least!) is to exercise caution at all times. The cost for this water is £110 per rod per week and permits are available from the Estate Office (0593) 5237. A good place to stay is the Navidale House Hotel (0431) 2258 in Helmsdale which can also arrange trout fishing on at least five lochs.

The Brora

South of the Helmsdale lies the Brora. This fine river has good early runs and February, which is when the season starts, can produce upwards of a hundred fish. The river is of two parts, the Upper and the Lower, which are divided by Loch Brora. The Blackwater, which joins the Upper Brora at Balnacoil, can also provide good sport and the average over the last five years is thirty-two salmon. As a spring river the best time is February to May, though providing there is enough rain to provide reasonable water levels, salmon and grilse fishing in June and July can be rewarding. It is also fine sea-trout water.

Conservation is a topic which is discussed at length by fishermen and other interested parties up and down the country—concrete results are somewhat more difficult to find. How refreshing it is, therefore, to find a river whose management are proving that actions speak louder than words. As a result, the fishing is improving. This will surely be to the longer term benefit of all. The season on the Blackwater closes early on September 1st to allow the fish a chance to get to the upper reaches for spawning. On the Brora all sea-trout caught before May should be returned and no hen fish may be killed on any beat after September 15th. On most waters spring fishing calls for fishing deep with a sinking line, but on the Brora the fish will often take a big fly such as a Collie Dog or Tadpole fished close to the surface on a floating line. This defies tradition and convention but it can work extremely well. The traditional methods, however, should also prove effective. If you are after sea-trout on Loch Brora you will find that Kenny's Killer more than justifies its name. A team of wet flies of such tried and trusted favourites as Black Pennell, Dunkeld and Peter Ross will stand you in good stead.

The Brora is certainly accessible to visitors and anyone booking well in advance should be able to get on this water. Ownership of the river is held by Sutherland Estates (0408) 633268, Gordon Bush Estates and Cadogan Estates. Gordon Bush Estates let the Upper Brora through the Roxton Sporting Agency (0488) 683222. They also let Balnacoil Lodge which sleeps up to twelve and overlooks the river. Cadogan Estates bought the north bank of the Lower Brora in

1990 and their letting is handled by Finlayson Hughes of Perth (0738) 30926. Sutherland Estates (which includes the Blackwater) let their fishing with their three sporting lodges, which can take parties of up to fourteen. Prices range from £550 to around £800 for four rods for six days and beats alternate with the Cadogan Estate water to provide variety. Sutherland Estates can also arrange stalking and grouse shooting, so there is always a chance of a McNab! Day tickets on the tidal water are available from Rob Wilson's tackle shop (0408) 621373.

The Fleet

The Fleet runs close by but is understandably overshadowed somewhat by its famous neighbour. The nine miles of this lesser known river which flows into the tidal waters of Loch Fleet, can fish well, depending on the water levels. However, if the river is low and good water is hard to find, the best bet is to head for the loch. This too is good sea-trout water and small flies of traditional patterns such as the Dunkeld and Zulu are effective. The river is privately owned, but fishing can occasionally be obtained through Bell Ingram in Bonar Bridge (0863) 2683. Rogart Angling Club also have a long term agreement with the Morvich Estate to fish a small section of the Lower Fleet which includes Polsons Pool and Davoch Beat. From May to October every Monday, Wednesday and Thursday is split into three eight hour sessions which cost £8 each. Permits are obtainable from the Post Office Stores at Rogart (0408) 641200.

Helmsdale Lochs

Lochs in the area include Badanloch, Rimsdale and Nan Clar to name but three. The Garvaults Hotel near Kinbrace (0431) 3224, which is on the road from Helmsdale to Melvich, has fishing on ten lochs and can arrange fishing on over twenty others. The best fish from the hotel's lochs was an eight and a half pounder pounder three years ago and 1991 yielded a five pounder. A short distance away at Forsinard one finds the Forsinard Hotel (0641) 7221 which has exclusive fishing on six lochs and can arrange fishing on a further fourteen These lochs are full of wild brownies weighing in generally around the 3¼lb mark. Anything over 2lb is a good fish. Because they are little known and off the beaten track these lochs offer unexpectedly tremendous sport as well as that elusive quality in these busy times, solitude. Now that there are so many trout waters in the south fewer people go to Scotland for a trout fishing holiday. However, when was the last time (if ever!) you caught over sixty fish in a day? As Tony Henderson of the Garvault Hotel will tell you, it is perfectly possible on the lochs in this beautiful and unspoilt area.

The Shins to The Ullapool

Before the advent of the new bridge over the Dornoch Firth anyone fishing the Helmsdale or more northerly rivers had to make the long detour via Bonar Bridge. However, this afforded the chance to see the Carron, Shin, Oykel and Cassley. There must be few places where one can see four such notable rivers within such a small area. Sadly, these rivers have all been affected by hydro-electric dams. No fisherman can but shake his head in sorrow at the ugly dam at the east end of Loch Shin which has reduced the river to a mere shadow of its former self.

The Carron

Driving to Bonar Bridge the River Carron is the first river one sees. Its character has been somewhat changed by the hydro-electric dam at its source, but this has had one beneficial effect, for the water level falls very quickly during a spate. This is a first class salmon river with about ten miles of fishing belonging to nine owners. Three falls make natural divisions of this river. The lower part is from the Firth to Gledfield Falls. The best time to fish here is considered to be March and April, for fish will stay below the falls until the water temperature rises above 38°F. The middle section is up to Morell Falls which fishes well in April and May. When the water temperature is above 42°F the upper reaches up to Glencarvie Falls will provide good sport from May to September. Prices vary according to beat and season and range from £150 for two rods to £4500 for four rods, including a comfortable lodge which sleeps eleven. Some beats do become available but the best ones are very hard to get on. Finlayson Hughes of Perth (0738) 30926 may be able to help you. As on so many rivers, September sees some fine runs. Spring, however is more likely to produce big fish and the best fish for 1990 was a 24lb beauty taken in April from the Cornhill beat.

The Shin

When Andrew Young had the fishing of the River Shin in the nineteenth century the cost was £12 a month and in 1849 Major Cumming caught twenty-two salmon in ten hours. His fellow rod, Mr Fitzgibbon, the fishing correspondent of Bell's Life, took fifty-two fish in fifty-five hours! It is worth remembering that these prodigious feats were done with the heavy tackle then in use. Anyone who has spent a day casting with a big split cane salmon rod can imagine how their shoulders must have ached at the end of the day—but oh, how pleasurably! Paradise Pool is justly famous for producing big fish. Sadly, this pool was washed away in the torrential rains of 1988 but the damage was quickly repaired. Just north of Invershin are the Shin Falls. This is one of the few falls which are easily accessible to man and motor and as a result they are a popular tourist attraction complete with roadside cafe. The sight of a salmon leaping is one of the wonders of nature and when they are running here you will see hundreds of them. One can but watch in awe at the strength and bravery of the fish as they try to leap the falls. Often they will hit a rock and fall into the pool below, but driven by some primeval instinct they will keep on trying until at last they lie spent and exhausted in the pool above.

A few miles further on the A836 is the town of Lairg. Here is the Aultnagar Lodge Hotel (054) 982245 and the Sutherland Arms Hotel (0549) 2291 which will provide a comfortable pillow and has fishing books going back to 1861—and what fascinating reading they make. This hotel has a lease on the River Shin and can also arrange fishing on Loch Shin and Loch Craggie. Loch Shin is the largest loch in Sutherland and being some twenty miles long, it is possible to get marked weather differences at either end. Due to the hydro-electric power sluices there are few salmon but it is good trouting water and there are Arctic char at the western end. There can be a very large mayfly hatch which will naturally produce superb fishing. Permits may be obtained from R. Ross in Lairg (0549) 2239, the only tackle shop for miles around. A day's bank fishing costs £3 and a boat with an outboard motor £20. The Overscaig Hotel (0549) 83203 on the north side of the loch offers guests free fishing on this and other lochs, including Loch Merkland.

Loch Craggie

There are three lochs in Sutherland called Craggie, meaning big stones or rocky. The one we are referring to here is situated three miles north-east of Lairg and factored by the Sutherland Arms Hotel. Here you will find some of the best trout water in Scotland. The average weight is just under the pound and the best fish for 1991 was 4½lb, but there are some very big fish. Fishermen should note that there is no bank fishing whatsoever and a day for two rods, including a boat, costs £24 with a bag limit of ten fish per boat. If your fellow rod gets more than his fair share then one feels justified in feeling a trifle peeved ... but such is life!

The Oykel

From its source in Loch Ailsh to Dornoch Firth, the course of the River Oykel covers some thirty-five miles and varies in character from tumbling rapids to gentle pools. It has long been famous as a prolific salmon water and is, as a result, hard to get on. George Ross (0549) 84259 is the fishing manager of the Lower Oykel fishings and people in their forties write to him hoping to get on when they retire! His wife, Irene, ties superb flies which are sold all over the world and if you have the opportunity of casting them on the river you are indeed a fortunate fellow.

The Lower Oykel runs from Oykel Falls to the Kyle of Sutherland. These seven miles are divided into four beats and here you will find such famous pools as George, Blue, Junction and Langwell. The Upper Oykel is from Oykel Falls to Eileag Burn and is also very difficult to get on. There is a long waiting list and the expression 'dead man's shoes' comes speedily to mind. The splendid Oykel Bridge Hotel (0549) 84218 handles the lets and may be able to help you. These four miles are divided into three beats which rotate at 6am. There are three rods per beat. Salmon run, on average, at about the 9lb mark and it is also good sea-trout water. Slightly more accessible is the stretch from Eileag Burn to Loch Ailsh. This water is let through the Inver Lodge Hotel (05714) 496 and is kept exclusively for hotel guests. These three miles are divided into two beats with two rods per beat and the costs vary between £25 and £50 a day. The best time is from July to September when it is not uncommon for two rods to account for a dozen salmon in a day. The average weight is 6lb and the best fish recorded in the last two years tipped the scales at 18½lb. Among the notable pools are Lornas Corner, Edmund's Pool, Keeper's Pool and the Laird's Run. Advance booking is essential. The hotel also has three beats on the River Kirkaig available at between £18 to £50 per day per rod. Furthermore, guests can take advantage of free fishing on Loch Ailsh and trout fishing on several other lochs. Trout fishing for non-residents is available at £17.63 a day including a boat.

The Cassley

Also flowing into the Kyle of Sutherland is the Cassley. This is a superb spate river which, given good water levels, provides excellent salmon fishing. June often sees a great grilse run. The upper reaches of this river down to Duchally are owned by the Balnagowan Estate (0862) 842243 which belongs to Mr Fayed of Harrods fame. This water can fish well from July onwards and is often fished by stalkers staying at the estate lodges when they want a break from the hills. From Duchally to within a stone's throw of March Cottage, the north bank becomes the Glencassley fishings, while the south bank is the Upper Cassley fishings, which are let through Bell Ingram of Bonar Bridge (08632) 683 per rod per week, at a cost varying from £55 in May to £200 in September. The Upper Cassley beats comprise some seven miles with thirty-seven pools, while rods on the Glencassley beats enjoy five miles and thirty-three pools. From March Cottage to the Achness Falls is the Glenrossal beat and below these falls is the Rosehall beat. The cost of a rod on the Glenrossal beat varies between £70 and £125 a week and on the Rosehall beat from £550 to £1050 per week, but that is for three rods and also includes the services of a ghillie. The Achness Hotel at Rosehall (0549) 84239 can arrange the fishing for you, but there is a waiting list.

Just north of Invershin is the turning for the A837. The road follows the course of the Oykel and is the nearest that many will get to this famous river! Continuing on this road will lead to Inchnadamph and Loch Assynt. The loch is some seven miles long and is good trout water. The average weight may be around half a pound, but eight and nine-pounders are not uncommon. Here you will often find Willie Morrison who, with seven years experience behind him, knows the moods of the loch well. The Inchnadamph Hotel (0571) 2202, of which Willie is proprietor, has five boats for the use of the guests and a day's fishing with an outboard motor costs £16. The Assynt Angling Club has fishing on some thirty-two lochs and further details can be obtained from the Tourist Information Office (0571) 4330. The Inver Lodge Hotel also has a single boat on Loch Assynt.

The Inver

The Inver is a short river and its six miles separate Loch Assynt from Inver Bay. It is here that in 1870, Dr Almond caught a monster 27lb 4oz brown trout: the largest fish taken from this river. It is divided into three beats with the top and bottom beat being owned by the Ben More Estate, while the middle beat belongs to the Bradford family. The top beat is let through the Inver Lodge Hotel (05714) 496 at a cost of between £18 and £45 per rod per day according to season. The beat is roughly a mile long and in a good season can produce upwards of a hundred salmon as there are several good pools, including the noted Black Pool.

The Kircaig

The Inver Lodge Hotel may also be able to arrange fishing for you on the Kirkaig which lies just south of the Inver and is on the boundary between Sutherland and Ross-shire. The salmon, as the Romans knew when they christened him, is a great leaper, but no fish could ascend the fifty foot Falls of Kirkaig so, although the catchment area of the river may be eighty square miles, it is only the two miles down from the falls that hold fish. The river is divided into three beats and only the lower beat will suit those of advanced years. The middle beat requires some agility, and on the upper beat, where the river becomes a raging torrent as it flows through the gorge, it is more advisable to wear climbing boots than waders!

Lochs Sionascaig & Oscaig

The A837 ends just south of Lochinver, but those with a sense of adventure will follow the secondary road to Inverpolly and Lochs Sionascaig and Oscaig (try saying these after a few wee ones!). This is the heart of the Inverpolly Nature Reserve and the unspoilt landscape of Wester Ross is some of the finest imaginable. Loch Sionascaig is some three and a half miles in width and set against the backdrop of Cul Mor, Cul Beag and Stac Polly which all rise above 2000 feet. The loch has many bays with half-pounders lying in wait. It also boasts scattered islands which are forbidden territory to anglers: teeming with wildlife they are a further attraction to a marvellous setting.

This is one of the few places left where, if you are lucky, you may see the majestic osprey. Rival he may be but there are no finer anglers than these magnificent birds. The loch is as deep as two hundred feet in places and these murky depths are the haunt of large ferox trout; one of 16lb 14oz was caught in 1989. Permits for this water and other lochs may be purchased from the Inverpolly Estate Office (0854) 82452. A day's boat fishing will cost £12, and an outboard motor can be hired for £8. Bank fishing is fly only and costs £3. The Garvie, which has a heritage as a sea-trout water, flows out of Loch Oscaig. The Summer Isles Hotel (085482) 282 can arrange permits for you to fish the loch, which offers good grilse fishing in high summer. A glance at the map will show you that this area is peppered with lochs and lochans nearly all of which will provide a good day's sport.

The Polly

The River Polly flows from Loch Scionascaig through the Polly Lochs to the sea at Polly Bay. There is a good run of grilse in the Polly from mid June onwards and in September 1991 the first ever salmon was taken on Loch Sionascaig. The fishing on the Polly is let on a weekly basis together with accommodation in Inverpolly Lodge (085482) 452. Prices range from £650 to £1210 per week.

The Ullapool & Loch Achall

A journey around the shore of Loch Lurgainn, which lies in the shadow of Cul Beag, will bring you back on to the A835 and a short distance south lies Ullapool. Apart from being able to take the ferry to the fishing delights of Lewis and Harris from here, there is also the River Ullapool and Loch Achall. The river is short and exciting and is divided into three beats. A day on the lower beat costs £5 while the cost for the upper beat is £15. Salmon on this river average around the 6lb mark and sea-trout, which can also be taken on Loch Achall and in the estuary, almost 2lb. Ullapool Angling Club issue permits through Ullasport (0854) 612621 on Argyll Street. All proceeds go towards stocking and Tom McDougall, the club secetary, has written a beginners guide to fishing in the area. Permits may also be obtained from the Highland Coastal Trading Company (0854) 612373. The main beat of the river, in addition to unique and remote salmon fishing on the Rappach River (a tributary of the Oykel River), is let through Rhidorroch House. The House, overlooking Loch Achall, sleeps thirteen. Fishing on the loch and numerous other hill lochs can be let with the House, details from (0854) 612548.

The majestic Loch Achall is abundant in brown trout and has some salmon and sea-trout fishing. There are three boats for hire and bank fishing is also allowed—all bookings through Ullasport (0854) 612621.

A precis of the joys of fishing in Scotland would not be complete without a word about the ghillie. A good ghillie is worth his weight in gold for no matter how often you may have fished a piece of water, there is always something new to learn. If you haven't fished the water before, the ghillie is an essential advisor and companion. They know if there are fish in a pool, where the lies are and what fly is likely to do the trick. As if that wasn't enough, they will also row for you. You can read all you like in books but there is nothing to beat the experience of the man on the spot who knows every mood of the water. They are men of many talents for they are often first class naturalists and can, if you are lucky, tie exactly the right fly for the particular state of the water. They are a fund of local lore and knowledge. Some people may be too proud to ask for their advice but they will really be poorer without it.

The Guinard & the Little Guinard

Coming south from Ullapool, the road follows the shore of Loch Broom. If you take the A382 coastal road you pass through the Dundonnell Forest. After skirting Little Loch Broom this road will bring you to Gruinard Bay, where the Gruinard and Little Gruinard end their journeys. These rivers are certainly more accessible today than they were in Victorian times. An old fishing guide suggests taking the train to Achnasheen, which is only fifty miles or so away and from there a coach service often runs for most of the rest of the way. There is no mention of the frequency of the service or how fishermen were to finally reach their destination! However, in those halcyon days there wasn't the pressure of modern office life and if one's holiday overran by a week or two it didn't matter. These are both spate rivers and while the salmon runs may not be what they were, there has been very good sea-trout fishing from July to September. The rivers are owned by Letter Erwe Estates (044584). Fishing is let with a cottage for around £800 plus VAT but there is a long waiting list here and no day permits are available.

The Gruinard drains Loch na Sealga which is famous for the fighting qualities of its brownies. There are salmon here too, and that tug on your line could be the start of a memorable fight as anyone who has caught a salmon on a trout rod will know! The Boat Pool is a favourite on the Little Gruinard where salmon average around 6lb and like its big sister, has good sea-trout water as does Loch Fionn. Trout here average half a pound although there are some bigger ferox. This loch is surrounded by mountains which funnel the wind down so rowing can be fairly strenuous, especially at the end of the day when a long pull may be required.

Loch Maree

Leaving Gruinard, the road meanders alongside Loch Ewe and then on to Poolewe. Do take a minute to stop and take deep breaths of the fresh Atlantic air—it's marvellously bracing and you also have the pleasure of a glorious Hebridean view if the weather's fair. The River Ewe drains Loch Maree and is one of the most celebrated examples of the long loch and short river systems. At just over a mile long the river is one of the shortest in Scotland. Fairly sluggish to begin with, the Ewe narrows. Many fine holding pools such as Hen, Manse and Tee Pools are produced, separated by white-water rapids. This river was first made famous by Sir Humphrey Davy who thought nothing of catching twenty or more salmon a day. However, times have changed, as they also have on Loch Maree. This is one of the most famous sea-trout fisheries in the world which in 1935 produced a record fish of 21lb. Up to the late 1960s double figure fish were not unusual but then came U.D.N. which pretty well wiped out these big sea-trout and catches declined. In recent years it has had other problems: escapee farm salmon are a threat to the native stocks, the netting of sand eels, which are the staple diet of sea-trout, not to mention seals. Indeed grey seals have often been sighted in the river and even at the head of the loch.

However, things are looking up for this famous water. In 1988 Frank Buckley took over as Fisheries Consultant and his tireless efforts have brought about many improvements. By involving the Duke of Edinburgh Award Scheme and other volunteers a hatchery has been built and the spawning grounds in the feeder burns, which had been choked, are now cleared. Dedicated work like this brings results and the last couple of years have seen a best salmon of 22lb, a sea-trout of 6½lb and a brownie of 4½lb, with fifteen fish being caught in a day by one boat. Given another couple of good seasons, the loch may even be restored to its former glory as the best salmon and sea-trout loch in the country. Dapping is the favoured technique on these fourteen miles of water which are over 300 feet deep in places, though trolling is permitted up to the end of June. The Loch Maree Hotel (044584) 288 has the fishing rights on about two thirds of the loch and its water is divided into ten beats. Boats are available and the cost for a day's fishing for two rods including a boat is £15 from April until the end of June, rising to £25 for July and August and £20 from then until the close of the season in October. From July to the end of October fly fishing only is allowed. Trolling and spinning, however, are permitted in April, May and June.

Between Loch Maree and Loch Carron is an area of unspoilt countryside which has many good lochs such as Loch Damph, Lundie and Bad an Sgalaig. Roads are few and far between but those prepared to walk for their sport will have a memorable day. There are also some very good small spate rivers such as the Balgy, Torridon and Badachro. Fishing these rivers is a real delight and emphasises the overall high standard and availability of fishing in Scotland.

Loch Glascarnoch

Taking the A835 across country from the Braemore Forest will bring you to Loch Glascarnoch where the fishing is free! This three and a half mile long water is owned by the Hydro-Electricity Board. If you are thinking that any fishing which is free must be of poor quality, then reconsider. Members of the Inverness Angling Club, who fish the water regularly, will change your mind. South of here and below Fannich Forest is the fine water of Loch Fannich which is part of the River Conon system.

The Conon

For many years, not only the River Conon but also its tributaries and lochs have been dammed for hydro-electricity and this has naturally, or should I say unnaturally, affected water levels. Two of the dams have salmon counters which show a consistently good average number of fish. The system is also a notable brown trout water, for it was from Loch Garve, at the top of the Blackwater, that a monster of 26lb was caught in 1892. Frasers Newsagents at Strathpeffer (0997) 21346 issue permits for the four beats on the Upper Conon which is owned by Loch Achonachie Angling Club, at a cost of between £5 and £15 per day, according to season, and spinning is allowed when the water is up. Permits for fishing this part of the river are also available from the East Lodge Hotel at Strathconon (0997) 7222. This hotel can also issue permits for the Blackwater and sometimes arrange for guests to fish the Brora, Glass and Beauly.

Most Conon salmon are originally from the Blackwater. The hens are netted and stripped at the top of the upper beat and the eggs are hatched in the Contin hatchery. Fishing on the Blackwater can be arranged through Lady Elisa Leslie-Melville (09974) 242 or Mr R. Smith (090855) 586, alteratively contact the Craigdarrock Lodge Hotel (0997) 421265 which is conveniently situated about four hundred yards from the middle beat. The Fairburn Estate own part of the Middle Conon and lets are available from the Estate Office (0997) 3273. Some of this section is timeshared during the summer and autumn (although not the south bank owned by the above) but from January to the end of June lets can be obtained from either Savills in Brechin (0356) 22187 or the Coul House Hotel, Contin (0997) 21487 at a cost of between £50 and £400 (excluding VAT) per rod per week according to season. If this is too expensive, Seaforth Highland Estate (0349) 61150 can offer you trout fishing at £3.50 a day or £12 a week and also lets out several holiday cottages.

The Lower Conon may not be the same quality of fishing but it is more affordable. It is managed by Dingwall Angling Club and the cost is £15 a day. Permits may be obtained from the Sports and Model shop in Tulloch Street, Dingwall (0349) 62346. These permits also cover Lochs Achanalt, Chuillin and Luichart.

The Glass

Between Dingwall and Alness is the River Glass. This river is not to be confused with the water of the same name which is part of the Beauly system. It is totally different in character, quality of fishing and price. The river rises in several hill lochs under the shadow of Ben Wyvis before flowing into Loch Glass. This part of the river and downstream to the gorge is privately owned by the Wyvis Estate. Black Rock Gorge is over a mile long and is an awesome spectacle, for there is a sheer drop of up to two hundred feet and in some places it is only six feet wide. If standing on one of the footbridges looking at the raging torrent far below doesn't make your head spin, the smell of the wild garlic will! This grows so profusely that it is harvested twice a year by the cheese factory in Tain. From the gorge to Cromarty Firth the river is known as the Allt Graad and this three quarter mile stretch is divided into three beats. Permits may be had for £7 a day or £25 a season from Alcocks Newsagents in Evanton High Street (0349) 830672. The river is stocked on an annual basis and is the type of water that offers the chance of an occasional salmon or sea-trout at a very modest cost.

The Alness, the Blackwater & Loch Maree
A few miles north of the Glass lies the well known Alness (or Averon, as it is sometimes known). This used to be prolific sea-trout water but, like so many rivers, it has seen a decline in recent years, but the salmon fishing has improved and now averages four to six hundred fish a year. The best year in recent times was 1985 when over eight hundred fish were caught. Conifer plantations have encroached on the banks of this river and its main tributary, the Blackwater, and have led to flash floods which have done some damage to the spawning grounds. However, improvements are in hand and the river is stocked every year. Sea-trout average 1½lb and salmon 6½lb, though September usually sees some better fish of up to 20lb. The river, which is largely owned by Novar Estates (0349) 830208, drains Loch Morie. This is good brown trout water and also offers the chance of char and ferox which run well into double figures; the best for 1991 being 15lb 4oz. A day's fishing costs £15 for two rods including a boat. Water from the loch to Strath Rusdale is also owned by Novar Estates. Alness Angling Club (secretary Brian Poe (0349) 883963) lease one beat. Permits cost £16 a day between July and September and can be obtained from Pattersons Ironmongers in Alness High Street, (0349) 88286. The Castle Water, which extends to Dalreoch Burn, is private and retained for family and friends. So, if you're a friend of the family—good fishing. If not either get acquainted or find pastures new! Below the burn, Novar Estates have four beats. The cost of the Novar Estates water ranges from £12 to £35 per day per rod, weekly lets are sometimes available and trout fishing on their three top beats below the loch cost £3 per day. The Coul House Hotel at Contin (0997) 21487 can also arrange for guests to fish the Novar Estates water. Needless to say the advice is, as usual, to book as far in advance as possible.

The three watchwords for a fishing trip to the Highlands are undoubtedly Preparation, Preparation and Preparation! Hotels and river owners want their guests to catch fish and are only too pleased to give advice on flies. However, it never ceases to surprise them how many guests either never ask or wait until they have arrived to find out which are the favoured flies. A phone call before you go could transform an enjoyable holiday into a successful holiday. It is well worth checking all your tackle and making sure you have plenty of spare casts before leaving home, so be prepared and check before you go. If this sounds somewhat patronising—please forgive me. I am only reciting a lesson learnt from personal and bitter experience!

The Beauly

The Beauly is a superb salmon river and as a result it is very, very hard to get on! It is easy to assume that the desire to own salmon fishing stems from recent times but the Beauly has always been a prized water. After the estate had been forfeited following the Jacobite uprising of 1715, Lord Lovat asked his friend the Duke of Gordon to present a petition to the King. The request was that one *lea rig* behind the castle might be given to him and his heirs in perpetuity. Amused by such eccentricity, King George I granted the request only to find that lea rig in fact meant the river! A century and a half later the Master of Lovat proved just what a bargain had been extracted by taking 156 fish in five days. That is an average of thirty-one fish a day and was achieved using a twenty-five rod!

The Beauly is still a prolific salmon river and an average of 7000 fish a year are counted at the two dams. Catches of forty fish in a day are not uncommon, so it is not surprising that when Lovat Estates put seven beats on the market in 1990 the asking price was over £10m. The purchaser, Landmatch plc, formed The River Beauly Fishing Company (0763) 241181 to manage the now syndicated river. All the management are keen fishermen and the managing director is William Midwood, whose family used to own the Naver. The company is undertaking a variety of conservation measures and its stocking policy gives us great hope for future years; it also has a first class consultant in William Shearer, the leading salmon biologist. In 1990 the Falls, Home and Downie beats twice produced over a hundred fish in a week. Favoured pools on these beats include Glide, Castle, Charlies and Greenbank. As with most time-shared fishing, it is possible for outsiders to get the odd week and further details may be had from the company. In spite of the river's prestige, you don't have to be a millionaire to gain coveted access to it. A day's permit from Morrisons (0463) 782213 in Beauly's West End will enable you to fish the tidal water from below Lovat Bridge to Wester Lovat Farm at a cost of £8 a day (except Thursdays and Saturdays). Alternatively, for £3.50 a day you can also fish the North and South Estuary, where spinning is allowed.

The catchment area of the Beauly extends to beyond the Great Glen in the North West Highlands and the whole system has been harnessed for hydro-electric power, resulting in many dams and power stations. I am not sure if there is a collective noun for dams but there are many fishermen who have seen the character of rivers changed beyond recognition and would term the situation a damnation of dams! In the interests of fairness it must be pointed out that dams do have their uses and can help to maintain reasonable water levels, thus making a river fishable for longer periods.

This appears to be a river of many components. From the new dam at Loch Mullardoch a tunnel carries the water through Loch Beinn a' Mheadhoin and thence to the River Affric which goes on to join up with the River Glass. Water from Mullardoch also forms the River Invercannick, which itself later joins the River Glass. The Glass is joined by the Farrar below Struy and, at the confluence of these two streams, the Beauly is born.

All these tributaries are outstanding salmon streams. Fishing of this quality is understandably hard to come by but Lovat Estates (0463) 782205 have six beats on the right bank of the River Glass. A week's permit will cost you in the region of £40 plus VAT per rod. Season tickets per rod vary from £1000 plus VAT for May up to August 24th, after which the cost is £1500 up to the end of the season on October 15th. L.A.H.Mure Esq. (0456) 5251 has two miles of the left bank of the Glass which are divided into three two-rod beats. Understandably these beats are quickly snapped up. F. Spencer-Nairn Esq. (0463) 76285 may be able to help with fishing on the Farrar and also let cottages.

Lochs Monar & Mullardoch

The Glen Affric Hotel (0456) 415214 issues permits for the fine trout waters of Lochs Monar and Mullardoch, where good bags of 20lb fish or more are possible in the right conditions. The cost of £25 a day includes a boat with a maximum of four rods. The hotel also has a fly casting school—this could be the chance to brush up your technique. It always surprises me that many first class shots will go to a shooting school before the start of the season to get their eye in again, yet once a fisherman thinks (and I repeat thinks!) he has mastered the art of casting he rarely bothers to seek expert guidance again. I know that at the start of every season my casting is pretty rough and it always requires a few days practice before the fly is landing where I want it to. Time at a casting school is never wasted, for one can always improve one's technique and learn new tactics.

The Torridon

The River Torridon is owned by the Loch Torridon Hotel (0445) 791242. A day on this river is available to guests at a cost of £13.50 a day. This is a flash spate river and can be quite reasonable fishing.

The question that every honest fisherman dreads having to ask, usually after a blank week, or even day, is where is the next salmon going to come from? The problem is that, like most other things, salmon fishing is a very inexact art. Trout, by way of contrast, are somewhat easier to assess. If a fish is rising and you can match the hatch there is a fair chance of catching him. As we know, salmon do not feed when they swim up a river, and as a result it is extremely difficult to predict taking times. It would appear nevertheless that early morning, around lunchtime and evening are the optimum times. This is the same pattern as trout and we all look forward to the evening rise and will often stay out until the light goes. So why is it a different story with salmon? Part of the problem is that, understandably, ghillies go home for their tea at around 5.30 pm! After a day on the river the thought of a bath, a dram and some good eating is a very appealing prospect—after all, this is meant to be a holiday! But if you want to catch a fish, I strongly urge you to fish on. It is surely no coincidence that many big fish—including Miss Ballantine's—were taken late on in the day.

The Ness System

The Ness System is the largest catchment area in the Highlands and at twenty-five miles long the loch is monster sized! However, the river is only about six miles long. It used to be regarded as the queen of Scottish rivers due to very productive yields and its great width. A fish that inhabits wide open waters will give a much better fight than his cousin in a small river, who has less water to manoeuvre in. Steam navigation and the Caledonian Canal were thought to be the culprits, for the decrease in salmon and the value of the fishing fell from £1100 p.a.—a considerable sum in Victorian times—to a quarter of that amount. This queen may have lost her crown, but the Ness is still a respectable salmon river.

As with so many other rivers, the spring runs are a mere shade of times gone by but this has been more than compensated for by the increase in the summer runs of salmon and grilse. The Ness is a wide river and early season spinners will use a ten-foot rod and when the fly comes into its own from June onwards, you will need a carbon rod of fifteen feet or more. At the end of a day's fishing with such a rod you will be more than ready for a bath and a large dram or two! Inverness Angling Club has three miles of both banks where fly, worm and spinning are allowed. The cost of a day's fishing is £12 and permits can be obtained from J. Graham & Co. the tackle dealer (0463) 233178. Above the club water is Ness-side where lets are handled by Angus Mackenzie & Co. (0463) 235353. These beats have produced some good fish, with a lady taking a twenty-four pounder in 1990 and in 1989 a gentleman of the cloth had a twenty-five pounder. Next is the mile or so of Ness Castle water where the agent is Mr R. M. Robertson (0542) 22411. Beyond this is the time-shared Laggan water which is factored by Mr G.S. Dawson

(031) 449 3973. Weekly lets may sometimes be available. Finally, there is the Dochfour Estate beats and further details may be had from the Estate Office (0463) 86218.

Due to its size, fishing from a boat on Loch Ness can prove hazardous if there is a wind whipping up white horses. The golden rule is, if in doubt, don't go out. While the fly works well for sea-trout, trolling with two spinning rods is the favoured method for salmon which can run up to 30lb. The fishing is privately owned but hotels such as Inchnacardoch Lodge Hotel (0320) 6258 and Whitebridge Hotel (0456) 3226 may be able to help. The Glenmoriston Lodge Estate, whose Head Keeper is Mr Alastair Mackintosh, also has two boats on the loch; including outboards they cost £30 a day per rod. In 1990 these boats accounted for sixty-nine salmon.

The Moriston

Glenmoriston Lodge Estate (0320) 51219 can also offer good trout fishing on twenty one hill lochs and eight miles of salmon fishing on the River Moriston. The cost of a day's fishing varies between £20 and £40 according to season. Mr Macintosh's own pattern, the Wee Tosh is particularly successful, but old favourites like the Hairy Mary and Stoats Tail work well. Seven miles of the headwaters of this river are owned by the Cluanie Inn (0320) 40238 and offer the occasional salmon at a cost of only a few pounds a day. One should not expect top class fishing but for a modest sum you are at least in the running for a catch. No permit is needed for fishing on Loch Cluanie. A boat for two rods and a day's fishing on the delightful Loch Ruthven can be had for £10 from R.Humfrey Esq. (0808) 3283. These 375 acres produce good fighting brownies averaging around the pound mark, which are often taken on the local favourite fly—the Badger.

The Enrick

The River Enrick rises in Loch nan Eun and flows alongside the A831 on its course through Loch Meiklie to enter Loch Ness at Urquhart Bay. The fishing is generally unexceptional but the scenery is gorgeous. Permission for the Enrick can be obtained from Mr R. Sorenson at Kilmartin Hall (0456) 476269. Mrs Elizabeth Taylor (0456) 476275, Kilmartin House, may not have any Oscars on her mantlepiece but she does issue permits to fish Loch Meiklie at £6 a day (9.00am—3.30pm) including a boat. This super little fly-only loch has beautifully marked pink-fleshed trout which average one pound and any under twelve inches should be returned.

Loch Quoich & the Garry

Loch Quoich covers some four thousand acres and is the kind of water where an outboard is essential. As with any water of this size, weather conditions are an important factor, but on the right day, the fishing can be excellent and may be had for £22 a day for a boat with an outboard and fuel. The Gearr Garry drains this loch and flows through Lochs Poulay, Inchlaggan and Garry. Tomdoun Hotel (0809) 2218 can arrange for you to fish all the waters and also has three and a half miles of salmon fishing on the north bank of the River Garry, which is free to hotel guests. Fishing the south bank is through Garry Gualach Ltd (0809) 2230, who run sporting holidays and can arrange shooting and stalking for you, should you wish to swap rod for rifle. A nymph fished on a sinking tip may well prove to be the downfall of a big 4lb plus Arctic char on Loch Garry which is also excellent trout water. Mr J. Morgan at Ardochy Lodge (0809) 2232 has rights for salmon and trout fishing but as he says, the loch is large and the salmon are few. R.B.Scott Esq., at the Invergarry Post Office (0809) 3201 can arrange for you to fish the Garry between Loch Garry and Loch Oich at a cost of £25 a day. The price also includes salmon fishing on Loch Oich, where trout fishing may be had from Glengarry Castle Hotel (0809) 3254 for free, although a boat will cost £5 for a half, or £9 for a full day.

Inexpensive salmon fishing can also be had on the River Shiel. £10 is the price for a day; contact Mrs Campbell (0599) 81282. A few miles west is Glenelg, which is just across the water from Skye. Here you will find the lovely Glenelg Inn, which arranges marvellous ceilidhs and a very original form of pub crawl, using inflatable dinghies! Before anyone writes to say that the Shiel cannot be so cheap, I would point out that this is the one that flows into Loch Duich.

The Shiel

The other River Shiel (forty miles south) that drains the Loch of the same name is a totally different kettle of fish! This is another example of the long loch and short river system. These rivers can produce those great days we all dream of. The river is only three miles long. By comparison, the loch is some eighteen miles in length and for its size it is one of the narrowest in Scotland. Although there can be excellent summer runs of salmon and grilse, the river is probably best known for its sea-trout fishing. Unless there is a breeze to stir the water, which is fairly slow, night fishing is likely to prove the most productive method. Catches may not be what they were thirty years ago, yet the loch still ranks among the best sea-trout waters. An old advertisement for the Shiel Hotel offers fishing for five shillings a day! Alas, today it is one of those rivers that is almost impossible to get on unless you are prepared to wait fifteen or twenty years before fishing such pools as Garrison, Grassy Point and Parapet. Still, if you are looking for a long term plan then this is a tremendous water. Write to: R.S.—L.S.D.F.B., c/o C. Kennedy Esq, Robertson Neilson & Co., 95 Bothwell Street, Glasgow G2 7JH.

Loch Shiel

Loch Shiel is much more accessible and what is more, it must also be one of the prettiest in Scotland. The Jacobite uprising of 1745 began here, for it was on the shores of Loch Shiel that Bonnie Prince Charlie raised his flag. This used to be very good sea-trout water but like so many others, has seen a decline in numbers caught in recent years. Because this is such a large loch, salmon are usually trolled for. Make sure you tackle up, as twenty-pounders are not uncommon and the best fish in recent years was a forty-two pounder. There are many sand and gravel bays which provide excellent spawning grounds and a good spot for a picnic lunch while admiring the soaring mountains that surround you. It is also good trout water with an average of three quarters of a pound, and two-pounders are not uncommon here. The Stage House Inn (0397) 83246 and the Glenfinnan House Hotel (0397) 83235 at the eastern end and Loch Shiel Hotel (0967) 85224 and Clanranald Hotel (0967) 85662 at the western end all have boats and can offer a day's fishing at around £15. Guests of E. Macaulay of Dalilea Farm (0967) 85253 will find the price of their accommodation includes fishing and boats with outboards. The Road to the Isles, (A830) can be found at the northern end of Loch Shiel and, if you travel west on this road, you will find two jewels, the River Ailort and Loch Eilt. A week's fishing, which includes both the river and the loch, costs £250 from Salar Management Services Ltd (0667) 55355.

Loch Morar

As we continue westwards we come to Loch Morar, which lies a few miles south of Mallaig. There is also a railway service to Mallaig, which must be one of the prettiest train journeys one could wish for. Not terribly practical for fishermen, but a marvellous journey— should the motor fail you. The loch is twelve and a half miles long and while there are salmon and sea-trout, it is mainly a trout water. A permit for bank fishing is available at £2.50 a day per person per rod and a boat with an outboard can be hired for £16.00. Permits may be had from Morar Motors or Loch Morar Adventure Centre (0687) 2164. The Morar Hotel (0687) 2346 has three boats for guests and can also arrange fishing on several hill lochs.

The Nevis

Returning eastwards one finds Fort William, where you can fish in the shadow of Ben Nevis—Britain's highest mountain. There is no better way to appreciate the grandeur of the mighty Ben than by fishing the River Nevis which skirts round it. Snow from the peaks above the glen help to maintain reasonable water levels for most of the season, although it can run low. It is essentially a spate river and thus all depends on getting the right conditions. On its day it can produce terrific fishing, especially for sea-trout which average about a pound, while salmon are about the 6lb mark. A day's permit costs £5 from the Rod and Gun Shop (0397) 702656 in Fort William.

The Lochy

The Nevis joins the River Lochy just before it flows into Loch Linnhe. The Lochy is the largest and best salmon river in the area and so very hard to get on. It is largely owned by the River Lochy Association, a group of private owners, and the waiting list is long. Wading can be particularly dangerous as there is a power station at the western end of Loch Lochy. If it starts to generate, the water level can rise very quickly, so it is safest to fish the larger pools from a boat. Beat 7, which stretches from the tidal waters to a mile above Fort William, is available from the Rod and Gun Shop (0397) 702656 at a cost of between £17 and £22 a day. This is good water which produces about 450 salmon a year, some of which exceed 28lb.

The Spean

Heading north from Fort William on the A82 will bring you to Spean Bridge with its famous war memorial. It was in this area that the brave Commandos did much of their training during the Second World War. In the days before fishing conservation was treated seriously, the headwaters and the feeder lochs of the River Spean were harnessed to provide power for the British Aluminium plant, which would have wiped it out as a salmon river were it not for its main tributary the river Roy. As a result, the best fishing is from Roybridge down to the Lochy. The Spean Bridge Hotel (0397) 712250 can offer guests fishing on the stretch between the old viaduct and Wade Bridge at a cost of £10 a day. The Rod and Gun shop may be able to help you get on other beats of this river and many other waters in the area. This is a good river where sea-trout average 1½lb and salmon 8lb; but it has a deserved reputation for producing big fish—a 37 pounder was caught in 1976

The Roy

Is there a river that has not had its character changed and harmed by man? Well, yes! There are thankfully a few and one is the Roy, which rises close to Loch Spey, the source of that great river from which it takes its name. How refreshing it is to find such a river that has been left to its own devices. The fish like it too—for nearly all salmon and sea-trout which run the Spean are heading for the Roy. It is very much a spate river and as there is no loch for it to drain it can make for a very frustrating time with weather against you. Permits may be had from the Roy Bridge Hotel (0397) 712236 and Stronlossit Hotel (0397) 712253 for £15 a day. Mrs Irene Pryke (0449) 741481 lets three beats which rotate and can also offer self-catering accommodation. There are two rods on each beat and currently the cost is £12 per day per rod.

Lochs Lochy & Arkaig

Fishing is free on Loch Lochy, which is the most western loch in the Caledonian Canal system. It is almost solely a trout water but there are five-pounders for those prepared to work at fishing this deep water. Boat moorings are controlled by the West Highland Estate Office (0397) 702433 who also issue permits for Loch Arkaig at £2 per day. Before the Caledonian Canal was built this loch abounded in salmon. An old game book records the following: 67 fish in a week, 289 fish in a month, 19 fish in a morning and one week only produced 3 fish, beside which is written 'disappointing'—all these fish were to two rods. If only all fishing was similarly disappointing!

For the intrepid wanderers among our brethren there are the Islands, each of which has its own unique delights and pleasures for the visiting fisherman. With ferries and air flights, communications are much easier than they used to be. In the early nineteenth century Colonel Jameson was invited to stay with a friend on Lewis to enjoy some fishing and stalking. At Ullapool the weather was against him and it was eight days before he could get across. The sport began in earnest and every day's entry for a period of five weeks records a good day with salmon, sea-trout, trout and stalking. The least successful day records two sea-trout of 1½lb and 2lb and a fight with a hefty salmon who broke him; whereas the best day produced eleven salmon, four sea-trout and some good trout. Getting back to the mainland was a problem and he had to wait three days for the weather to improve. On his way back to Lancashire the axle of the coach broke. The local laird invited him to stay and so much did he enjoy the trout fishing, that it was two weeks before he made his departure. Those were the days!

Just across the Firth of Lorne is Mull, one of the most beautiful islands of the Inner Hebrides. Here you will find pine forests, wild moorlands, deserted beaches, mountains and the famous fossil tree preserved in the lava of Ben More millions of years ago. You are unlikely to find gold, but it is certainly there! A Spanish ship carrying a large quantity of gold to pay troops sank off Tobermory during the time of the Armada. But despite many attempts no-one has yet found the wreck. From a fishing point of view there are good spate rivers for salmon and trout and several noted trout lochs.

The Aros
The Aros is perhaps the best known river for it was here that in 1911 a 45lb salmon was taken on Ash Tree Pool after a six hour fight—the main run on this river, which is just under five miles long, is in July but this may be later if there is a hot dry summer. Salmon average 7lb and it is also noted for its sea-trout which usually tip the scales at around 1½lb but run up to 3lb.

Loch Frisa
Nearby is Loch Frisa where salmon and sea-trout are often seen but seldom caught. It is, however, an excellent trout water and being quite dangerous by island standards, is best fished from a boat. Do be careful if the wind is up for the loch can be quite bold. Permits are available from the Forestry Commission (0680) 300346 at £2 per day for bank fishing or £15 to include a boat. The Forestry Commission also issue permits for the River Lussa with its famous Pedlars Pool. This is very much a spate river and fish may take some time to ascend the waterfall at Tor Ness. Most of the bigger fish, including a thirty-four pounder, have been taken below the falls. Salmon and sea-trout are about the same size as in Aros and it is widely regarded as one of the best rivers on the island.

The Forsa, the Ba & the Coladoir

Arguably the best fishing is to be had on the River Forsa. At ten miles long it is the longest river and has some forty pools—double figure fish of up to 18lb are caught, though the average is around 8lb. Like so many of these island spate rivers it rises and falls very quickly and is best fished when in spate. Another fine river is the two and a half mile long Ba which is privately owned. There is a big pool near its mouth at Killiechronan where you can often see salmon and sea-trout waiting to run—an invigorating sight. The River Coladoir has four miles of pools broken by gentle falls and offers good sea-trout fishing and the occasional salmon. Another fine sea-trout water is the River Bellart on which it is possible to catch a dozen in a day. But those will often be finnock (small sea-trout) and once you have caught enough for supper, you are urged to return any further catches so as to conserve stocks for the future.

Lochs Torr, Ba & Assapoll

At the northern end of the island is Loch Torr which was purpose-built for fishing in 1899. This is a fly-only water which is stocked with rainbows and brownies and produces the occasional salmon and sea-trout. If trouting is more your thing then do try the three Mishnish lochs which lie between Dervaig and Tobermory or lochs Pellach, Meadhoin and Carnain an Amis.

Loch Ba, like the river of the same name, is let by Killiechronan Estates (0680) 300438. This loch fishes very well for salmon and especially sea-trout—double figure fish are not uncommon! Sguabain is Gaelic for windswept and the loch certainly lives up to its name. Weed is a problem here so take care when playing your fish. At the southern end of the island on Ross of Mull is Loch Assapoll where salmon average 8lb and sea-trout 2lb. This is superb fishing and the loch is also famous for its brownies which run up to 7lb.

Tackle and Books in Tobermory (0688) 2336 can arrange for you to fish most waters as can many hotels like the lovely Western Isles Hotel (0688 2012) which is also in Tobermory.

The Laggan & the lochs of Islay

Just south of Mull are the islands of Islay and Jura, names to conjure with for any lover of malt whisky. Most salmon fishing on Islay is privately owned, but not impossible to attain. The cost for a rod per week is in the region of £240 and fishing begins on the 1st of July with the salmon running to a reasonable average of 7¼lb. This great little spate river does not really require wading as you can fish from the both banks. The Islay Estate has various four rod packages for the Rivers Sorn, Grey and the Laggan. In addition, fishing on many lochs, including Loch Gorm can be had, the latter is very shallow so watch out for rocks when boating. Salmon fishing averages at about £400 per four rods per week from Mr B.Wiles at the Headkeeper's House, Bridgend (049681) 293. The Machrie Hotel (0496) 2310 in Port Ellen has great brown trout fishing on the Machrie Burn and is also a good centre for any holiday. The Port Askaig Hotel (049684) 245 organises bookings for the Dunlossit Estate. As well as three beats on the river Laggan they have six very good trout lochs with

Ballygrant, Lossit and Allan providing the best fishing. Wet and dry flies both do well and bank fishing costs £4 for an evening, £8 for a half and £12 for a full day. Incidentally, you will not need your hiking boots, as these three gems are accessible from the road.

The Lussa

Walking boots of some description are something of a must for Jura. This wild and wonderful island has only one road, which finishes at the cottage where George Orwell completed *1984*. Fishing on this island, famed for its stalking (*jura* is gaelic for island of deer) is predominantly for brown trout. However, the River Lussa when in spate can produce interesting salmon and sea-trout fishing. Contact Mr C.Fletcher at the Ardlussa Estate in Ardlussa (0496) 82323.

The Machrie

Across from Kintyre we come upon the delightful isle of Arra, more renowned for breathtaking scenery than its game fishing and dominated by the 2868 foot high Goat Fell. However, the Machrie river can produce good sport, especially from dusk onwards and the salmon tend to average around the 6lb mark. Contact Mr J.T. Boscawen at the Strathtay Estate Office, Boltachan, By Aberfeldy, Perthshire (0887) 820496. Prices vary between £90 and £145 per rod per week. For the River Iorsa and its loch contact the Dougarie Estate Office (0770) 84259.

Skye Waters

Separated from Mull by the Ardnamurchan Peninsular—the most westerly point of the mainland—is Skye and its romantic associations with Bonnie Prince Charlie and Flora Macdonald. Being relatively easy to get to, it is popular with tourists and likely to get much busier with the proposed new road bridge. Ullinish Lodge Hotel (0470) 72214 has the rights for the River Ose and the upper four miles of the River Snizort and fishing is available to guests at between £10 and £15 a day depending on conditions. Fishing on the lower eight miles of the Snizort is available to guests of the Skeabost House Hotel (0470) 32202 at a cost of £10 per day. Both hotels can also arrange trout fishing on lochs as can the Misty Isle Hotel (0470) 22208 on the shore of Loch Dunvegan. This is run by experienced fishermen who can also arrange sea fishing. Permits for the Uig Angling Association water on the River Hinnisdale are available from the bar of the Ferry Inn (0470) 42242 at £15 a day. As one would expect, these are spate streams and rain is the all important factor. Portree Angling Association can offer visitors a wide choice of loch and some river fishing and permits may be had from Jansport in Portree (0478) 612559 for between £3 and £5 a day.

Scots and fishermen consider that Lewis, Harris, North Uist, Benbecula and South Uist make up the Western Isles. If you have the opportunity to visit, do go. They are a fisherman's paradise. There is outstanding salmon and sea-trout fishing and literally hundreds of trout lochs. The Islands' remoteness ensures that you can enjoy your fishing in perfect tranquillity, disturbed only by the sight of red deer on the hills or rare birds like the red-necked phalarope. I strongly advise you to make sure your fly box is suitably filled before coming here as tackle shops are few and far between. The Stoats Tail is a popular choice for salmon, while for sea-trout I would take traditional patterns such as the Peter Ross, the Mallard and Claret, Silver Invicta, some Zulus, a Wickham's Fancy, a Goat's Toe and my old favourite, the Muddler Minnow.

The Grimersta & the lochs of Lewis

Lewis has several hundred lochs full of hard fighting wild brownies which can go up to 6lb. The Grimersta is a great river by national as well as island standards, and one of the most prolific waters you could wish for—fifty-seven fish taken on the fly in one day is a record that will take some beating. The fishing is owned by a syndicate which was formed by Lord Leverhulme in 1922 and is managed by Grimersta Estates Office (0851) 72358. The river itself is only some two miles long, above which is a chain of lochs culminating in Loch Langavat which, at seven miles long, is the longest on the islands. It is fly-only water except for Langavat where spinning is also permitted. A favoured technique is to fish a very small fly on the point and something much larger like a Muddler Minnow tied on a size 6 as a dropper. There are four beats, and such famous pools as Bridge, Battery, Captains and Sea Pool. While Autumn may be the best time, May and June can produce catches of up to fifty fish a week but are not so predictable.

The Laxay

There are three miles of the River Laxay above Loch Valtos and one mile below it. River fishing is mainly on the three pools of the lower section which are appropriately named Top, Middle and Lower: the loch is divided into beats each with a boat and a ghillie. Sea-trout average 1½lb and salmon 7lb though a 33lb fish was caught back in 1933. The Creed is another good river. Its five miles are divided into four single rod beats which rotate on a daily basis while its loch is fished by two boats. The river flows through Lady Levers park with its magnificent rhododendrons and noted pools include Fall, Bond and Junction. A day's bank fishing permit costs £10 from the Stornoway Trust Estate Office (0851) 702002, and £16 will pay for a boat and one rod. The Blackwater fishes well especially on the lower section which has some good holding pools. It is aptly named for the river is rather peaty and you will probably find that a fly with some orange or yellow will work best. The Uig is very much a spate river but if you hit it in the right conditions it can be very good. It was near here that the famous 12th century Lewis chessmen were found. Scaliscro Estates (085175) 325 can offer salmon and sea-trout fishing on the Rivers Creed and Blackwater and six lochs including Langavat. It also offers trout fishing on nine other lochs. The trout fishing is superb. Take for example Loch Fhreunadail where the trout average half a pound and the best day's log was fifty-five. The premier loch in my opinion is Loch Bruiche Breivat where they average ¾lb and run to 4lb plus. The most successful day record here was one hundred brownies and two Arctic char! Trout fishing on Lewis is superb but do be prepared to walk or hire an argocat to get you across country.

Harris Waters

Harris is world famous for its tweeds and no visit would be complete without a visit to see how they are made. Guests of the North Harris Estate (085986) 200 can stay at Amhuinnsuidhe Castle which is the most westerly castle in the country and enjoy fishing on eight large lochs where salmon range from 5lb-8lb and sea-trout 1lb-5lb, though there are bigger fish as the records are 18¾lb and 11lb. Other good fishing on Harris includes the Scarista and Horsacleit which is very much a spate stream. The Rodel Hotel at Leverburgh (08598) 2210 offers guests good salmon, sea-trout and brown trout fishing on a number of lochs. Ardvourlie Castle (0859) 2307 is a great place to stay if you are fishing in the area. Here on the shores of Loch Seaforth you can see otters and if you are lucky golden eagles. The lunches are both sumptuous and scenic. It is not unknown for an eagle to time his fly-past as you are seated—a marvellous diversion, wouldn't you agree?! Fishing for guests can be arranged on the nearby Aline Estate which boasts some first class water.

Loch Nan Geireann

Lochmaddy Hotel (0876) 3331 is the place to stay for fishing North Uist and Benbecula or if you wish to be independent from the hotel, the North Uist Estate Office (0876) 3329 will be able to help you. There are many first class trout lochs and the Skelter System offers salmon and sea-trout fishing. At the northern end of the island is Loch Nan Geireann. Here, at low tide, there is a tidal pool where you can see salmon and sea-trout leaping and splashing in the clear shallow water, a sight that will delight any fisherman.

Lochs of South Uist

The Lochboisdale Hotel (0878) 4332 manages most of the fishing on South Uist, which has some of the best Hebridean fishing. Two-pound trout are the norm rather than the exception when fishing Grogarry Loch which fishes well from the bank as well as from a boat. Other good lochs include Bornish, Kildonan and Stilligarry. Lochs Howmore, Ollay, Fada and Roag are known for their salmon and superb sea-trout, which run up to 8lb and are often over 4lb. It is also worth emphasising once more the scenic beauty of these islands, field glasses are almost as important as your hip flask.

Although Orkney is only six miles across the Pentland Firth from Caithness, it was part of the Viking Kingdom of Norway and Denmark until 1468. The islands are rich in history, something the locals are proud of. Here you can see the standing stones of Stenness, a small circle dating from the third millenium BC. Close by is Maes Howe, the finest chambered tomb in Western Europe built before 2700 BC. It houses the largest collection of runic inscriptions to be found in any one place in the world! Beneath the waters of Scapa Flow are the remains of the seventy-two German Naval vessels scuttled in 1919. It is also the only place where you will see a round hazard sign for otters crossing the road.

Loch Harray

From a fishing point of view this is some of the best trout water in the world. At 2528 acres Loch Harray is the largest Orkney water. With an average depth of eight feet and rarely exceeding fourteen feet it is perfect trout water. There are good hatches of midges, olives, sedges and later on daddy-longlegs while an abundant supply of freshwater shrimp helps to give the flesh a lovely pink colour. Although a seventeen-pounder was caught thirty years ago they average about three quarters of a pound. However, these fish will fight like nothing you have met before and many an experienced angler has been convinced that he must be into at least a two pounder from the way it has fought and has been surprised to find that when brought to the net it is only a one pound fish. These fish are very surface active and fast risers so quick reactions are needed. The Merkister Hotel (0856) 77366 is an ideal place to stay as the manager, Angus MacDonald, is a local expert.

Lochs of Orkney

Loch Swannay may be only a quarter of the size of Harray but it is a favourite with the locals and produces fish of 2lb and more with amazing regularity. Good baskets in recent years have been ten fish for 17½lb, four for 8¼lb and three for 12½lb—need we say more?! Loch Stennes is famous for the record 29lb fish taken at the turn of the century and today fish of 5lb-7lb are caught quite often. This is the one loch where it is worth casting a fly over the weed beds as these make good cover for trout avoiding the attention of the seals present throughout the year. It also serves as a larder, for these trout are piscivorous—one fish's bulging stomach revealed a twelve-inch eel, fifteen spined stickleback, lugworm and coalfish, as well as more normal samples of diet like midge, snails and daddy-longlegs. Two other good lochs are Boardhouse and Hundland, which often fishes well in bright conditions. There are also several other smaller waters. Good Orkney flies include Black Pennell, Zulu, Invicta, Soldier Palmer, Dunkeld, Alexandra and local favourites like the Loch Ordie. There are no rivers and the only lochs for sea-trout are Stennes and Kirbister, but sea-trout can be caught in the bays and shorelines of the coastline. Further details may be had from the Orkney Tourist Board (0856) 872856. The Orkney Trout Fishing Association have a beat on Loch of Skaill. The trout here average at around 2lb. Muddlers and Whickams Fancy are recommended flies and all you have to do to enjoy this fishing is join the association! As a visiting angler you can expect to pay £10, unless you are a pensioner, in which case £6 will cover the cost. Further details may be had from the Secretary, M. Russell Esq. (0856) 76586

Lochs of Shetland

The Shetland Islands are closer to Norway than Scotland and for hundreds of years were allowed to run their own affairs without interference from the mainland. Then oil was discovered in the North Sea and the islands were developed. However the trout are still there and there are hundreds of lochs with good fighting brownies of up to 8lb and more; an added bonus for fishermen is that there are no midges here. Favourite lochs include Tingwall, which is regularly stocked with native-bred fish, Benston where the average is 1½lb and Girlsta which produced the 12½lb record for Shetland.

The outer islands have good fishing too. Whalsay has three first class lochs including Huxter. Unst has Lochs Cliff and Snarravoe and good sea-trout fishing at Burra Firth and Dales Voe. Yell has sea-trout and brownies in Loch Papil. Even tiny Fetlar has three lochs and you may see a snowy owl.

As on Orkney, salt water spinning in the Voes is the thing for sea-trout and a strip of mackerel belly on the treble may help. The same flies as suggested for Orkney should do the trick though you might care to add a Ke-He. All this fishing is available for £10 for a season, £7 a week or just £2 a day by joining the Shetland Anglers' Association whose secretary is Mr A. Miller (0595) 3729. The Association publishes a particularly useful booklet which includes maps, hints on technique and specific information on over one hundred lochs. Alternatively, the Shetland Isles Tourist Board (0595) 3434 will be able to help and advise you.

Speyside

Speyside is an intoxicating area not only by virtue of its glorious river but also as a result of the number of distilleries in the area. Driving down Strathspey you will happen across the source of many a famous whisky. High street brands mix with lesser known labels, making for a veritable treat. The local tourist board have coined the area the Whisky Trail and according to a local gossip it is impossible to lose one's way even though the route is badly sign posted. 'Follow the bodies!' he said. Perhaps the answer is to take an extended holiday so you can do justice to at least some of the unique malts of this area.

The Spey

From source to mouth some hundred miles long, the Spey begins in the small Loch Spey near the River Roy, not far from Loch Lochy. From the loch it is joined by small burns from Corrieyairack Forest. These burns present a problem, for as they tumble down the steep slopes they wash away the soil from the forestry plantations and, as a result, the spates are much more pronounced. When in spate the water is very coloured, in fact almost black. The Upper Spey has been harnessed for hydro power but at Blargie it is joined by the River Mashie and from here begins to take on its true character.

This is Jacobite country. As you look at Cluny Castle, which was rebuilt in the nineteenth century, spare a thought for Cluny Macpherson. Following the failure of the 1745 rebellion, this clan chief hid for eight years in the hills above and had to suffer the ignominy of watching 'Butcher' Cumberland's troops razing his ancestral home to the ground. Also in the area are the ruins of Ruthven Barracks, scene of one of the few Jacobite successes. It was here that the interestingly named Gordon of Glenbucket defeated the government troops. How different history might have been had Bonnie Prince Charlie not turned back at Derby and retreated north. Harried all the way, the retreat became a rout until the desperate last stand at Culloden. Alas, claymores were no match for muskets nor was the fierce but poorly organised clan loyalty very effective against the regimented discipline of the government army.

For over fifty years, the Scots and English sympathisers had lived in hope of seeing a restoration of the Stuarts. Their hopes had been raised when Dutch William—William of Orange—died after a fall from his horse, which stumbled on a mole hill and gave rise to the Jacobite toast 'To the little gentleman in black velvet'. After the failure of the 1715 rebellion they continued to drink to the health of the King across the water out of the beautifully engraved Jacobean glasses with their secret Stuart motifs. All these hopes died at Culloden: this was one of the bloodiest battles fought on British soil and the rapacity with which survivors were hounded down, and the clan system destroyed, put paid to the last aspirations of those who espoused the Stuart cause.

But enough of history, what of the fishing? Some of the estuary nets have been bought off, and hence the fishing has improved. That's all very well—you might say—but how do I get to fish? Surprisingly, despite the Spey's reputation, fishing is possible if you know where to go. The best beats are expensive and are impossible to get on. However, various hotels, fishing clubs and estates offer days or weeks that can be taken up if you book early enough. The clubs often have various restrictions. For example, Aberlour Angling Club requires that visitors fishing their one mile stretch stay the night(s) prior to fishing in one of the village's three hotels. They also have a bag limit of two fish per day—one above the bridge and the other below. Any further fish caught have to be handed over to Munro's Tackle Shop to be sold 'for the good of the club and the village'. This does not happen very often! The following is a list of contacts that will be able to help you to fish this majestic river:

(For Badenoch A.A.) A. & L. Donald, Main Street, Newtonmore (0540) 3242; Speyside Sports, Grampian Road, Aviemore (0479) 810656 (new Abernathy A.A. stretch, £15 per day, £45 per week excluding Sunday); Alvie Estate, Kincraig (0540) 651255 or Dalraddy Caravan Park (0479) 810330 (three beats, £20 per day and £96 for a weekly salmon ticket, £10 a day for trout); Lynwilg Hotel, Aviemore (0479) 810209 (three miles and four lochs); The Paper Shop, Kinguissie (0540) 661207 and Ashdowns (0540) 673242 (a stretch of the Spey from Kinguissie to the dam, full day £3.00), Rothiemurchus Estate, by Aviemore (0479) 810703 (three beats, £15, £20 and £25 per day, plus two stocked and two wild lochs); Craigard Hotel, Boat of Garten (0479) 83206 (Abernathy A.A. six and a quarter miles both banks at £15 per day); The Boat Hotel, Boat of Garten, (0479) 83258; Allens, Boat of Garten (0479) 83372 (also Abernathy A.A.); Caledonian Angling do personalised packages from the simple to the luxurious (0479) 82363.

Strathspey A.A. have a seven mile stretch with several permit issuers in Grantown; Mr and Mrs Hayward at Mortimers (0479) 2684 (£100 for seven days), Spey Valley Hotel (0479) 2942, Seafield Lodge Hotel (0479) 2152; Strathspey Estate, Grantown (0479) 2529 retain three beats available for weekly hire by parties; Nethybridge Hotel, Nethybridge (0479) 82203; Blairfindy Lodge Hotel, Glenlivet (0807) 590376 let the Carron/Laggan Beat for one week each year at £2500 plus VAT for five rods (can also arrange rods on the Avon); R.& R. Urquhart (0309) 72216; Aberlour A.C. have outlets in the town, for example: J.A.J. Munro in the High Street, Aberlour Hotel (0340) 871287; Lour Hotel (0340) 871224, Dowans Hotel (0340) 871488; the favourite, Craigellachie Lodge (0340) 881224; Linc Holdings Ltd (0205) 79444; Orton Estate (0343) 88240.

Loch Insh

The next feeder stream of any consequence is the Truim and then, at Newtonmore, the Spey is joined by the Calder, while below Kingussie we find the junction with the Tromie. Sadly, both the Calder and Tromie have been dammed for hydro power. Just above Kincraig it flows through Loch Insh whose shallow waters contain large quantities of trout and salmon, along with more than adequate supplies of pike and arctic char. The loch also contains a watersports centre with canoeing, windsurfing and sailing but this hasn't prevented some forty salmon being caught from approximately one hundred and twenty boat lettings. The largest of these, weighing in at an impressive 23½lb was taken by the Director of Loch Insh Watersports and Skiing Centre, Clive Freshwater (05404) 272, who will prove a fount of information and assistance for prospective visitors.

In the church at nearby Kincraig is St Eunan's bell. This masterpiece of celtic bronze work was carried in front of funeral processions fourteen hundred years ago. Below the loch are the junctions with the Feshie, another victim of afforestation, and the Druie. After passing through old villages it is quite a surprise to come to Aviemore with its clusters of chalets and modern hotels. Most incongruous. On our way to Fochabers we have often watched skiers coming down the runs and thought that skiing and salmon fishing would make an unusual biathlon event! A couple of miles further the A9 is the fork for the A95 and the quaintly named village Boat of Garten, so called because a ferry was the only means of crossing the river until the bridge was built.

The Nethy & the Dulnain

The next tributaries to join the Spey are the Nethy and Dulnain. Strathspey Angling Association has twelve miles of the River Dulnain. This is first class salmon fishing and also offers sea-trout, grilse and brown trout. As one would expect, it is fly-only except when the water is high, when spinning is allowed. Permits at a cost of £100 a week may be had from Mortimers in Grantown (0479) 2684 but you have to be staying locally.

After this we journey on to Grantown-on-Spey. This is the seat of Clan Grant and the capital of Strathspey. Although a popular tourist resort it is also well known to fishermen for it is here that Arthur Oglesby (who has probably forgotten more about salmon fishing than most of us will ever learn!) runs his excellent fishing courses. From Grantown to the estuary is the best fishing on the Spey with a succession of big deep holding pools broken by stretches of white water rapids. These pools can be deceptively dangerous and the greatest possible care should be taken when wading. Due to the fact that the river is so fast, the slightest slip can produce tragic results. There are far too many fishing accidents and while it may be tempting to wade a little further so that one can cover more water it is just not worth the risk.

The Avon

At Ballindalloch the Spey is joined by the Avon, known as the Aan by locals. To whisky drinkers the Avon is famous for its tributary the Livet, source of that lovely malt, Glenlivet. Because the Avon's source is in the granite and quartz slopes of the Cairngorms it is crystal clear and so demands a careful approach to avoid alerting the fish. The Ballindalloch beats are prime salmon fishing, especially Junction Pool which has also produced a notable 8lb brown trout. There are many famous names hereabouts, Upper Pitchroy, Lower

Pitchroy, Phonas Water, Knockando, Laggan and Carron, Wester Elchies Kinermony, Aberlour, Easter Elchies and Craigellachie. All are superb fishing but are expensive as well. In 1989 a mile of north bank fishing on Faster Elchies which had six named pools, was put on the market at an asking price of £900,000!

At Craigellachie, you can watch salmon and sea-trout running the rapids to Bridge Pool by standing on Telford's bridge. A mile or so downstream the Spey is joined by another stream whose name is well known to whisky drinkers, for the Fiddich is the home of Glenfiddich. It was the steep wooded sides of this valley, combined with the need to be able to cover the big pools, that led to the development of Spey casting. This method keeps the line in front of you at all times and is worth learning as it can come in useful on many other rivers.

The Gordon Arms Hotel at Tomintoul (0807) 580206 can offer guests two miles of fishing on the Avon at £17.50 a day, £90 for six days. Also there is the Richmond Arms Hotel (0807) 580209 which can offer guests fishing on over six miles of this gin-clear water at a cost of £135 a week. R.G.Heape Esq. at the Ballindalloch Estate Office (0807) 500205 can offer fishing on six miles of the Avon. This water averages 166 salmon and 226 sea-trout a season. Both the Gordon Arms and the Richmond Arms can offer fishing on the Livet. If you're under fourteen, permits to fish the long stretch of the Fiddich leased by Mortlach Angling Club may be had for £4 a day from TV Services in Dufftown (0340) 20527. Any older than that and you can expect to pay £7.

The Lossie
A few miles west, along the coast, we find Lossiemouth and the River Lossie. This river is overshadowed by its famous sisters the Spey and the Findhon but is the type of water that offers the occasional salmon at a modest cost. It is also a good sea-trout water for, while salmon average around 150 per season, sea-trout catches in recent years have varied between 1179 and 3166. Summer is the time for sea-trout and autumn for salmon. As it flows through arable land the bed of the river is muddy and pools tend to be small and deep. The course of this river from its source in Seven Sisters Spring to the Moray Firth is some thirty-four miles. On its journey it skirts the town of Elgin. Here you can see the ruins of the cathedral known as the Lantern of the North. This term does not derive from evangelical fame but the fact that it was repeatedly burnt to the ground! Permits to fish the upper waters may be had for £10 a season from Mr W. Macdonald, President of the Dallas Angling Association (0343) 89367 provided you are staying in the parish. Incidentally, salmon do get up this far if there has been enough water for them to ascend the rocks at Kellas. A little way south of Elgin is Glen Latterach Reservoir (0343) 86234, where a full day's bank fishing (with no bag limit) will cost only £2.60.

The Findhorn
Continuing west along the A96 brings you to Forres and the River Findhorn. This is top quality salmon fishing in beautiful surround-

ings. Many years ago the then Earl of Moray netted Sluie Pool and took over 1300 salmon in one night—an early demonstration of the detrimental effect of netting. The course of the river was much changed by the tremendous floods of 1829 when the river rose by over fifty feet in places causing widespread loss of life and livestock. It still rises very quickly when in spate and can rise by as much as two feet in ten minutes, so do be careful. The river's source in the Monadhliath Mountains is some sixty miles from the Moray Firth. Apart from the occasional conifer plantation, the river is very open down to Dulsie Bridge. Below here, the river thunders for some twenty miles through a gorge with sheer sides over two hundred feet high in places. The river relies on snow melt to maintain its level and this cold water usually stops fish running beyond the gorge before May. However spring fishing in the gorge can produce twenty and even thirty-pound fish. July is the time for grilse and as one would expect September is the best time for the upper river. It is a hard river to get on and you may find yourself on a long waiting list. The following may, however, be able to help you. J. Mitchell, Tackle Shop at Forres (0309) 672936 has access to private beats on one and a half miles at a cost varying from £200 to £300 per week per rod. Cawdor Estates (0667) 7666 let some of their beats. Mr D. McConnell of Moray Estates Office (0309) 672269 has a waiting list but serious enquiries for the future will be considered. Logie Estates (0309) 611208 lets beats at a cost of £935 per week for four rods, though there is a waiting list. R.& R. Urquhart (0309) 672216 let the Coulmony Beat at a cost of £50 per rod per day. Muckrach Lodge Hotel (0479) 85257 at Dulnain Bridge has two miles on one bank. This water holds four rods and the cost of a day's fishing is £30 a day and a ghillie is available.

The Nairn

A few miles to the west lies the River Nairn. This is an area rich in history. Here you will find Clava with its Druidical remains, Jacobite ghosts on Culloden Moor, and Cawdor Castle—immortalised in Shakespeare's *Macbeth*. The source of the river is high in the mountains, south of Loch Ness. Parts of the upper river suffer from salting but downstream there are many good deep holding pools, although the bankside bushes and trees can cause a few casting problems. However, being a narrow river it is not too difficult to cover the water. May and June are the best months for sea-trout fishing which can be superb, while August and September are best for salmon. It is a productive river, and though spring runs are not what they were, salmon are caught in March and April. S. Newbould Esq., of the Nairn District Salmon Fishery Board (0667) 53495 may be able to help you get a day on one of the private beats. Nairn Angling Association has eight miles of fishing upstream from the harbour. Permits for this water cost £10 a day or £35 a week and may be had from Pat Fraser, Radio, TV & Sports Shop, Nairn (0667) 53038. Clava Lodge Holiday Homes (0463) 790228 have a mile and a quarter of the south bank, costing £4 per rod per day.

Lochindorb

Should you not be lucky enough to get on one of these rivers, you might care to have a day's trouting on Lochindorb. Bank fishing is free but is only permitted on the north eastern quarter of the shoreline where the public road runs immediately adjacent to the loch. There are six boats for hire, available for a morning, afternoon or evening for £5. Hire of a boat from 8.00am to 5.00pm costs £9 and a full day—8.00am to 10.00pm—costs £10. Contact Mrs Young (0309) 651270 for details. Lochindorb means 'lake of the small fish', and the wild brownies here average between a half and three quarters of a pound. The loch is self-stocking but has relatively poor feeding with the result that there are large numbers of small trout present. For this reason there is no restriction on size of trout killed. With a breeze from the south or west rippling the surface you will do well to fish a team of dark pattern flies—good baskets may result.

Loch Morlich

Slightly better fish averaging around the one pound mark can be caught on Loch Morlich. This is near Aviemore so don't expect good catches until the snow melts and the water warms up. May is the recommended month. At three quarters of a mile long, it fishes particularly well from the bank but don't discount hiring a boat as trout up to two and a half pounds are regularly caught. The loch is shallow, with fish covering the entire area and the loch also has a watersports facility. Permits cost £3.10 a day or £11.50 a week (£1.50 and £6 junior prices) and can be had from the Forestry Commission Warden (0479) 861271 and the Loch Morlich Watersports Centre (0479) 861221. The manager of the watersports centre is a keen fisherman himself and will gladly point you in the direction of other lochs he fishes.

One of the obvious but nevertheless perilous hazards of spring fishing is that grand old British institution, the weather! Ocean racing has been compared to standing under a freezing cold shower while tearing £50 notes and the same could be said of spring fishing—hopefully the notes would be of a smaller denomination. While March can produce times when shirt sleeves are the order of the day it can be and often is, bitterly cold and naturally January and February are less hospitable. Yet being British we think nothing of it and are prepared to pay large sums of money for the pleasure of being frozen to the marrow! There is often a howling gale either blowing straight into one's face or down one's neck just to make casting that bit more challenging. To add to the pleasure there may be rain or sleet coming down the valley in almost horizontal sheets. But of course there is always the chance of a fish, providing one's hands are not too numb to play him.

The Ythan

The river Ythan (pronounced eye-than) is truly a peach of a river for it used to be famous for its pear-mussels and it is believed that the large pearl in the crown of Scotland came from the river. It is also one of the best known sea-trout fisheries and catch figures more than justify its reputation. Added to this, it is one of the few rivers where salmon are on the increase. From its source in a spring-fed well in a schoolmaster's garden at Strabocie to the estuary at Newburgh the Ythan flows through about thirty-one miles of rich agricultural land. Newburgh is less than fifteen miles north of Aberdeen which with its airport makes fishing in this area very accessible for us and European fishermen. The airport has daily services from Paris and Amsterdam so don't be surprised if some of your fellow rods are French or German or Swiss as they know this is the finest sea-trout fishing in Europe and you can't keep quiet about something as good as the Ythan.

Such is the fame of the estuary fishing that the river itself tends to be overloaded, but those in the know are aware that there is good fishing to be had here at a reasonable cost. Fyvie Angling Association has three miles of the upper river where a day's fishing up until 31st August costs £5. Permits are available from the Vale Hotel, Fyvie (0651) 891376. The Buchan Hotel at Ellon (0358) 20208 has a mile at £10 a day and the Aberdeen Angling Association also has some water. All netting has been stopped for over ten years now, and if the salmon runs continue increasing the prospects for the future are excellent.

For most the Ythan means estuary fishing. This of course is tidal water and so not so dependent on rainfall as further upstream. At high tide it is rather like a lake and then at low tide it changes into a small river. Here you will see sea-trout splashing and crashing about all over the water; a sight which is sure to get the pulse racing! The water is fished from both bank and boat depending on the state of the tide. On an incoming tide, especially when it is half way up, most rods will prefer to fish from a boat while bank fishing is at its best from when the tide begins to ebb. There are seventeen pools and fishing is by fly or spinner. Fly is the most popular method but it will often be presented on a spinning rod because of the need to cast a fairly long line. Also there is quite a lot of weed which is much easier to remove when using spinning tackle. Popular flies for traditional fly fishing include Peter Ross, Dunkeld, Zulu, Golden Butcher and the special Ythan fly of Eddie Forbes, the fishery manager who has done so much to improve things. Most spinners will use an Ythan Terror which is an imitation minnow of blue and silver with some feathers on the end. This water is owned by the Udny and Dudwick Estate and has recently been leased for a twenty-one year period on a time share basis which can if required include a cottage. Ythan Valley Fisheries (0358) 689052 will be able to give you further information on this scheme and let you know if there is a spare day or week. Day permits for the eleven-acre fishery, three miles north west of Ellon, cost £12 per day, with reductions for OAPs, juniors and larger parties. Some may say statistics are boring, but this water has a record of 17lb and 10lb plus fish are regularly taken. There was of course the day in 1953 when two rods had sixty-three fish for 169lb in two and a half hours! The average is two pounds, but these silver tornados will feel three times that weight and they fight like demons. Just to complete this fishing paradise the area is a nature reserve and bird sanctuary with large colonies of eider duck.

The Deveron

While quite a lot of the Spey is difficult to get on, the Deveron which is twenty miles or so east is much more accessible to the visiting fisherman. The river is some sixty miles from its source at the foot of Hill of Three Stanes to the coast at Banff and Macduff. Unusually for a river of this size there are no lochs in the system and, so being a spate river, rain can play an important part in the fisherman's luck. However it is not that chancy for in an average year it will produce at least 1000 salmon and a similar figure for sea-trout, while a good year will yield 2500 salmon and 3000 sea-trout. It is also a big fish water which produced a fifty-six-pounder in 1920, but even this was eclipsed by Mrs Morrison's magnificent sixty-one pounder in 1924. The fish in recent years may be of more modest proportions but within the last five years there has been a thirty-four-pounder and quite a few over twenty pounds, while the average is around ten pounds.

From its source the Deveron flows to Carbrach village after which it rushes through the gorge formed by the steep banks of Meikle Firbriggs and Daugh of Corinacy. It is then joined by Black Water and flows through Glenfiddich Lodge Beat, Lesmurdie and Beldorney (which averages sixty salmon per season). The latter is let by Bell Ingram of Aberdeen (0224) 644272 at £110-£130 per rod per week. Next come the Edinglassie and Invermarkie beats and the Huntly Angling Association water. Salmon fishing on these upper beats is fairly dependent on water levels but there is very good trouting to be had. Brown trout of 3lb and more are often caught and there are a few rainbows which have escaped from the fish farms. Best bets fly-wise include Gold and Dunkeld.

At Huntly (the start of superb salmon fishing on the lower beats) the Deveron is joined by the Bogie. This tributary which rises near Rhymie village offers good fishing for the salmon and sea-trout on their way to the spawning grounds in the headwaters. Then there are the Huntly Lodge, Castle Hotel, Corniehaugh (with its famous Still Pool) and Avochie beats which regularly produce salmon of the 15-20lb class. The Castle Hotel at Huntly (0466) 792696 has one and a half miles of double-bank fishing on which hotel guests have priority. The cost varies between £10 and £15 per day, and £40 and £150 a week, depending on the time of year. The Huntly Angling Association (0466) 792291 can offer fishing on six miles of both the Deveron and the Bogie at £30 a week, £40 a month or £50 a season—a day permit costs £15 but must be bought and used on the same day. At Inverisla the river is joined by the Isla which attracts few spawning fish as upriver access is difficult. The next beats downstream are Woodsie, Conieclugh, Rothiemay Castle, Upper Mayen, Mayen House, Redhill and Carronhaugh. The weir at Connieclugh halts the passage of fish when water temperatures are low and several large fish have been taken here. Rothiemay has the well known Sunnybrue pool and both this beat and Mayed can be fished by guests of the Forbes Arms Hotel (0466) 81248 at a cost of between £5 and £25 a day according to season.

Continuing our piscatorial voyage downstream we come to the Glennie, Turtory Ardmeallie, Church, Boat of Tortory, Marnoch Lodge and Euchrie beats. Noted pools here include Falconers, Bridge and Islands. Then it is on to beats such as Netherale, Carnousie, Forglen, Mountblairy, and the excellent Montcrofter. In 1987 Netherale produced a superb sea-trout of 14lb and Mountblairy as well as yielding The Fish (61lb), has also produced the best fish in recent years. Below Turriff the flow of the river is reduced due to abstraction for drinking water and some of the lower pools can silt up. However, the District Fishing Board is doing its best to clear them.

Finally the river flows into the sea between the towns of Banff and Macduff. Recently fishing has been fairly poor here, especially in summer, when water is low and an over abundance of weed growth prevails. As one would expect with a river of this size there are a number of owners and the following may also be able to help you. Jay-Tee Sports of Banff (0261) 815821 issues permits at a cost of £5 per day and £10 per week (Monday to Friday) for the Banff and Macduff Angling Association Water. Sea-trout here average at 1½lb-3lb, and there is a bag limit of twenty per day. Tickets for the Turriff Angling Association (fly-only) are available from Ian Masson Fishing Tackle (0888) 62428 at a weekly cost of £50. In the spring the Association has five private beats where a day will cost between £6 and £10. The Drummuir Estates (0542) 81225 water is usually booked well ahead but some spring lets are available and it may be possible to get a day later on in the season; the cost of a week here for four rods varies between £215 and £345. Salar Management Services (0667) 55355 let the Avochie Beat and Scotia Sporting Services may be able to help with other beats. The County Hotel in Banff (0261) 25353 can arrange fishing for guests. If you prefer to take a cottage Mr G. Manson of Huntly (0466) 792482 may be able to help and also looks after eight beats of the middle stretch where the cost varies between £5 and £27 a day. A limited number of weekly tickets occasionally become available due to post-Easter cancellations. The Montcrofter Fishings are handled by Savills in Edinburgh (031) 226 6961. Good trout flies are March Brown, Black Pennell, Grouse and Claret and Greenwells Glory, while favourite salmon flies include the Stouts Tail, Garry Peg and Munro Killer.

The Don

The Don flows into the North Sea at Bridge of Don which is just north of Aberdeen and the Dee. Despite their proximity the two rivers are very different in character for while the Dee is one of the great Highland spate streams, the Don wends its way at a leisurely pace through water meadows and good farmland rather like a southern chalk stream. It used to be said that 'a mile o' Don's worth two of Dee unless it be for fish or tree'—a reference to the plantations on the upper Dee. It is perhaps unfair to compare the fishing, for few rivers can compete with the Dee and the Don is certainly among the finest salmon and trout streams of Europe, particularly now that the nets have been bought off. It is also one of the few rivers which still has a good spray run. Trout fishing begins in April, with a heavy run of fish in September and October.

This is another area that is rich in history and you will tread the same roads as that pioneer of Highland roads, General Wade, the brilliant but ill-fated supporter of Charles I. Monymusk House used to have a relic of St Columba that was carried in front of the Scottish Army at the Battle of Banockburn in 1314. The spectacular ruins of Kildrummy Castle, a victim of the 1715 Jacobite rising, bear mute witness to the capture of Robert the Bruce's brother in 1306, while Pictish cairns are evidence of an even older civilisation.

There are some sixty-three beats on this river whose source is Well of Don on Little Geal Charn in the far off Grampian Mountains. Its head-waters are fast flowing but below Inchmore its progress starts to become more sedate. In this beautiful moorland setting you can hear the cry of the golden plover and watch pied wagtails. At Cock Bridge it crosses the A939 which can often be blocked by snow in winter and here it sheds the Highland burn character of its infancy and becomes a more mature river. The Colquhonnie Hotel at Strathdow (0975) 651210 has seven beats on which a days salmon fishing can be had for £15 and a day's trouting costs £7. An added attraction of the Don is that it is one of the best trout streams anyone could wish for. Trees may test our casting abilities but in the water beneath their leafy shade lie brown trout—frequently over 2lb. There is also a hatchery at Stathdon which releases 750,000 fly a year into the headwaters to ensure good fishing for the future. Near Candacraig House is the Pot of Poldullie, which is the favourite pool for trout fishermen and can produce lovely 3lb plus brownies. Then it is on to Deskry and Glenbucket Castle. At Glenkindie are the ruins of Towie Castle and the Glenkindie Arms (0975) 641288 whose beat costs £10 a day for salmon fishing or £6 for trout. Downstream are the Kildrummy Fishings; managed by Mr T. Hillary (0975) 571208, this is one of the best upper Don salmon beats and costs £10 for a daily permit. Tickets are also available form the Kildrummy Castle Hotel (0975) 571288.

At Bridge of Alford the river opens out and becomes a lady of more majestic proportions. Permits for here may be had for £8 or £4 a day (depending on whether salmon or trout is the quarry) from the Wardens office of the Grampian District Council (0975) 562107. Retaining the municipal theme, Gordon District Council (0467) 20981 control the Haughton Fishings at Alford, with a daily salmon permit costing £11 for an adult between May and September, £5.50 for a child. For the rest of the season daily tickets cost £13 and £6.50 respectively. W. R. Murray of 27 Main Street (0975) 562366 also handle booking for the Moonhaugh House beat which holds three rods—advance booking is recommended. Just below are the Castle Forbes and Monymusk waters. It is no coincidence that Castle Forbes was once known as *Putachie* (gaelic for trout), as many consider these waters with the famous Dam Pool to be the best trout fishing in Scotland. Forbes Estate Office (09755) 62524 has five beats where trout fishing may be had for £7.50 a day or £45 a week. A week's salmon fishing costs between £90 and £120 plus VAT, depending on the time of season. Locals and visitors staying in the area can get a £5 reduction on the price of a daily salmon permit, which otherwise costs £25. Forbes Estate Office do not offer a season ticket. The Grant Arms Hotel at Monymusk (0467) 7226 offers over ten miles of salmon and trout fishing on the Monymusk Estate water at £22 a day or £95 per rod per week. All red salmon must be returned to the river, as must trout under eight inches. The hotel is run by Colin Hart, a great fisherman, and its water includes the well known Paradise Wood.

It's downstream again to Kenmay where Messrs J.J. Watson (0467) 20321 issue permits for Inverurie Burgh Water at £10-£12 a day (£6 Trout only)—they can also arrange for you to fish the Manar beat for between £10 and £12 per day, and the Ardmurdo Beat at £8 per day for two visitor rods. Sunday fishing is allowed on the River Ury. On the Kintore, J. Copland (0467) 32201 can arrange salmon and trout fishing by the day at around £11 or £32 for a week with children, OAPs and disabled people paying half price. In Aberdeen, J. Somers & Son of The Tackle Shop issue permits for the town's Angling Association's ten miles of water at £15 a day for salmon and £4 a day for trout.

Among others who may be able to help you is Mr McIntosh (0975) 651302 who lets the Tornashean Water. The Banchory office of Strutt & Parker (0330) 24888 lets the Tillypronie Estate water and cottages are available. Mrs Petrie (0975) 571342 issues daily permits at £10 a day for salmon, £6 for trout. The gamekeeper Mr Steven Sharpe can arrange for you to fish a good hill loch for £12 a day including a boat. Kemnay Fishings can be contacted through Mrs

Milton (0467) 42220 and offer daily salmon permits for £12 and trout for £6. The sporting agencies may also be able to help. Macsport in Kildrummy (0975) 571377 have two miles where a day costs £20 plus VAT. Ian Black of Meadowland Sporting (0224) 724286 can also arrange fishing on the Dee and mixed sporting holidays. Scotia Sporting Agency (0339) 886891 have access to Don and Deveron beats where the cost ranges from £20 to £50 a day.

The lower river tends to suffer from pollution and poaching, but the latter wouldn't happen if the fish weren't there so don't ignore it! Popular salmon flies for the Don are Munro Killer, Stoats Tail, Harry Mary, Shrimp Fly, General Practitioner and Garry Dog, while one of those big brownies may be tempted by a March Brown or Greenwells Glory.

Grampian Waters

There are not many lochs in the area and the only one of any size is Loch Strathbeg. There is no bank fishing on the loch, but a day with a boat can be had for £6 for one person, £7 for two people, or £8 for three from the Post Office in Crimond (0346) 32229. Sadly, the quality of fishing here has deteriorated in recent years and fishermen who are more concerned with the day's catch are turning to some of the excellent stocked waters in the area. Crimongate Fishery (0346) 32203 is five miles south of Fraserburgh off the B9033 and has a six-acre lake well stocked with brownies and rainbows in a lovely rural setting. A full day's fishing, with a five fish limit, will cost £15. A short journey west, meanwhile, will bring you to Fedderate Reservoir. This is a 250 acre loch which is amply stocked with rainbow and brown trout. If you are not lucky enough to fish the estuary water at Newburgh you can console yourself with a day on Ythan Valley Fisheries' eleven-acre lake, which is also stocked with rainbows and brownies and is only a few miles upstream at Ellon.

In the earlier part of the nineteenth century few people visited Scotland and before the age of the railway or reasonable road surfaces, large areas were inaccessible. However, Queen Victoria's purchase of the Balmoral Estate was largely responsible for changing public attitudes and the novels of Sir Walter Scott, with their talk of daring deeds and descriptions of magnificent scenery that awaited the visitor, added the romantic flavour that the Victorians enjoyed so much. Osborne on the Isle of Wight may have been a popular holiday resort for the Royal Family but it was Balmoral that held the special place in Victoria's heart. 'It seems like a dream', wrote the Queen, 'to be here in our dear highland home again. Every year my heart becomes more fixed in this Paradise.'

The Dee

From the wells of Dee, some four thousand feet above sea level in the Cairngorms, to the sea at Aberdeen the course of the Dee is some eighty-five miles long. As with the Spey, snow melting at its source helps to give and maintain good spring and early summer water levels. This is one river that does not suffer from being hydro-ised and there are no natural or artificial obstructions until we reach the Linns above Braemar. The fishing is even better now that the Atlantic Salmon Conservancy Trust has bought out the netting stations at the mouth. As a result several beats have broken all past records and the sea-trout catch has trebled in three years. There are over fifty miles of first class salmon fishing on this exceptionally clear water which still has a good spring run. This, of course, is excellent news for fish and fishermen but what of the more distant predators? Today, catches in all our waters are vastly affected by deep sea netting. This is particularly commonplace in the migratory routes near the Faroes, Greenland and the like. It is a desperate situation and little seems to be being done. Life goes on however and in our simple way, rod in hand, let us return for a morning's fishing.

The Dee tumbles down from its lofty birthplace through Glen Dee. Here we find Chest of Dee where the river crashes down a steep staircase of broken rocks and pools. After a heavy rain or snow melt you can hear the river's angry roar for some distance. Next on to White Bridge where salmon rest after their fight through the Linn of Dee. There is a path from the road to the Linn and you can watch salmon as they leap or lie in the pools gathering strength for their continuing journey. Below the Linn, the Dee widens into a broad crystal fed stream with Scots pine adorning its banks. Nearby is Mar Lodge, built by Queen Victoria for her eldest daughter, Princess Louise and her husband the Duke of Fife. Braemar Castle is another interesting edifice. It was burnt to the ground twice in under thirty years; firstly, in 1689 as a result of the Earl of Mar's failure to support the Jacobite cause and then in 1716 by the Duke of Argyll's forces because the Earl had led the Jacobite troops at the battle of Sheriffmuir. The Earl was known as 'Bobbing Johnnie' for his habit of changing sides, but he always seemed to end up on the losing one. At Invercauld Robert Louis Stevenson wrote most of *Treasure Island.* Nearby, Queen Victoria leased Gordon House until she bought it in 1848 and employed the services of the local architect in Aberdeen. After some rebuilding and enlarging, the house was renamed Balmoral.

Ballater is a favourite place for visiting fishermen for nearby are such famous beats as Birkhall, Monaltrie, Glenmuick and Abergeldie. At Countrywear in Bridge Street (03397) 55453 you can see the cast of the famous 42lb fish caught by Arthur Wood in 1926. As well as inventing the greased line method of fishing, this great sportsman grassed 3490 salmon from the Cairnton Fishings beat between 1913 and 1934. Countrywear also issue permits for the Mar Estate Water. This beat which is some six and a half miles long holds four rods and costs £20 per rod per day. They can also arrange for you to fish the Glebe Pool beat for £15 a day. Between Ballater and Aboyne the Dee is joined by three tributaries—the Gairn, the Muick and the Water of Tanar. The banks and surrounding hills are thick with Scots pine, birch, alder, willow and oak. Timber used to be a major Deeside industry with logs being floated down river to the Aberdeen mills. This must have played havoc with the fishing. Below Aboyne the river loses the impetuosity of its highland youth and flows gently through fertile farmland. Around Banchory, where the Dee is joined by the Feugh are such well known beats as Cairnton, Woodend, Commonty, Blackhall, Crathie, Invery, Park and Drum. Banchory is the centre for fishing the lower Dee and here you will find the Invery House Hotel (0330) 24782 which can arrange for guests to fish the Commonty beat at a cost of between £350 and £520 plus VAT per week, including a ghillie. In 1991 an Austrian doctor staying at the hotel had two twenty-pounders, and one of twenty-six pounds. The hotel also has sea-trout fishing on the Feugh which flows through its grounds. The Banchory Lodge Hotel (0330) 22625 has three quarters of a mile of double-bank fishing for guests at the same price as Invery House, also including the services of a ghillie.

Between 8000 and 13,000 salmon are caught every season on this superb river where the average fish weighs 8lb. An unusual feature is that all but six of the forty-five beats are single-bank and it is one of the very few rivers where spring fishing is still the best. Although spinning may be permitted most rods will prefer the fly and a Blue Charm, Logie, General Practitioner or Jeannie may do the trick. As one would expect with fishing of this quality, it is not an easy river to get on. However the sporting agencies may be able to help you. Graham Scott at Highland Trophy (0339) 886465 has access to various beats where the cost ranges between £250 and £1000 per week. Meadowhead Sporting (0224) 724286 and Macsport of Kildrummy (0975) 571377 may also be able to help. Glen Tanar Sport and Leisure (03398) 86451 normally let their water on a weekly or fortnightly basis but day permits are available in August and they also have a well stocked ten-acre loch. If your ambition is to have your own fishing then time shares on the Ardoe and Myrtle beats are for sale through Savills' Edinburgh office (031) 226 6961.

The North Esk

Some forty miles South of Aberdeen on the A92 we find the town of Montrose and the North and South Esk. The North Esk is a fine river which now that some netting has been suspended is likely to improve. Actually, so far only two netting stations have been discontinued and those only temporarily, however, it is hoped that this will become permanent and that other nets will follow. The sources of the river are the waters Mark and Lee, two streams which come tumbling down the Grampian Mountains to join forces at Invermark and form the North Esk. It then flows through the beautiful heather and rowan landscape of Glen Esk and here you will find beats such as Invermark and Millden. The Dalhousie Estate Office (0356) 624566 lets the Millden Fisheries beat where the weekly cost for three rods ranges from £75 to £660 and day tickets are sometimes available. The estate also lets well-appointed cottages which can sleep up to six.

Downstream lies Craigoshina and then it is on to Burn Loups and the Gannochy Estate (0356) 47331 water. This is usually let by the week but days are sometimes available. The Estate also has a number of cottages available. After Loups the river flows through fine farmland in the succession of long holding pools. The North Esk District Fishery Board has done a great deal to improve the river and Burn Loups is now the only obstacle fish face in the course of their run. The entrance to Glen Esk is guarded by Edzell Castle with its beautiful gardens of rambling roses and orderly box hedges. West Water—which with its good spawning grounds is an important feeder—joins the Esk at the famous Junction Pool which has produced many fine catches of salmon and sea-trout.

There are many well known beats such as Arnhall, Strachthro, Pert, Gallery, Morphie and Craigo to name but a few. However, this productive river which can often produce a fish on opening day is very popular and you may have to join the queue before casting a Blue Charm or Thunder and Lightning on this water. However, Mr G. Luke (0674) 73535 the secretary of the Montrose Angling Association may be able to sell you a permit at a cost of between £8 to fish their eleven and a half miles on a Thursday, Friday or Saturday as a guest of a member providing you can prove you are a whisky drinker and not a lager lout! Scotia Sporting Agency may be able to help with several beats while Joseph Johnston and Sons (0674) 72666 issue both daily permits and weekly lets. The Morphie Fishings have recently been time shared and a few units are still available from Savills (031) 226 6961. The North Esk is very much a spate river and as one would expect spring and autumn tend to be the best times. However, the summer months can see good runs of grilse and sea-trout depending on the water level. Sea-trout average around 2lb and salmon 9lb though twenty-pounders are caught every season.

The South Esk

The South Esk is also a spate river and as there are no feeder lochs in the system, the headwaters are of little interest to the fisherman. But it is a totally different matter after the White Water joins the river at the head of Glen Clova where some fine sport can be enjoyed. The Clova hotel (0575) 5222 has three miles of double-bank fishing which holds eight rods. Spinning and bait as well as fly are permitted on this water which costs £13 a day. Downstream from the glen there are some good holding pools and the river broadens out when it meets the Prosen Water just beyond Cortachy Castle. From here down to the Montrose basin is very good fishing, particularly for sea-trout which average two and a half pounds, but most seasons produce at least one six-pounder. Famous beats include Careston, Finavon, Kinnaird and House of Dun. One of the best stretches is the Finavon Castle Water. There are two miles of double-bank fishing and two and a half miles of single-bank divided into three beats, Castle, Indies and Balgarrock Meadows which share more than thirty pools and lies between them. The manager is Miss Dawn Darling (0307) 85344 and prices for these outstanding beats may be had on application. Mr H. Burness (0575) 73456 is the secretary of Kirriemuir Angling Club which has seven miles of double-bank fishing where a Dunkeld or Blue Charm may produce the magic tug. Spinning is also permitted and locals use a Toby, Devon or Mepps. The cost here is £50 a week or £10 a day but no day tickets are issued on a Saturday.

Lochs Nan Eun & Bainnie

These are two fine hill lochs, on which a day's fishing will be rewarded by a bag of up to a dozen hard fighting wild browns. Good flies for these lochs are Black Pennell, Soldier Palmer and Peter Ross tied on a size 12 or 14. Bainnie is a fairly level two and a half mile walk from the A93 just south of Braemar. The walk to Nan Eun is also fairly level, but it is nine miles! So it could be an idea to hire a four-wheel drive vehicle even though the last two miles are still on foot. The effort is well.worthwhile for the trout are genuinely wild and there are majestic Grampian peaks all round. Permits may be had from either the Invercauld Estate Office (0339) 741224 or the game keeper, Mr R. Hepburn (0250) 885206. The season for this fly only water is March 12th to August 11th and the cost is £5 a day or £25 for the season.

Despite the huge amount of research, all too little is known about the sea habits of the salmon. It is a commonly known fact that they return to the rivers of their birth to spawn, and this is where netting becomes an important factor. Stake nets are bad enough and it is encouraging to see how many of these are now being bought off, but it is difficult to avoid the feeling that the drift-net industry must shoulder a fair degree of responsibility. Huge nets six hundred yards long trap the fish on their return to spawning grounds. The north east coast drift net fishery employs just under five hundred people, while fishing in Scotland supports five thousand jobs and is valued at £50 million a year. So with up to £320,000 being asked for a week's time share on the Tay, isn't the fisherman entitled to expect a reasonable level of fish in the river? Something has got to be done and I urge you to support the associations which are trying to change this disturbing state of affairs.

The Tay

To see what the Tay can produce you only have to walk to Hardys in Pall Mall, for there in a case is a cast of THE fish. At 6.15pm on October 7th 1922 Miss G.W.Ballantine, spinning bait—a dace—was taken in Boat Pool on the Glendevine Water. Nearly two hours later (8.05pm to be exact) it was landed. In 1820 the Earl of Howe is said to have landed a fish of 69lb on the Tweed, but this is somewhat legendary and at 64lb Miss Ballantine's fish holds the official record. In April of the same year Major Baker Carr took seventeen fish in a day which varied in weight from 9lb to 30lb. Back in Victorian times the Duke of Atholl regularly used to take six or seven salmon before breakfast. But perhaps this is not surprising considering the catch records of the time. Take 1843 for example, when returns show that 35,126 salmon and 43,617 grilse were killed, and the river wasn't fished anything like as hard as it is nowadays. What a river!

Perth was formerly the capital of Scotland and was fortified by the Romans, who were so awestruck by the mighty Tay that they compared it to the Tiber. But, as Sir Walter Scott wrote in 'The Fair Maid of Perth':

> 'Behold the Tiber,' the vain Roman cried,
> Viewing the ample Tay from Baiglies side;
> 'But where's the Scot that would the vaunt repay,
> And hail the puny Tiber as the Tay?'

The Tay drains more than 2200 square miles of country and carries the largest volume of fresh water in the British Isles. It begins its 114 miles in the hills near Tyndrum on the west coast. Two feeder streams, the Dochart and Lochay, merge to become Fillan Water. This then tumbles past Crianlarich and on into Loch Dochart where, perched on an island, the ruins of Dochart Castle still keep watch over the narrow pass into the glen. It is joined by the wild waters of Benmore Burn as it threads its way though boggy ground and on to Loch Iubhair. Then it is on to the falls of Dochart at Killin which is on the western shore of Loch Tay. Salmon rarely ascend the falls until the temperature is right, which is not usually before May. Loch Tay is some fourteen miles long by three quarters of a mile wide and is over four hundred and fifty feet deep in places. Trout average three quarters of a pound but three and four-pounders are taken regularly, while big ferox lurk in its murky depths. The shallow areas of the east and west ends are probably the best fishing and, as on all big lochs, a ghillie is an indispensable asset. Trolling is likely to be the most successful method, especially in the spring when the average fish is a hefty 17lb. Above the western shore are the ruins of Finlarig Castle, seat of Black Duncan, the Earl of Orchy. The well preserved dungeons and beheading pit are ample evidence that the Earl lived up to his nickname. Overlooking the northern shore is the 3984 feet lofty eminence of Ben Lawers. From the summit of this mountain on a clear day you can see both east and west coasts. Its slopes are covered with rare mosses and lichens such as mossy cyphel, Alpine forget-me-not and campion.

The Ardeonaig Hotel (0567) 2400 is the only hotel on the south side of the loch and is halfway along the shoreline, yards from the ancient ruins of Mains Castle. It is the ideal place for a fishing holiday, as with one of the hotel's five four-rod boats you can cover both the east and west ends of the loch. Moreover, if you feel like a break from fishing you can always try the hotel's nine-hole golf course. Other fishing hotels are Clachgaig Hotel (0567) 2270 which has three boats and Croft-na-Caber (0887) 830236 which also has a water sports centre. Permits for a day's trouting can be had for £3 from the Kenmore Post Office (0887) 830200. The Kenmore Hotel (0887) 830205 has three boats for loch fishing and two miles of river fishing which is available to guests at £11 a day and non-residents at £16.25 a day. On January the 15th, which is the first day of the season, fishermen are piped down to the water and a bottle of whisky is cracked over the bows of one of the hotel's boats. Most rods will troll using Rapallas, Kynochs or Tobies. This method may not suit the purist, but on the other hand it does catch fish! Now that many of the downstream nets have been bought off and the Lochay has been improved, catches on the loch should improve in a few years time.

The Lyon

A short distance downstream from Kenmore is the junction with the River Lyon, one of the Tay's biggest tributaries. Like the Lochay this river has been hydro-ised and the dam at the eastern end of Loch Lyon prevents fish from reaching the loch and spawning the headwaters. The hydro scheme has, however, created some good deep holding pools and fish now spawn in the river's tributaries and its lower reaches, with the best fishing on the lower seven miles down to the junction with the Tay. Much work has been done to improve the Lyon in recent years. Spawning grounds have been improved and it is being stocked with fry. It is a superb river to fish with large deep holding pools, cascading falls, and white water runs.

There are some particularly attractive pools on the Fortinglass water and here in the churchyard you can see the oldest tree in Europe, a 3000 year old yew. Although the back end of the season is likely to be best, the Lyon also produces good springers. The Coshieville Hotel (0887) 830319 has the first one and a half miles of water above the junction. This water has six pools, taking four rods and a boat is available for fishing Castle Pool. A day's trouting costs £5 while salmon fishing varies between £10 and £15. Two and a half pound trout are not uncommon here. The Post Office House (0887) 866221 at Bridge of Balgie issues daily permits for fishing some of the upstream beats.

Between the junction with the Lyon and Aberfeldy are the Tay's Farleyer and Bolfracks beats. It was from here that the Black Watch began its road to fame and glory in 1740. Until that date it had primarily been used to keep the peace between feuding Highlanders. However, war with Spain had broken out and troops were needed. It was decided that the regiment should be force marched to London and rumour spread that they were destined for the West Indies. Travelling south of the border was a big enough wrench for men who had never left their homeland before, but the West Indies with their lethal fevers was the worst of possible fates (my how things change!). Some of the men deserted but those that were captured were shot in the Tower of London. However, the regiment was sent to Europe and at Fontenoy opposing officers dropped handkerchiefs to signal that fighting could commence.

At Aberfeldy, where the Urlar Burn joins the Tay, is the Farleyer House Hotel (0887) 20332 which can usually arrange fishing for guests, although it can be expensive. The Weem Hotel at Weem (0887) 20381 has privileged access to one and a half miles of good water for guests. If you think that all fishing on the Tay is expensive Mr and Mrs J. Garbutt of Grandtully (0796) 482207 have a pleasant surprise for you. They have a mile of single bank fishing above the Kinnaird beat where the cost of a day is £7. Now you may think that at this price the fishing must be mediocre at best and that a £40 a day stretch is likely to make more productive use of your landing net. If you do, you are missing a great opportunity, for a twenty-five pounder was recently caught on this water and the average weight is around ten pounds.

The Tummel

As one might expect with such a big river as the Tay, many of its tributaries are fine salmon rivers in their own right and one such is the Tummel, which joins the Tay at Logierait. Although its character has been effected by the hydro dam at Faskally, this is good fly water and April sees some fantastic rises of trout to hatching olives. To whet your appetite there is a fish pass with a viewing gallery at Pitlochry. The Angling Club here has the fishing of the right bank and those hoping to fish are asked to write to the Secretary. Alternatively, you could try the Atholl Estate Office (0796) 81355 which has fishing on the Tummel, Garry and Tilt, or stay at the impressive East Haugh House Hotel (0796) 473121 which has leasing arrangements on various beats of the same three rivers and also the Shee. Salmon prices vary between £35 and £100 per day and trout between £2 and £5.

Much of the Tay has wooded banks and, added to its considerable width, it is often much more practicable to fish it from a boat. While it may be tempting for the bank fisherman to wade so as to cover that little bit extra water (which is sure to hold a fish), wading can be extremely dangerous as this is a fast flowing river and the pools can be very deep. The conifers surrounding Dunkeld House are thought to be more than two hundred years old and are particularly striking. The town in medieval times was the religious centre of Scotland and you can see the tomb of Robert II in the cathedral. To most fishermen, Dunkeld is synonymous with the fly of the same name. This brightly coloured little temptress has proved the undoing of many a fat trout, and one that has personally brought a degree of luck. The river is joined here by the Braan whose Black Linn falls are impassable to salmon. Just below the town are the Birnam Woods of *Macbeth* fame, while downstream is Glendelvine where Miss Ballantine caught her fish. Now that some of the nets have been bought off, Dunkeld is seeing much better runs of seatrout. Dunkeld & Birnam Angling Association have two combined beats and day permits are available for £2 from Kettles of Dunkeld (0350) 727556. A good place to stay is the Stakis Dunkeld House Hotel (0350) 727771 which has two miles of double-bank fishing. The hotel is in the middle of its four beats, which hold twelve rods and the services of two ghillies are available. Hotel guests understandably have priority but bookings from non-residents are welcome. Mr M.C. Smith (0350) 727593 lets the Dalguise Salmon Fishings, which are one and a half miles of double-bank at between £20 and £35 a day according to season. Not far downstream is the Kinloch House Hotel (0250) 884 237 which can arrange spring and summer fishing for guests on two beats, where the cost ranges from £60 to £200 a day.

Below Glendelvine are Kercock and Meikleour, after which the Tay is joined by the Isla at Islamouth. This is superb fishing but very expensive! The Tower of Lethendy fishings at Meikleour have recently been timeshared on ninety-nine year leases with a top price of £350,000, and that's just for one week. Both the Isla and its tributary the Ericht, which has good spawning beds have a justly deserved reputation for producing excellent fishing. Richmond & Co. (0382) 201964 manage the Gauldry beat on the Isla where a week for four rods costs £400. Also on the Isla, Mrs Henderson (0828) 7226 can arrange for you to fish about one and a half miles of single bank, which has four named pools at between £15 and £25 per rod per day. Spinning tends to be best on the slack water here, but there are some nice runs which take the fly well.

On the Ericht, the Bridge of Cally Hotel (0250) 886231 water costs between £20 and £25 a day; Ian Stewart (0250) 872968 is the ghillie and can give you further details. Or you can try Finlayson Hughes (0738) 30926 who let the Craighall Rattray beat where you can enjoy such pools as Witches, Cauldron and Pipers Cave. There is a tradition of spinning on the Tay, partly because of its size and also because it is an early spring river and spun baits allow you to get down better and fish the Tay water. But where streams and pools can be covered by fly it is well worth a try. Beats such as Islamouth and Benchil have excellent fly water. However, you will need a big rod, for although a fifteen-footer may cover some of the upper beats, an eighteen or twenty-footer will be needed for the bigger pools. On the big pools another alternative to spinning is *harling*. This involves trailing three lures on set lengths of line from a boat. With this method the boatman does all the work and the fisherman just has to wait until the rod bends and the reel plays its merry tune. This may seem boring but Miss Ballantine, to name but one, found it rather effective!

The lower beats are superb and very difficult to get on especially at prime times, unless you are lucky enough to be invited as a guest or happen to be a millionaire. The Tayside Hotel at Stanley (0738) 828249 has access to time shared beats from May to July, where a day can be had for £20. Perth District Council (0738) 439911 owns some fishing and, if you can prove you are a resident of this fair city you can purchase a permit at £5 for five years. If you can prove you live within fifteen miles of the city you are eligible to join the Perth and District Angling Club. Applications for membership can be had from the local tackle shops and the fishing on the club's water can be excellent and is great value compared to the expensive adjoining beats.

If conditions are favourable, just west of Pitlochry there is excellent loch fishing to be had on lochs Tummel, Rannoch and Dunalastaire Water, where you will find the Dunalastaire Hotel (0882) 2303. The eastern end of Rannoch is guarded by Schiehallion, 'The Fairy Hill of the Caledonians'. However, it is fat trout and not fairies that you will find here where the murky depths, more than 300 feet in places, hold quantities of large ferox—seven pounders are not uncommon. Much of the loch's banks are crowded with conifers and the shallower margins of the western shore are the best fishing areas. A day here with such flies as Greenwells Glory, March Brown or Blue Zulu should produce a good basket of three quarter pound brownies, while for the big ferox, trolling is the best method. The loch is fed by the outflow from Loch Laidon, which lies some six miles to the west and where a day spent fishing its attractive bays can produce twenty or more large bags of lively trout of between a half and three quarters of a pound. Loch Rannoch Hotel (0882) 2201 is a good place to stay for fishing these lochs or exploring Rannoch Moor, whose waterlogged peat with tufts of cotton grass and coarse sedges is alive with the calls of snipe, curlew and grouse. Permits for Loch Tummel are obtained from the Pitlochry Tourist Information Centre (0796) 472215 at £3 per day and £10 per week (trout, pike and perch only).

The Tay is a colossus among the waters of the world. It may have reported decreasing catches, and this is a worrying sign, but it is still a symbol of strength, power and beauty. Scotland is a land rich in scenic wonders and there are few more compelling sights than the waters of the Tay and her tributaries. There may be finer waters in Canada, Scandinavia or even Scotland but few, if any, have the stature of the Tay—a symbol of salmon and of Scotland.

Many scribes have pondered long and hard over the special appeal of loch fishing. One of the things I enjoy about fishing is getting away from the hustle and bustle of town life and being able to enjoy the solitude of the countryside. Standing in a line of fellow anglers fishing some supposed 'hot spot' is not my idea of fun. Don't misunderstand me, I have had many happy days on stocked water and enjoyed some good tussles with rainbows. However loch fishing is a totally different phenomenon. The fish may be small but they are wild and I would rather face a hard fighting half pounder than a number of one pound 'stockies' which often have little or no flavour to their flesh.

Loch Lomond

Having described one of the joys of loch fishing as being able to enjoy the quiet and solitude of the country you may think it inappropriate to discuss Loch Lomond. After all it is only a short distance from Glasgow and there is a main road along the whole of the western shoreline. It is also a major tourist attraction. However, Lomond is a big water covering some twenty-seven square miles and this, combined with its many small wooded islands, ensures that there is ample room for both tourist and fisherman. One of the fascinating aspects about Lomond is the difference in character between its north and south ends. This is principally because it is a product of the Ice Age. There is a geographical fault line running from Arden to Balmaha and the loch differs dramatically below the village of Luss. Above this point it is narrow, steep-banked and as deep as 450 feet in parts. South of Luss the loch broadens out and gets progressively shallower as you near Balloch at the southern end. This is important from a fishing point of view for, while twenty feet of water may suit sea-trout, salmon prefer much shallower water, a depth of between five and eight feet. The great banks of silt and sand such as Pilot Bank above Ross are the product of glacial deposits from the Ice Age.

As it is such a vast expanse of water, bank fishing is pretty unproductive and the only really practical method of fishing is from a boat, drifting gently between the islands. In medieval times mainlanders used the islands as a sanctuary for themselves and their livestock. This however, was no guarantee of safety from the marauding Norsemen. In 1263 King Haakon sailed his galleys up Loch Long and then carried them overland to Lomond—no mean feat! Here they were relaunched and the islands were systematically plundered. Several centuries later the islands were used to house drunkards and lunatics, but all is quiet now except for the piping of birds.

The most likely way of catching a salmon is to *troll.* This involves using three rods with two carrying lures some twenty-five yards behind the boat and a short stiff rod, usually called a poker, fishing some ten yards nearer in. The start of the season will see natural baits such as the golden Sprat and at the beginning of June, artificials like Rapallas and the Kynoch Killer are favoured. This method calls for some smart action when you get a take. The first thing to do is to head for deeper water, then to wind in the spare lures and start playing the fish, as rapidly as possible.

May sees the beginning of the fly season when a team of traditional flies such as Black Pennell, Peter Ross and Dunkeld will be used, for this is also good sea-trout water. Among the local favourites are the Turkey and Gold and the Burton. Dapping is also a popular technique but because Lomond is so big and regularly fished by the locals, you will find that everyone has their own method and their own favourite fly. Among the islands, Inch Moan and Inch Fad are popular but the best advice on a likely place will come from those who hire out the boats as they will know what's been happening. Macfarlane & Sons of Balmaha (0360) 87214 hire out boats at £12 a day for two people or £20 to include an outboard. More than two people will pay £14 or £25. April 13th 1991 was a lucky day for one of these boats which took a lovely twenty-seven pounder from the 'Stables', near Ross Priory. Permits and advice can also be obtained from The Balloch Hotel (0389) 52579, Ardlui Hotel (03014) 243 and The Tarbet Hotel (03012) 346. R.A. Clement & Co of Glasgow (041) 221 0068 issue permits on behalf of the Loch Lomond Angling Improvement Association. The cost of a day's ticket is £9 while a week is £27.

The Fruin and the Endrick

The Loch Lomond Angling Association is also responsible for fishing on the rivers Fruin and Endrick. Public access, however, is restricted to full members of the Association. A subscription ticket costs £115, together with a £25.54 joining fee. These permits cover salmon and trout; eight to twelve ounces is the average for trout which will be found all along the shores, though the northern end is likely to be more productive.

The source of the River Endrick is in West Stirlingshire and flows into the loch near Balmaha. The upper part of the river is not worth fishing for, although the salmon is a mighty leaper, no fish can ascend the ninety-foot Loup O'Fintry falls. Below the falls there are some good pools but downstream there are more falls, the Pot of Gartness, and salmon need the right level of water to ascend them. Below the Pot is the meeting with the Blane, which is the main tributary and the junction pool known as the Meetings of Lynn is a favourite spot. Below Drymen the river flows through rich pasture and woodland and can be a bit sluggish. It really requires a good spate to provide exciting fishing; but then pools such as Oak Tree and Coolies Linn can produce salmon of around 10lb and sea-trout which average around 2lb. It takes the right conditions to get fish into the river and many find that trolling on the loch by the mouth of the river can produce excellent results.

The Leven

Despite the mass of water in the loch, the Leven which connects it to the Clyde is relatively slow moving due to the barrage at Balloch.

As is to be expected from being so near a big city, the river is heavily fished. This is also because it can be very good as Mr S.Burgoyne will tell you, for in July 1989 he caught a magnificent sea-trout of 22lb 8oz. This river is also controlled by the Loch Lomond Angling Improvement Association and day tickets can be had for £12.50 while £57.50 is the cost of a season's ticket.

Loch Leven

Heading north over the Forth brings you to the start of the M90 and in a short while you are alongside Loch Leven. This water is world famous and many international fishing competitions are held here. Its reputation derives from the superb hard fighting qualities of its brownies which have been used to stock waters all over the world. It is fair to say that in recent years catches have fallen and also that the trout seem to feed off the bottom. This is a perplexing change and one which will surely keep the experts busy for some time. As a result of these developments many rods are now using sinking lines, but as most of the loch is shallow you don't have to go down too far. Despite such problems this is still one of the great trout waters and you will find that traditional small double-hook flies such as March Brown, Dunkeld, Invicta, Black Pennel and Soldier Palmer can be effective. One of the attractions of the loch is the size of the trout, for they average around one and a quarter pounds and three pounders are taken regularly. The best fish in recent years has been 6lb 6oz. It should also be noted that boats are essential on this water. Permits can be had from Loch Leven Fisheries at The Pier (0577) 863407, where you can also hire boats and it is a good idea to book in advance. The day is divided into two sessions; 10.00am to 6.00pm, which costs £21 and 6.30pm to 11.30pm for £28. There is an afternoon session (2.00pm to 6.00pm) for £14, and at weekends dawn (which can be 2.30am!) to 9.00am costs £24. The Loch is not only a tremendous water, it is also a most beautiful one. Imagine the scene as the sun comes up—you have fished hard and had good results, the occasional joke has rudely disrupted the lapping of the water on your boat. This is what life is about; a holiday with your head buried in the sand in Southern Spain is unlikely to evoke such gratifying memories. Make no mistake—to enjoy a dawn on Loch Leven is a memory you will treasure.

Continuing still further north on the M90 towards Perth brings you to Bridge of Earn. It is a mistake to regard the River Earn as a tributary of the Tay for it flows into the Firth below the tide. This is, however, not a bad salmon river and some say better than the Tay for sea-trout which average 2lb and can be over 7lb. The Earn flows out of Loch Earn which is a good water-sports centre. There is trout fishing on the loch and permits may be had from St Fillans and Loch Earn Head Post Office (0764) 685309 who can also hire you a boat. The cost of a

day's fishing on the loch is only £3 but that reflects the quality of the fishing. The lower river tends to be slow and sluggish but upstream from Kinkell Bridge at Strathallan it is a pleasing streamy river with some good pools. The Earn Angling Improvement Association has been doing sterling work to improve fishing here.

The river is now being stocked with native fish and all but two of the nets have been bought off. The fact that two miles were recently sold for £570,000 will give you some idea of the quality of the fishing. A day on the Lawers Estate Co. Ltd. (0764) 670050 water costs £50 and season tickets are available. This beat is a little awkward to reach but well worth the effort. Rather more affordable is the Crieff Angling Clubs water which costs £8 a day for salmon or £3 for trout (which can be excellent). Permits from Mr J.Boyd's newsagent shop in Crieff (0764) 653871 and it is advisable to book ahead for weekends as Sunday fishing is allowed.

The Forth & its Tributaries

Fly fishing on the River Forth? Incredulity would be the natural reaction of many a southerner brought up on images of factories discharging waste into the river. The ill-informed might argue that there was no point in going and that you might just as well try a day's salmon fishing on the Thames, as the result would be the same. How wrong can you be! In 1988 over 1000 salmon and grilse were taken from the Town Water at Stirling alone. The Scots really care about their fishing and a tremendous amount of work has gone into improving the rivers. The Forth is one of the great success stories and the river and its tributaries, the Teith, Allan and Devon, also have good runs of sea-trout. The good news story continues for the spring run is actually increasing. Opening day, February 1st 1991, produced a twenty-five pounder at Callander and April has seen several fish of around thirty pounds. A day's permit for the Forth costs £23.25 and a seasons ticket is £85 which strikes me as being good value for money. They may be had from Country Pursuits (0786) 834495.

Mr D.Crockart (0786) 473443 can also arrange a day for you on the Blue Bank Fishings on the Teith where the cost varies between £11 and £32 a day. James Bayne of Callander (0877) 30218 also issues permits for the Teith and the Town Water at a cost of £15 a day.

The Devon still suffers from some pollution, but this is reflected in the cost of £3 a day or £12 for a season and it can fish well in the Autumn—contact Devon Angling Association (0259) 215185.

The Allan, where a day costs between £10 and £25, is beginning to be very good for sea-trout and are increasing. Tickets may be obtained from McLaren Tackle (0786) 833530. In Bridge of Allan, meanwhile, Bridge of Allan Reservoir (0786) 834495 offers boat fishing for trout at £12 (boat hire covers two people).

Central Region Waters

There are a number of stocked fisheries in the area. Examples of enjoyable fishing available are Carron Valley Reservoir (0786) 442000 where a week day ticket costs £19.30 (£5.80 for the hire of a boat), Lake of Menteith (08775) 664 (the comfortable Lake Hotel), near Aberfoyle, where a full session's boat fishing costs £22 per boat, and Loch Dochart at the northern tip of Loch Lomond. Fishing here is either bank or boat and details can be obtained from either Muirlaggan Farm (0877) 4219 or Portnellau Lodge House (08383).

If you fancy a change from rainbows what about American book trout? Unless you have fished in the States, which has some great trouting areas like Montana, you may not have come across these fish before, but of all the stocked varieties they are the ones most likely to put up a memorable fight. There are two fisheries in the area which are stocked with them: Mill Dam and Loch Monzievaird and permits can be had for them from Kettles in Dunkeld (0350) 2556 and Mr Groot of Crieff (0764) 3963.

Oban to Kintyre

Despite its undoubted beauty, this is a region that has suffered from the demands of twentieth-century man. Over fifty per cent of Argyll has been ravaged by forestry. Of course it is understandable that any landowner wishes to maximise the return from his holdings, but surely afforestation on this scale here and also in many other parts of Scotland is ill-conceived. Tax concessions have played a great part in these schemes but what is their purpose? No doubt the mandarins of Whitehall looked at the balance of trade in timber and decided we should try and become more self-sufficient. A glance at the map indicated sparsely populated areas of Scotland and the decision was made.

The Awe

The River Awe is one of those rivers affected in recent times by the dubious benefits of man's intervention—in this case by a sixty-foot dam. Before this development, the river truly justified its name with its roaring torrent of fast flowing pools and deep rocky runs. It was renowned for producing fish of awesome proportions; in 1921 Major Huntington had a fifty-seven pounder while four years later, his wife had one of fifty-one pounds. There are a number of other fifty-pounds plus fish recorded, while twenty-pounders were a weekly, if not daily, occurrence. While it may no longer be a glass case river it is still very, very good and a day or, if you are lucky, a week on one of its seven beats will be a treasured memory. As it drains, Loch Awe is half- river half-estuary, after which it tumbles down the Pass of Brander before assuming a more gentle pace, with banks decked with silver birch and oak, flowing through rich meadows to join the salt water of Loch Etive. Over three thousand fish a year are counted through the barrage and further good news is that UDN, which has plagued the river for more than twenty years, is on the decline. Bell Ingram (0738) 21121 can arrange for you to fish the Barrage Beat at a cost of approximately £210 although availability is unsurprisingly limited. Mr Campbell-Preston of Inverawe Fisheries (08662) 446 may also be able to help you cast a fly on the illustrious river. The cost per rod is £30 a day or £140 a week and three charming cottages are available for letting. As one would expect with a river of this quality, it is a fly-only water where the early season will see large tues fished on a sinking line. As the water warms up rods will change to an intermediate floating or sink tip depending on their preference. Flies tend to be fairly small, and black is the favourite colour, so a size 10 Stoats Tail, for example, would be a popular choice.

Loch Awe

Loch Awe is a long thin ribbon of a loch which has become very popular as, in addition to salmon, sea-trout and brown trout, its waters also hold ferox of monster proportions, perch, char, pike and escapee rainbows from a fish farm. I cannot help thinking that in some cases not enough thought has been given to the operation of fish farms. Escapees can cause havoc with stocks of fly and, small as they have been here, this can result in some big fish. One rod took nineteen rainbows in a day with five of them over 7lb. Nineteen eighty-eight saw several double figure fish with a best of 14lb, while two years earlier a massive rainbow of 21lb 4oz was taken by Mr Graham. The ferox are rather more elusive but they are huge. One was washed up on the shore with a partially eaten belly which still weighed in at over 21lb. Then there is the monster 37lb 8oz fish of Mr W. Muir which was caught in 1866. Trout fishing is good and at present free, though the riparian owners have applied for a protection order so that it can be properly managed and stocks conserved. Sea-trout fishing is not what it used to be, but this is a common tale of woe on west coast waters. Most salmon are taken from the northern end and fishing round the islands is likely to be most profitable. Because trouting is free, it is sad to say that there are quite a few who don't bother to obtain a salmon permit. This is not fair on those who do or the riparian owners. Needless to say, anyone fishing with a suspicious looking trout rod should be reported.

A day's ticket only costs £2 and for £20 you can hire a boat with an outboard. Tickets can be obtained from the Ardbrecknish House at Dalmally (08663) 223. The loch can be dangerous water for it is nearly three hundred feet deep in places and the wind can whip down it, so always wear a life-jacket. Although it is very popular it is still easy to find a quiet, secluded spot as the loch is some twenty-five miles long. It is an attractive setting with wooded shores and islands such as Fraoch Eilean, where you can see the ruined castle of Lorne, a delightful sight. Fishing in its compass is an exhilarating experience.

The Orchy

The reason why most salmon are taken from the northern end is that they are bound for the spawning grounds of the River Orchy. This river drains Loch Tulla and its ten mile journey takes it through Glen Orchy which, with its famous Iron Bridge Falls, must be one of the prettiest glens you could wish to find. The barrage on the Awe has affected this river, as salmon which used to enter the river in March and April will not be seen in any number until the beginning of June and July through to September. As a result, these are now the best months. Salmon tend to be held back by the falls until the June spates and pools below the falls such as Pulpit and Gut can be particularly rewarding. Those wishing to fish the upper river may care to stay at the Bridge of Orchy Hotel (08384) 208 which has a beat reserved for hotel guests. Some of the best fishing is the Craig Beat which has recently been time shared. There are twenty-one named pools on these two miles and the five yearaverage is ninety fish. The owner of the Upper Craig Beat is Mr L. Campbell (08383) 282 and day tickets are available at a cost of between £12 and £22. Croggan Crafts (08382) 201, the tackle and country clothing shop in Dalmally, has daily permits for five privately owned beats and others where the cost ranges between £14 and £25 a day. Carraig Thura Hotel (0838) 2210 can offer guests fishing on its own water. The Dalmally Beat is managed by West Highland Estates of Oban (0631) 63617. Their chalets, which sleep 4, cost between £160 and £200 a week and the fishing costs between £70 and £125 per rod a week according to season. Incidentally, the hotels are also available for non-fishing holidays. Spinning is probably the best method of fishing the rocky gorges near the falls, but much of the river deserves to be fly-only water, especially as the fly works so well.

Loch Fyne Waters

South east of Loch Awe are the salt waters of Loch Fyne and its spate rivers. Argyll Estates (0499) 2203 can arrange fishing for you on the Rivers Shira, Aray and Dubh Loch at a cost of between £600 and £1000 per week, which includes self-catering accommodation in a lodge and fishing for four rods.

The Aray is a good salmon and sea-trout water and provides an attractive setting on its lower reaches where it flows through the park surrounding Inverarary Castle. The ornamental gardens and ornate bridges here are in marked contrast to the heavily wooded upper beats. The afforestation causes rapid changes in water levels and the ability to spey cast will ensure that you don't lose too many flies in the trees.

Both the Shira and the Fyne are victims of hydro schemes but offer good sport. Fishing on the Fyne was owned by Lord Glenkinglas but has now been divided between his sons. The four beats are owned by Ardinglas Estate (0499) 6261 and Cairndew Estate (0499) 6255. The season starts at the end of June and extends until the first week in October. A week's fishing for two rods costs in the region of £800 and though it is a popular river those who investigate well in advance may be lucky. Loch Shira is really a bay of Loch Fyne, while just above it is Dubh Loch in whose tidal waters you may also find grey mullet. Salmon usually rest in Dubh in July and August before running the river in September. On the western shore of Loch Fyne is Douglas Water. This little river is twelve miles long but impassable falls three miles upstream from the Loch confine fishing to the lower river. There you will find ten good pools with Roman Bridge Pool probably being the best. Day permits can be had for £6 from Argyll Caravan Park (0499) 2285.

Loch Eck & the Eachaig

On the opposite shore is Strachur and taking the A815 south brings you to Loch Eck and its river the Eachaig which connects it to Holy Loch and its naval bases. The Eachaig may be under five miles long but there are forty pools divided between three beats. Although famous for both the number and size of its sea-trout—1989 saw a 15lb 8oz fish taken on Ashtree Pool—it is also good salmon water. Further details may be had from Salar Management Services Ltd. (0667) 55355. The Loch is a narrow water some six miles long and up to a hundred and forty feet deep, and largely surrounded by forestry. As well as salmon, sea-trout and brown trout, its waters hold some powan, a rare relation of the grayling, and I am sure some ferox must stalk its depths. Permits can be had from the Whistlefield Inn (0369 86) 440 where a day including the use of one of the hotel's three boats with an outboard, which can hold up to six rods, costs £20. Fly works well at the northern end where the Cur flows in but trolling will produce good results, in all parts. Talking of good results the best salmon and sea-trout for the 1990 season were 19lb 6oz and 8lb 1oz respectively. It is also very good trout water as the average weight of 2lb proves.

Purdies, the tackle shop in Dunoon (0369) 3232, issue permits for the Dunoon and District Angling Club who have fishing rights on several small rivers and lochs in the area. In the way of clubs, the Oban and Lorn Angling Club have twenty-three lochs, most of which are easy to get to though a few involve a cross country hike. Anglers Corner (0631) 66374 will issue you a permit if you pretend you live within twenty five miles of Oban (southerners will have to brush up on their accent!)—the first year including joining fees costs £22. A further £5 will get you a boat permit. Lochgilphead and District Angling Club has the fishing of several lochs and rivers and permits for these are available from The Sports Shop (0546) 2390

Kintyre Waters

The A83 runs south of Lochgilphead into Kintyre. There may be an airport at Campbeltown but the long detour, which involves driving round the head of Loch Fyne, ensures that the visitor will be able to enjoy the peninsular's lochs and little rivers in perfect peace. Having said that, because of its remoteness, there is a certain free and easy approach to fishing on some rivers. This especially applies the further south you go and it has been suggested that those wishing to fish the Breackerie or Connie Glen Water, which lie at the southern tip, could be well advised to ask the local poachers in case they interfere with their poaching operations! A similar spirit exists on Machrihanish Water. The Lussa flows from its Loch through a pretty glen to enter the sea at Peninver. Even here there is no escape from hydro schemes and the erection of a dam, with no compensating flow on the Loch has severely altered the character of the river, where the best fishing is on the bottom beats. The river still manages to produce around 400 salmon a season and it is also good sea-trout water. At £8 a day or £80 a season it must be some of the least expensive salmon fishing available. Permits for the Lussa, which produced a best fish of 14lb in 1991 may be had from Inland Fisheries of Peninver (0586) 552774.

The Add

Perhaps the best river in the Kintyre district is the Add. Several tumbling burns continue to form this river and in the upper reaches there are steep rocky pools. The river becomes more sedate as it nears the Crinan Canal and the flow fades away; in fact the last two miles of the river are tidal. This is another river which has suffered from both a hydro scheme and afforestation which give it a Jekyll and Hyde character as one day there will be a flash spate while another day it may be almost dead for there is little compensatory flow. The upper reaches are owned by David Bracey of Kirnan Hotel (0546) 605217 while the lower river is owned by Robert Malcolm Esq. of Dunhrune Castle (05465) 283. The river is divided into three beats, Minard, Kirnan and Poltalloch. Both Kirnan and especially Poltalloch fish well and, although Mr Malcolm does not let his water on a regular basis, a day's fishing can be had for about £10.

Reasons why people choose fishing as their preferred pastime are almost as diverse as the places in which they practice their sport, but high on the list must rank the chance of escape from the rigours of the daily grind into some of the most beautiful countryside imaginable. You may think this an odd remark with which to preface this section, which takes in Glasgow and its industrial heartland, but in Scotland you are never far away from the countryside. Despite the geographical size of this area there is little fishing of note. There are few lochs, but none that can compete with the fame of their more northerly sisters. However, as one would expect in such an industrial area, there are a great many reservoirs. There are some good trout fisheries and Drew Jamieson of the Lothian Regional Council in Edinburgh (031) 229 9292 (ext. 3849) is the best person to advise you on them.

The Clyde

There is of course the Clyde—to most sassenachs the Clyde conjures up images of shipyards and heavy industry. Or it did before the economic climate changed. So what do we expect now—a deserted and polluted wasteland? Wrong, wrong and thrice wrong! There is excellent fishing to be had here. There is some first class trout water and salmon and sea-trout are being re-introduced. This is clearly a river of the future and, though the pre-industrial revolution glory days which saw salmon of over 40lb and sea-trout of 14lb may not return, it seems likely that good salmon and sea-trout fishing will be restored. The reasons? Well, purely and simply, something has been done about the situation.

The Clyde River Purification Board has done much hard work, as have the various clubs, such as the United Clyde Angling Protective Association. The work has included cleaning, restocking, creating and improving pools as well as buying out estuary nets. Conservation is not new here, for the UCAPA was founded in 1887 and has always been at the forefront of fishing improvements.

Many people associate the Clyde with Glasgow alone but the river is some eighty miles long. Its source is in the Lowther Hills, not far from the Wells of Tweed, and its upper reaches abound with half and three-quarter pound trout. On its way the river broadens out and so do the trout! Two-pounders are regularly caught on some of the lower reaches such as Crawford, Hazelbank and Crossford. Permits for the Lamington and District Association water may be had from Brydens Newsagents (and tackle shop) at Biggar (0899) 20069 for £4 a day (half-price for OAPs). The average weight here is one pound and, just to whet your appetite, May 1991 produced an eleven-pounder! Permits for the UCAPA water may be obtained from tackle shops or the secretary, J. Quigley Esq. of Wishaw (0698) 382479.

Perhaps the reason that the Clyde is not better known is that the Scots are a canny race and understandably believe in keeping a good thing to themselves! But take a tip, the Clyde offers very good trouting at present and, judging by what's happening, I am sure it will be a good salmon and sea-trout water given a few more years.

The Garnock & the Irvine

South East of Glasgow on the A736 is the Ayrshire coastal town of Irvine and it is here that the rivers Garnock and Irvine share a common estuary. A further attraction is that if you fancy a change from fishing, the renowned golf courses of Prestwick and Troon are both a few miles away. Mind you, there are many others, and playing these Open courses is sometimes more difficult than finding good autumn fishing! The source of the Garnock is east of Largs and its course is some fifteen miles long, making it one of the country's smallest salmon rivers. Despite much excellent work, the river still suffers from pollution and there have been some tragic occurrences. That there are still a reasonable number of salmon says much for the resilience of this river's stock. All the same, it can produce a memorable day and hopefully things will improve. A day on the Eglinton Angling Club water can be had for £10 a day from Jameson's Ironmongers at Kilwinning.

The Irvine has a varied life in its twenty-five mile journey to the sea. It flows through agricultural, industrial and urban areas. Hopefully pollution is a problem of the past. Much work has been done by a local improvement association and the river now shows consistent good sport, especially since the nets have been bought out. The lower reaches of the river were damaged in the eighteenth and nineteenth centuries by the erection of dams to provide power to drive a variety of mills. The mills are now disused but the dams are still intact and impale migrating fish at low water. The river is also well stocked with trout and a day's permit for the Dreghorn Angling Club's three miles of water costs £5 and is obtainable from Alysons's Flower Shop in Irvine (0294) 76716. This club also has fishing in the Annick Water. This is a delightful little trout stream where spider patterns such as a size 12 or 14 Black and Peacock or Black Spider do consistently well.

Loch Thom

Those who like their loch fishing might care to try Loch Thom. The Loch lies north of the Garnock at the head of the Naddsdale Water and is a short distance south of Greenock. At just under 500 acres, this is not a big water, nor does it hold particularly large trout, for the average weight is around the half pound mark. However, it does offer good fishing at a modest cost. A day costs £2 and a week £6, permits are available from Brian Peterson at The Fishing Shop in Greenock (0475) 888085. It is one of the waters that should be fished with very light tackle and skimming a moth imitation across the surface around dusk can make for some exciting moments.

One of the greatest of many mythical enigmas surrounding the art of fishing is the incredible success achieved by the fairer sex. Miss Ballantine represents perhaps the most celebrated example, but through the years there has been no doubt that ladies have a consistent knack of catching salmon and often big ones at that. To rub salt in the wound, they will often succeed in the exact places where men have failed. I have heard many stories of men who have returned disconsolate to the hut after trying a good pool without a sign of a fish. They have duly passed the rod to the wife, only to see it bent over within a few minutes and the inevitable excited cry of 'fish'!

The Ayr

The Ayr is the largest river in the county and has a wide catchment area. As a result its spates are less flashy and, like the Nith, take longer to get started and last longer. It is, however, another river that has been a victim of the Industrial Revolution. A great deal of the pollution problem here comes from disused coal mines. On top of this, there are several sewage and other discharges in the area. There are dams and weirs that used to power the now redundant mills and there is a fair amount of poaching—this is one factor that cannot be blamed on the Industrial Revolution! Despite such problems it is still a good river and when the difficulties are resolved, it could be extremely good. On top of the problems created by man, the fish have had to contend with UDN, which so devastated the spring stock that the early run has never really recovered. At present August, September and October are likely to be the best months and most locals will choose to spin or worm. A Yellow Belly Minnow or Zebra Toby can often prove successful for the spinner. There are parts of the river which take the fly well and favourites include the Brown Turkey, Blue Charm and Stinchar Stout.

The river is some thirty-nine miles long from its source on Wardlaw Hill to the popular seaside resort of Ayr. A wide and shallow river, it can be prone to flooding in its lower reaches. The best salmon and sea-trout fishing is from the weir at Catrine down to the estuary. Perhaps the most attractive stretch is from Failford to Stair.

Salmon average around 6lb and sea-trout 1½lb. All the river fishes well for trout and it is stocked every year. The Sorn Inn at Sorn (0290) 51305 which is just up from Catrine has a small stretch. Linwood & Johnstone, the newsagents (0290) 50219 in Mauchline, issue permits. The Failford Inn at Failford (0292) 541674 has two and a half miles and the cost here on a weekday is £5.

The Doon
Just south of Ayr is the River Doon. This river drains Loch Doon and the A713 follows much of its course from Glen Ness to the sea. It is a difficult river to get on as much of it is either privately owned or syndicated. However, the Skeldon Estate sometimes issue day tickets for their water, which has twelve named pools and it can be worth contacting the Estate Manager (0292) 56656.

The Stinchar
Continuing our coastal drive south on the A77 will bring us to Ballantrae which some people will associate with Robert Louis Stevenson's famous novel of Jacobite times. To fishermen, however, it is famous for being at the mouth of the Stinchar. In recent years the Doon has fished well but the Stinchar is the most productive river in Ayrshire. Unlike other rivers in the county, the river has not suffered from pollution for it lies well away from industrial areas and towns. As a result the water is remarkably clear and this well-managed river with its fine holding pools is one of the best fly waters in south-west Scotland. Many would argue, indeed, that it is a crime to fish it using any other method.

The source of the river is Loch Linfern in the Carrick Forest and in its twenty mile journey to the sea it is joined by its tributaries, the Duisk, Muck and Water of Tig. Loch Linfern is fairly small and as there are no reservoirs the river has spate characteristics. Afforestation, which covers much of its catchment area, has made the situation worse. Heavy rain in late autumn can bring the river into flood but it does not take long to fine down to a good fishing level. Although there is no stocking programme and still some netting, salmon and sea-trout spawn throughout the length of the river and its tributaries. Very few salmon enter the river in the early months of the season and July, with its good grilse run, is really the start of the season. Summer sport is dependent on rain, but can produce some great days and this is also the time for sea-trout. As rain becomes more predictable with the approach of autumn the tempo increases. September and October are often the finest months.

Some of the best fishing is on the Duke of Wellington's Knockdolian Estate which can produce up to 700 fish a season. A popular fly here is the appropriately named Duke's Killer. On the first occasion that the Duke tried it he hooked four fish! As one might expect this is a difficult beat to get on, but if you are prepared to take a summer week while waiting for a back-end one, it may be worth contacting the Estate Office (0465) 88237. Some water round Colmonell is owned by the Church of Scotland and forms part of the Rev. Jones glebe. The fishing here is handled by Mrs G. B. Shankland of Barnfoot Farm (0465) 88220. The upper stretch is fly-only and a day's fishing will cost £12 per person per rod. Spinning is allowed further down where the price of a day permit is £10. The Dalreoch Estate has one and three quarter miles of mainly double-bank fishing where a daily permit costs £35; it is available until the end of August, after which it is let on a weekly basis at a cost of approximately £190 per rod per week. A self-catering lodge is sometimes available. Permits can be obtained from the head keeper Mr D. Overend (0465) 88214. Bob Anderson of the Bardrochat Estate (0465) 88202 may also be able to help.

Stinchar salmon average around 8lb and sea-trout 1½lb. There are also some rainbows which have escaped from fish farms that run up to 3lb. It is not a large river and a single-handed ten- foot carbon should prove adequate for summer fishing and can also be used for sea-trout. A double handed fourteen-footer will be required when the river swells with late autumn rain. The most popular and effective fly is the Stinchar Stoat, which is much the same as a standard Stoat's Tail except that the hackle is orange rather than black. Another popular fly here and on many other waters is the General Practitioner which was first tried by the late Colonel Esmond Drury.

The Nith

Dumfries and Nithsdale is an area of much historical interest. Much of Robert Burns' work was written while he was working as an exciseman at a time when smuggling was a major local industry. His farm at Ellisland and house in Dumfries are now museums. Other buildings of note are the ruins of Sweetheart Abbey and Caerlaverock Castle with its nature reserve. At Sanquhar you can see Britain's oldest post office. Robert the Bruce murdered his rival John Comgh during the struggle for Scottish independence at Dumfries, and Arbigland is a popular spot with American tourists. It was here that John Paul Jones, the founder of the American navy, was born.

It is also an area of much piscatorial interest for here is the River Nith, Solway's crowning glory and one of the finest salmon and sea-trout rivers in Scotland. Sea-trout catches have averaged 3400 in recent years, and in 1989 the rod catch for salmon and grilse was 3641. These figures would have been better still were it not for the activities of poachers. The average salmon was around 9lb, grilse about 5lb and sea-trout 2lb. The best months are September, October and November and the Burgh Water in Dumfries produces about twenty fish a day. This is also the time for big fish which can be up to 30lb, although no fish today is likely to compete with the reputed sixty-seven pounder caught by Jock Wallace, the poacher, on the Barjarg water in 1812!

The Nith is born in Ayrshire, but its life at its source near Dalmellington is short lived as it enters Dumfriesshire at Kirkconnel and then flows on past the main centres of Sanquhar, Thornhill and Dumfries to join the Solway Firth. Above Sanquhar there are long stretches of sluggish canal-like water. The only white water to be found is in Drumlanrig Gorge but there are many excellent holding pools. Above Thornhill are seven miles of double-bank fishing divided into four beats, all owned by the Duke of Buccleuch whose seat, Drumlanrig Castle, is nearby—quite a lot of fishing around Thornhill is controlled by the Mid-Nithsdale Angling Association. Lower beats include such famous names as Closeburn Castle, Friars Carse, Portrack and Barjarg.

The river has many feeders and tributaries but the principal one is Cairn Water which joins the Nith below Lincluden College. The Cairn has some great fishing, especially in the small pools between Moniavie and Dunscore. The pool below Cluden Rock acts as a temperature barrier to fish and, unfortunately, as a magnet to poachers. The Cairn has other attractions besides salmon, for the Dumfries and Galloway Angling Association planted out 10,000 sea-trout fry in 1987. The same year saw the introduction of 3500 brown trout some of whom are now up to 2lb. This is a water which needs the autumn rains as in a hot dry summer it can be very weedy and shrink to a mere trickle.

The outbreak of UDN in 1967 did tremendous damage to the spring stock and so spring runs are really a thing of the past, but fishing below the caul in Dumfries at this time of the year can be productive. Flies that are well worth trying are Colonel's Wood, Castledykes and Slae Bushes.

The Nith is a spate river and, with no feeder lochs in the system, results are heavily dependent on rainfall. But rain is a mixed blessing since Upper Nithsdale is the victim of large scale afforestation. After heavy rain the river can be very coloured and it can be two or three days before serious fishing can begin again. Initially, worm will be the most productive method, while the next day will be suitable for spinners and then you should revert to fly. Because of its character most rods equip themselves with fly, spinning and worming tackle. It is a medium sized river and thigh waders will enable you to cover most waters.

Popular flies include the Hairy Mary, Blue Charm, Shrimp Fly, Stoats Tail and of course that local favourite, the Brown Turkey. In high water a two-inch Yellow Dog tube fly can prove deadly, but many will be spinning with a similar size or slightly larger Devon Minnow, in colours such as black and red, blue and pearl, green and yellow and brown and gold. In high water, sea-trout are also taken on a worm or a spinner such as a Mepps or small Toby, but in reasonable water levels fly is the most popular method. Two flies are normally fished on the leader as Nith sea-trout are often tempted by a bushy dropper such as a Black Pennell. Good patterns here are Blue and Silver, Wickham's Fancy, Greenwells Glory and Peter Ross. Later on in the evening and before dawn a team of spider patterns often works particularly well.

The Nith is an exceptional river and well worth a lot of effort to get on. Amongst those who may be able to help you are the Mid-Nithsdale Angling Club, where the cost is between £15 to £25 a day or £70 to £125 a week. Permits can be had from S. & I. Milligan of Thornhill (0848) 330555. Ian Milligan is a fount of local information and can be contacted for further details. The Killylong Estate (0387) 720415 has three-quarters of a mile of double-bank fishing: autumn fishing here is well booked with a waiting list, but summer sport is available. Nithsdale District Council (0387) 53166 charge £30 a day—visitors are only allowed to fish Monday to Friday. The Dumfries Office of Smiths Gore (0387) 63066 are the agents for the Blackwood beat. A week on the Buccleuch Estates (08486) 283 water costs between £100 to £800 plus VAT, but that is for two rods. They also offer day permits for the Linns beat for between £12 and £40 plus VAT. Further details from the Estate Office. Mr E. Tagg of The Blackaddie House Hotel at Sanquhar (0659) 50270 handles fishing on the Ryehill beat where the cost is between £15 and £35 a day and he can also arrange for you to fish the Upper Nithsdale Angling Club's water, two pools of which are right outside the hotel. There are no lochs which really stand out in this area but there are many good small lochs and stocked fisheries. Enquire locally for what would suit you best.

Many novices consider the wild Highlands of Scotland to be the exclusive terrain of game fishing. How wrong can they be! The Nith is a marvellous river and although the autumn beats are both expensive and popular they are well worth trying for.

The Annan to the Tweed

One of the most disturbing yet most neglected aspects of fishing is the increasing number of accidents related to the sport. I suppose this is not really surprising as fishing is becoming increasingly popular. However, I cannot help thinking that a number could be prevented by common sense and a little forethought. Wading can be dangerous, especially on some spate rivers where the water level can rise very quickly in a short space of time. Personally, I carry a wading stick and will always ask local advice, as even shallow river beds can be deceptively dangerous. I cannot understand those who don't wear a life jacket while boat fishing on big lochs. They always restrict one's movement a little but big lochs, especially those where the wind is funnelled between mountain sides, can rapidly change character and become dangerous places.

The Annan

A few miles east of the Nith is the Annan which is a good salmon river and even better for sea-trout. Its source is on the slopes of the delightfully named Devil's Beef Tub from whence it flows to Moffat. This attractive little town is just off the main road that connects Carlisle and Glasgow and was one of only two spa towns in Scotland. However, the only waters we are interested in are those that take the fly and the Beattock House Hotel (06833) 402) at Beattock, which is just below Moffat, issues permits for the Upper-Annandale Angling Association Water.

Downstream from Moffat the river is joined by Evan Water and Moffat Water. The tributaries are far bigger than the Annan at this stage of its journey. Some would argue that the true source of the river is Loch Skeen, at the top of the Moffat Water, just above the beautiful Grey Mare's Tail waterfall, which you can see from the A708. This is a river that has many picturesque names and among its tributaries is the Water of Milk. Others join it on its way to Annan and the Solway Firth: Kinnel Water, Dryfe Water and Mein Water.

Beats on the Annan include the Annandale Estate, Halleaths with its deep slow-moving pools, Royal Four Towns, Hoddom with its famous Goats and Kirkyard Pools and Newbie which is now time-shared. Permits for the Castlemilk Water, which includes the Royal

Four Towns beat, may be had from the Estate Office in Lockerbie (05765) 203. The cost of a day ranges between £17.72 and £28 plus VAT. Regular permit holders are given priority over visitors and no visitor permits are issued for Saturdays in October. Rather less expensive is the Hoddom and Kinmount Estates Water, whose Water Bailiff is Miss Marsh of Hoddom (05763) 488. The Warmanbie Hotel at Annan (0461) 204015 has a small stretch for hotel guests. Those wishing to fish the time shared Newbie beat are advised to contact the water-bailiff Mr Mick Aprile (0461) 202608.

The Annan is a spate river and forestry drainage from its catchment area naturally leads to fast run-offs and coloured water. In normal conditions it can be on the sluggish side and gentle hand-lining is the way to make the fly swim. Due to its colour in spate, worming and spinning are popular methods but it is good to know that a number of beats have a fly-only rule. The Annan used to have a good spring run but this has declined and springers are now usually taken below Milnbie. A wet summer can make for some exciting days, especially for sea-trout which average around 2lb, although most seasons will produce better fish of over 6lb. For salmon, autumn is the best time, when several 20lb plus fish will be recorded and the average is a high 12lb.

The Border Esk

The Border Esk is aptly named—not only does it cross the border but part of it and its main tributary the Liddle actually form the border between England and Scotland. Although its mouth and lower reaches are in England, the middle and upper reaches and principal tributaries are all in Scotland. The river is formed by the junction of the Black Esk and White Esk just below Castle Oer. After this it is joined by a number of tributaries, the main ones being Meggat Water, Ewes Water and the Wauchope, before reaching the town of Langholm. From this point south the A7 runs alongside the river as it collects the Tarras Water and below Canonbie it is joined by the Liddle, which has its source in Kielder Forest. This is a noted salmon and sea-trout water in its own right. At Longtown, road and river part company as the Esk heads for the Solway Firth and just north of Metalbridge it receives its final tributary the Lyne, before spilling over the mud-flats of Rockcliff marsh.

There are some wild brown trout in the river's upper reaches and tributaries, but these parts can take some getting to, so be prepared for a little rock climbing. For people who love a little extra adventure this is, however, a marvellous way to start the day and when you are finally fishing you feel alone, satisfied and totally at ease.

Autumn is the best time for salmon. Though they average ten pounds, a superb twenty-two pounder was caught in 1993 Popular flies are the Blue Charm and a Silver Doctor. The Garry Dog is the local favourite.

Afforestation on the upper reaches of the river and its tributaries can make for variable water levels with occasional flash floods. Much of the river between Langholm and Canonbie is tree-lined so the ability to spey cast will be a useful asset. Do be careful when wading for although some pools are easy to wade, others are deceptively deep, so do make a thorough reconnaissance before going out at night.

Night fishing of course means sea-trout and this is the Esk's main claim to fame, indeed it is one of the great sea-trout waters. In most seasons over 5000 of these shy warriors are taken with some topping the 8lb mark. Locals tend to use a double handed twelve-foot rod, but a single handed ten-foot carbon will enable you to cover the water and, being more sensitive, will give you a better feel when the action begins. A floating line is the best for the dusk rise, after which it may be advisable to change to a sink tip or intermediate. Popular flies are the Mark Brown and the Black Spider.

There is something magical about night fishing. First there is the dusk rise with sea-trout plopping all over the pool. As night approaches things become quieter and the flat surface of the water is only rarely broken by the rings of the rising fish. After this there is the fun of stalking fish or casting over the likely lie you noticed earlier in the day. When day breaks it is time to head for home and proudly display the results of your night's work. That at least is the theory! I would add that rods are particularly asked not to take too many herling—young sea-trout—so as to conserve stocks for the future.

The river is largely owned by Buccleuch Estates and most of it is controlled by the Esk and Liddle Fishery Association. Day permits cost between £6 and £30 and further information may be had from the Factor, G.L. Lewis (03873) 80202 or Mr George Graham, the Head River Watcher (03873) 71416. The Cross Keys Hotel at Canonbie (03873) 71205 also issues weekly permits.

The Tweed

The Wells of Tweed are a few miles north of Moffat and the Annan and it is here that the Tweed commences its illustrious journey to the sea at Berwick-Upon-Tweed. Its prominence is perhaps best summed up by the fact that it is the only river I know that has its own telephone line! In fact the aptly named Tweedline has three numbers, (0898) 666410 for fishing reports and prospects, (0898) 666411 for river levels which are updated daily and, most importantly from our point of view, (0898) 666412 which is the number for last minute rod vacancies.

Sparkling burns like Carr Water and Tweedhope Burn join the Tweed as it flows north to Tweedsmuir, which was the childhood home of John Buchan. There is very good trouting here and the

Crook Inn at Tweedsmuir (08997) 272 has its own stretch which is free to residents. This hotel also issues permits for the Peebles Trout Fishing Association water which costs £6 a day. Talla and Fruid, which once used to swell the infant river, have now been dammed to provide water for Edinburgh.

After being joined by Biggar and Holms water, the rough moorland banks give way to a more noble setting of pastures and parklands. By Peebles the river is joined by the swirling peaty Manor Water and the Lyne, another reservoir victim. Just west of Peebles is Neidpath Castle, whose walls bear the scars of Cromwell's artillery.

Peebles, with its famous fifteenth-century bridge, is where salmon fishing really begins. Blackwood & Smith (0721) 20131 handle lets for the Peebleshire Salmon Fishing Association, which is an association of fishing proprietors who allow fishing by permit. Day permits cost between £25 and £35 a day or £115 for the season. Fish average around nine pounds.

Below the town the river skirts Kailzie Gardens and the dense conifers of Cardrona Forest and here you will find such beats as Haystoun, Horsburgh Castle and Traquair. Traquair House, the home of Maxwell Stuart, is Scotland's oldest occupied home and legend says that The Bear Gates will never be opened until a Stuart sits on the English throne again. Innerleithen is famous for its textile manufacturing and just downstream at Walkerburn is the Scottish Textile Museum.

The Traquair Arms Hotel (0896) 830229 can offer good autumn fishing on four beats for £4 a day. The Tweed Valley Hotel at Walkerburn (0896) 87636 has some private beats in beautiful surroundings, where the cost of a day's fishing varies between £25 and £40. Many of their guests are regulars, but the proprietor, Charles Miller, can sometimes arrange for his guests to fish other beats. The best fish taken in 1992 by guests was an 18³/₄lb salmon. This hotel also has two miles of private trout fishing on the Tweed and two lochs, one with wild brownies and the other with stocked rainbows, which can be fished for £7.50 a day.

The Ettrick

Below Innerleithen the banks are again victims of conifer plantations. Here are beats such as Caddonfoot, Sunderland, Thornilee, Elbibank and Peel, as just north of Selkirk it is joined by the Ettrick which marks the beginning of the Middle Tweed. The Ettrick is a good salmon river in its own right and, like its tributary the Yarrow, is noted for its trout which go up to 3lb. Buccleuch Estates at Bowhill (0750) 20753 issue day tickets for their water on the Ettrick, Yarrow and Teviot at a cost of between £15 and £30 a day.

Ettrickshaws Hotel at Ettrick (0750) 52229 has two miles of single-bank fishing on the Ettrick, which is available free to guests or to anyone else at between £15 and £20 a day. The water here is a spate river and fishes well late in the season. At Selkirk there is a statue to that intrepid Victorian explorer, Mungo Park, who discovered the source of the River Niger in Africa.

Gala and Allan Water join the Tweed above Melrose, where the heart of Robert the Bruce is reputed to be buried in the ruins of the Cistercian Abbey. A Roman fort stands guard over the town and river and from its lofty position on Eildon Hills, would also have given a clear view of Dere Street, the main England to Scotland road in those days. On this stretch will be found such famous beats as Drygrange, Maxton, Merton, Rutherford, Gledswood, Bemersyde and Ravenswood.

From where the Leader Water joins the Tweed at Leaderfoot is what is widely regarded as the best salmon fishing in the world. In 1730 the Earl of Home caught a 69lb 12oz salmon and 1866 produced one of 57lb 8oz. Fish of such majestic proportions, or anything like them, have not been seen for many a year, a fact which may well be connected with the drift net industry. Nowadays most Tweed salmon are around ten pounds or slightly better, with the odd thirty-pounder occasionally falling to some lucky rod. Nearby is the small town of St Boswells where Sir Walter Scott and Earl Haig of First World War and Poppy Day fame are buried. As one might expect, water of this quality is extremely difficult and expensive to get on. However, if you are lucky enough to be able to afford it you might care to buy one of the weeks on the Lower Floors beat which the Duke of Roxburghe is selling on a thirty-year lease through Savills' Edinburgh office (031) 226 6961.

The Teviot

At Kelso we find the most famous pool on the river—Junction. This is where the Teviot joins the Tweed and, despite the fact that a week here for five rods is over £17,000, it is booked for years in advance. The Teviot is another tributary that is a fine salmon river in its own right—it has such good pools as Ferry Stream, Lower and Quarry which have all produced fish of over 20lb. Mr Bill Wright of Hawick (0450) 85252 has his own beat for two rods on the Teviot and may be able to organise other fishing, including the Tweed when available. Tweedside Tackle of Kelso (0573) 25306 can arrange days on various private beats subject to availability, and also issue permits for the Kelso Angling Association Water.

There are some famous beats between Junction Pool and below Coldstream, where the Tweed receives the Till. Among names to conjure with are Sprouston, Birgham, Carham, Wark, Cornhill and

Lennel. From the junction with Eden Water the Tweed forms the boundary between England and Scotland. The Till is also a fine salmon and sea-trout water. Its headwaters are sparkling burns which tumble down the Cheviot Hills and it is only at Chillingham Castle, with its famous wild white cattle, that it becomes the Till. Many rods fortunate enough to fish the beats in this area stay at either the Ednam House Hotel (0573) 24168 or the Crown Hotel at Coldstream (0890) 2558. Coldstream has military connections other than the famous regiment of Guards which bears its name, for just south of here is the site of Flodden Field.

From Till junction the Tweed progresses at a stately pace with deep pools, wide rapids and streaming round the many islands. It is here that you will find the famous Lady Kirk and Norham beats. Norham Castle was painted by Turner and Sir Walter Scott termed it the most dangerous place to be in England.

Whiteadder & Blackadder

A mile east of Paxton the border crosses the river which is now wholly in England and, shortly after this, it receives its last tributary, the Whiteadder. The upper reaches of this river have been dammed and flooded, forming a reservoir to provide water for Edinburgh. It is, however, good trout water. The Allanton Inn at Allanton (0890) 818260 issue permits for the Whiteadder Angling Club Waters, at a cost of between £10 and £20 a season. Its tributary, the Blackadder, offers good sporting trouting and a season ticket may be had from the Cross Keys Hotel at Greenlaw (03616) 247 for £5. Below Whiteadder junction the Tweed is affected by tides which ebb and flow, shifting sands and mud, until the river enters the North Sea at Tweedmouth.

Trying to book fishing yourself on the Tweed can be a headache to say the least. There are many beats and good tributaries but there is also a lot of competition for them and, as you can imagine, many people return year after year. You could spend several days on the telephone and get nowhere Alternatively you could save a lot of time by ringing the sporting agents.

Ted Hunter of Anglers Choice in Melrose (0896) 823070 has access to some private beats. James Leeming of Kelso (0573) 470280 was a land agent in the early eighties but soon moved towards becoming a fishing agent. He had access to eleven private beats in 1993, where the cost varied between £25 and £500 a day. E. MacDonald Sports of Peebles (0721) 20979 (formerly I. Fraser Sports) is an excellent tackle shop and issues trout permits. However, Mrs Lena Fraser carries on her late husband's salmon fishing as Fraser's Salmon Fishing and Hire Ltd (0721) 722960. They have two beats which are let from £30 a day.

As on so many rivers, the spring run is not what it used to be. Most springers are taken below Kelso, because fish will stay below the caul until the water temperature has risen. Summer fishing can, as one would expect, be rather chancy. However, a wet autumn and its attendant spates will see thousands upon thousands of fish running the river. Autumn fish average around ten pounds but twenty and thirty pounders are not too rare. This is a big river and you need to have as long a rod as you can comfortably handle and I would suggest either a fourteen or fifteen footer. Although some pools are very deep, most fish are taken in fairly shallow water and a medium or intermediate sinking line should suffice. Popular flies include the Garry, Willie, Gun, Comet or patterns such as the Munro Killer, Hairy Mary and Stoats Tail for summer fishing. The best advice is to go to one of the tackle shops like Anglers Choice in Melrose and find out the latest thoughts on flies, times and locations of recent catches.

Megget Reservoir & St Mary's Loch

For those who like their stillwater fishing, taking the A707 south from Selkirk will bring you to Megget Reservoir and St Mary's Loch. Megget covers some six hundred and forty acres, is two hundred feet deep in places and—for the statistician—holds on average thirteen and a half thousand million gallons of drinking water! Tibby Shiels Inn (0750) 42231 issue permits which cost £2.90 a day for bank fishing and boats are available.

There is a modest stocking programme every year and Arctic char are being introduced on a small scale as an experiment. This brown trout water is fly-only and traditional wet flies work well as do nymphs. Dapping is becoming increasingly popular. As this is over 1000 feet above sea level it can be very cold so do not forget to take an extra sweater. Anglers Choice of Melrose (0869) 823070 issue permits for St Marys Loch costing £3 a day for fly fishers or £5 a day for spinners and those using bait. This price differential probably says quite a lot about the availability of this water. The large loch also holds perch and pike and there is a watersports centre. I understand spinning is popular and the trout average a good pound, but I must confess that the idea of trolling for trout with a spinner does not appeal to me. Perhaps that is because I am still dreaming of getting a week on the Tweed! Incidentally, two other contacts for visiting anglers are W.S. Renton (Berwick) 3060268, who controls Watch Water Reservoir, and Mr T. Hardie (Galashiels) 2345, of Galashiels Angling Club.

IRISH SEA

SOLWAY FIRTH
CARLISLE
A596
DERWENT
A69
S. TYNE
PENRITH
A66
EDEN
CHEVIOT
KIELDER
CONGM MOSS
EHEN
LAKE
A595
DISTRICT
A6
CONISTON WATER
WINDERMERE
KENDAL
KIRKBY STEPHEN
LUNE
MORECAMBE BAY
HODDER
RIBBLE
BLACKPOOL
M55
CALDER
M6
M61
LIVERPOOL

For many the North conjures up images of industrial slag heaps and pit villages. What they fail to appreciate is some of the most rugged and remote and the most beautiful scenery in the country. The North is not short on water—no drought here. In fact Northumberland actually exports this precious commodity to the Middle East. The Pennines, the Lakes, the deserted coastal areas and the wild moorlands all provide a haven for the angler. Fishing is here aplenty, and it is never dull.

Cumbrian Rivers

North West Water, who control much of this area's waters are making commendable efforts to upgrade the waters in the region. Restricting netting on the Solway and banning the use of drift nets in the River Eden are just two examples of recent improvements. The hope is, clearly, to see increased runs of migratory fish and we wish them and the NRA all good fortune in this endeavour.

The Eden

The Border Esk, which in part marks the Anglo-Scottish border, has been considered in our Southern Scotland section and, as a result, the first great river we should consider is the Eden. The river runs for some seventy miles. At its estuary and for its first twenty miles there is some fine salmon fishing, but sadly the sea-trout fishing could only be described as indifferent.

A few miles south of Carlisle we find a productive stretch under the control of Warwick Hall. This stretch has done quite well for salmon in recent years, and as you can imagine, the fishing is extremely popular. There are two people who will be able to help you here; Don Haughin at Keeper's Cottage (0228) 560545 and Major Murphy (0228) 561918 at The Annexe. Both are situated at Warwick Hall itself. If you apply by November, Major Murphy will consider you for day rods the following season. The address is The Annexe, Warwick Hall, Carlisle, CA4 8PG

The Eden is particularly rich in natural food and another location where excellent cuisine can be found is in the Tufton Arms Hotel (0768) 351593. The performance of this stretch of the water is largely determined by water levels and, given a good period of rainfall, salmon run up to the Appleby area before the close of the season. Indeed, the spawning grounds are not usually reached until very late in the season. Appleby is one such spawning area but it is also good for brown trout. The remaining fifty miles of the river are dominated by some really excellent trouting. The Tufton Arms itself has good access to some first class water on over twenty-three miles of river and salmon fishing can be arranged from here too. Fishing for guests of the hotel costs between £6 and £12 per day and you also have the option of fishing two picturesque tarns, which are well stocked with rainbows. The salmon and sea-trout fishing, on estate water lower down the river, ranges from £15 to £50 depending on the season and the beat. The Tufton Arms can arrange tuition aimed at both the beginner and the more experienced fisherman who is seeking to brush up certain aspects of his technique. These courses are a delightful way of enjoying your fishing, combining practical guidance with some fishing on the glorious Eden. For the racing enthusiast, the Greystoke Estate is now a renowned training centre for racehorses. Despite the many sporting attractions, we must also emphasise the natural beauty of the Eden Valley, which boasts a rugged charm and a wealth of wild life.

The Eden differs from many English rivers in that there are very few stretches retained for private use and a number of fishing clubs have access to good water. So it may be of help to indicate some useful contacts. The Upper Appleby fishings, which are controlled by John Pape, are well worth noting. This is a fine stretch for brown trout. It includes five miles of double and single-bank, with a maximum of four rods at any one time. The brownies here are wild and furious and a battle royal often ensues to the delight of all lovers of the sport. Permits are £12 per day and are available from Mr Pape's shop, Appleby Shoe and Sports (0768) 352148. Mind you, you'll be lucky to snare the man himself as he's a passionate practitioner of the sport, runs some superb practical courses for small groups and is also the local chiropodist!

While Appleby may be something of a centre point for those seeking to fish the Eden, Carlisle Angling Association have approximately seven miles of double-bank fishing as well as some tidal waters. There are two principal points to note here. Firstly the value is excellent. Secondly all legal methods are allowed. A permit for the season would cost in the order of £15 for brown trout and sea-trout. A day ticket for salmon fishing will cost £10 up until the end of August, when weekly permits are available at £20. All the necessary permits can be obtained from the excellent tackle shop McHardy's (0228) 23988 in South Henry Street, Carlisle.

The Lazonby Estate, a little way north of Carlisle, has approximately four miles of single-bank fishing which ranges from £10 to £25 per day. This comprises the lower and upper beats, both of which hold four rods. There is some good salmon fishing here. In 1990 a 29lb beauty was taken from the Hollingstown Pool on the lower beat. Bookings are taken in advance but you need to be quick off the mark to be successful. Please contact Mrs Boyd (06974) 72453 for further details. The Estate can also organise some delightful beck fishing and the moorland streams are also great fun, especially for the beginner. They also provide good sport in the middle of the summer when other fishing is less good. There is a lodge available for hire and guests here receive discounted rates on fishing. Those of you contemplating a move to the area should consider a seasonal rod, which gives you one day's fishing per week at a cost of £300 for weekdays or £350 for weekends. Spinning is permitted on the Skye Foot beat.

Returning to a somewhat more tranquil scene, we should consider the Penrith Angler's water which is both varied and good. Some five different tickets are available here but perhaps the best value means of enjoying the fishing is to purchase a general weekly ticket. This costs in the region of £40, which covers two miles of fishing on the Eden and stretches of its tributaries, the Lowther, Eamont (also note Hornby Hall (0768) 891114 which has has 2½ miles single-bank on the Lower Eamont) and Petteril. Contact the Gun and Tackle Shop in Penrith (0768) 62418 for further details. Incidentally, the proprietor, Mr Rosling, is an experienced fisherman himself and also a mine of local knowledge. If you buy a couple of permits here you will be making a solid investment as this will hopefully give you the opportunity to pick his brains and receive some excellent advice. The Eamont is some twelve miles in length and joins the Eden just south-east of Penrith.

The Eden stretches through some really unspoiled land and the Kirkby Stephen and District Anglers Association has some super fishing upstream, some four miles from its source. Here, you find broad grouse moors and beautiful, if somewhat remote, open countryside. The Association's water is approximately twelve miles in length and provides a rich variety of fishing. Runs contrast with the many pools and the river itself changes tempo, flowing fast and free, then slowing to a more sedate pace. The average weight of fish ranges from a half to three quarters of a pound, but fish weighing between two and three pounds are not uncommon. There are some excellent lies to be found and trout and grayling fishing are both good at the confluence of the River Belah. Day tickets cost £15 per day and are available from Robinsons in Kirkby Stephen (0768) 371519.

The Eden is a marvellously scenic river yet there are many challenges to its depths. It is a real delight to those who class themselves in the true sportsman's league. The brownies are particularly tricky customers. They have been harried by mink, heron and other predators all their lives and have no intention of succumbing to your fly without putting up a good fight.

The Derwent

To the west is the River Derwent, a prime salmon water and one of Cumbria's most important river systems. It runs for some thirty miles and its source at Scafell lies amidst the most beautiful scenery. The river flows through the Borrowdale Valley, passing into Derwentwater and Bassenthwaite Lake before it reaches the Irish Sea at Workington. Poaching used to be an enormous problem on this water but the water bailiffs and the NRA have now got the situation pretty well under control. The best months for sea-trout tend to be July and August.

An excellent early start was made to the 1991 season with a 12lb fish being taken in early June. Salmon fishing seems to be at its best between July and October. The run may start in late June but this depends on the spring rains and the subsequent water levels. The average weight is in the 9lb region but usually a few fish are taken around the 24lb mark. In 1990 one rod successfully caught some forty-two fish in two splendid September days. The brown trout fishing is good and the bigger fish tend to be lower down the river. A large section of the river is owned by the Leckonfield Estate. The fishing is handled by their subsiduary, Castle Fisheries (0900) 826320. The Estate issues a limited number of permits for salmon, sea-trout and brown trout and the chap to talk to is the redoubtable Stan Payne. He has put some twenty years of service into the Estate and knows the scene intimately. The fishing is normally let to the same people. However, at the time of enquiring some weeks were available. There are six rotating beats of two rods per beat, the cheapest day rod is in the order of £35 and a weekly rod for a renowned time of year (September) would cost £850. Ghillies are also available at a cost of £25 per day. The Derwent is essentially straight forward to fish and wading is no problem. The more successful flies tend to be Stoats Tail, Garry Dog and Shrimp Fly.

There is also some town water, details of which can be obtained from the local tourist board (0900) 822634 in Cockermouth. The fishing is available on both banks and the right bank stretches from Derwent Bridge to Harris Mill Bridge and the left spans the water between High Sand Lane and Low Sand Lane and also from the junction of the River Cocker to the prominent N.W.E.B. pylon. The permit charge is £4.50 per week for visitor. Perhaps the best place to stay is the Trout Hotel (0900) 823591. The hotel have the fishing rights on the water behind them but acknowledge that the good beats are available through Castle Fisheries. Keswick Anglers Association have a two and a half mile stretch which runs from Portinscale to High Stock Bridge, in addition to water on the River Greta (a less significant salmon and sea-trout river.) Day permits for salmon are £20 and £5 is the charge for trout. Weekly tickets range from £80 to £25 for salmon and trout respectively. This section of the river flows through farmland which is surrounded on all sides by the Cumbrian Hills. The river can be quite fast flowing in places with good pools, allowing for some splendid wet fly fishing with traditional flies. Permits are available from Field and Stream in Main Street, Keswick (0768) 774396.

There are a number of stretches where your charm is as important as your casting ability. Workington Anglers Association and Cockermouth Anglers Association are essentially private clubs requiring you to be guests of members. We recommend you scour the local pub for that elusive catch. The fortunate fisherman will find water on a three mile stretch which runs from Carmeadow Bridge to the sea. If the water is below the two feet four inches gauge you must use a fly but if it rises to three feet, or the water is dirty or coloured, a worm can be used. Cockermouth and District Anglers Association allow members six guest days per year and they make use of a four mile stretch running through Cockermouth and wooded farmland. Cockermouth is the birthplace of two very different characters; the poet Wordsworth and the mutineer Fletcher Christian of The Bounty. A less renowned son of the area is Mr D.W. Lothian, who is a dab hand at fixing your clocks and also has a fair range of tackle (0900) 822006.

The Cocker

The River Cocker is a significant tributary with good runs of salmon and sea-trout and some first class brown trout fishing. Tickets are available from the Gun Shop in Cockermouth (0900) 822058. The

National Trust also have some water and information is available from Wordsworth House (0900) 824805. This is a super place to visit and, although fishing is not the best in the world, there are some opportunities. In addition, there are a number of becks in the Derwent system which offer a certain amount of free fishing. Coldale and Newlands Becks, which flow into Bassenthwaite Lake are super stretches, as are the River Greta and Mosedale Beck. You should always seek permission but, essentially, fishing is free and accessible, set amidst beautiful scenery.

The Ehen

A little way north of the River Calder, we come to the River Ehen which drains Ennerdale Water through Cleator Moor, flowing into the Irish Sea between Seascale and Nethertown. Egremont Angling Association runs about seven miles of desirable bank fishing and also has fishing on Ennerdale Water. A £30 permit allows reasonable salmon and some fine trout fishing. Salmon tend to be best from June to August and permits are available from the Rod and Gun Shop in Egremont (0946) 820368.

The Kent

The River Kent meanders steadily through from Kentmere Reservoir which is located north of Staveley. Its principal tributaries include the Gowan and Sprint. The river flows through some of the most beautiful countryside in Britain and is a delight to fish. Despite an unfortunate poisoning the river still provides the game fisherman with some quality sport. The better salmon and sea-trout fishing generally takes place later in the season—from September—and it is fair to say that the river is generally more renowned as a brown trout fishery. There are a number of stretches that can be fished by the nomadic angler, as well as some waters that become available—if you're lucky. There is a two to three mile stretch of private water owned by the Levens Hall Estate. The fishing is excellent here but there is a waiting list. What's more, only season tickets are issued. If you are interested, write to The Estate Office, Levens Hall, Kendal, Cumbria. Another private stretch of about one mile which offers some good value day permits (£3–£5 per day), is found a short distance below Lower Levens Farm. Permits here are available from Olde Peat Cotes, Sampool Lane, Levens, Nr Kendal, Cumbria.

Burnside and District Angling Association has some four miles on the main river which also encompasses the confluence of the River Sprint. Permits can be purchased from either the Burnside Post Office (0539) 726114 or the local boozer, appropriately named the Jolly Angler's Inn (0539) 732552. Although this stretch is some thirty miles from the sea, some impressive 30lb catches have been recorded in the area! All legal methods of fishing are allowed, but here's a tip for you; bright orange lures do particularly well.

Staveley is some eight miles from the Kent's source which flows from Kentmere Reservoir. Staveley Anglers Association has five miles of fishing available and permits are obtainable from D. & H. Woof in the Main Street, Staveley (0539) 821253. The cost of the permit is £10 for a week. This allows fishing for salmon, sea-trout and brown trout. The salmon run does not tend to peak until late

October. A fine freehouse in which to hear some good fishing tales is the Eagle and Child, Staveley (0539) 821320. The tenant here is Lenny Sosnowsky, a keen fisherman of Russian descent, who has many a yarn, and pulls a fine pint and, furthermore, hosts the local Fly Dressers Guild. This celebrated fishing pub is situated at the confluence of the Rivers Kent and Gowan and is a splendid place to visit. Permits for about twenty nearby tarns of the Windermere and District Anglers Association are also available here.

The largest association on this fine river is the Kent Anglers with approximately eight miles of fishing—five miles stretching downstream of Kendal and three miles upstream, with free town water in between. This is available to visiting fisherman for between £15 and £20 per day and £40 and £60 per week according to the time of season. Fly, spin and worm are allowed, although most members prefer to fly. Other methods catch too many young fish! Permits are readily available from either Kendal Sports (0539) 721554, 30 Stramongate, Kendal or Mr V. Carlson at 64 Kirkland (0539) 724867. Kendal, home of the mint cake, is a lovely town from which to commence any outdoor pursuit. Interestingly, Kendal has one of the few surviving snuff mills and the castle is famous for being the former home of Catherine Parr—the last of the wives of Henry VIII, who actually outlived him.

The Lune

Closely stalking the direction of the Kent a few miles east is the River Lune. This is another river with a good reputation for seatrout and salmon, running some forty-five miles from its source in Ravenstonedale Common, about six miles south of Kirkby Stephen, to its mouth at Lancaster. This important river passes through some celebrated scenery and the angler has the double delight of some fine fishing with a wonderful backdrop.

The Kirkby Lonsdale A.A. water near to Tebay and down to Kirkby is particularly well stocked with brownies. As the river becomes wider and deeper the fish become larger. Weekly tickets are available from the Tourist Information Centre in the Main Street (0524) 271437, next door but one to the Royal Hotel. Prices range from £35 to £50 per week.

There is also some good fishing for wild brown trout around Sedbergh. Lowis' in the Main Street issue weekly tickets. Although there are still nets in the estuary, there is some fine salmon fishing in the lower reaches of the river. Mrs Anne Curwen (0524) 770078 sells day tickets on behalf of the Lancaster and District Anglers Association. For salmon and brown trout, prices will vary depending on the day but are usually between £10 and £18. Visitors should note, however, that permits are only issued on weekdays. This is not a major worry as there are all manner of other opportunities for fishing locally. Mrs Carwen also sells tickets for the NRA's Halton Fishery which cost £8 per night (8.00pm to 4.00am). Mr Shallis at the Halton Stores and Off Licence (handy for all night vigils) can also supply day permits for the Halton beats and day and night permits for the Skerton beats. This is excellent value fishing and sea-trout are, despite the ravages of UDN, well worth going for. The waters vary, with the upper beat sluggish in character, while below Forge Weir the river offers fast runs and a succession of rocky pools. If you are planning to fish at night it is critical to familiarise yourself with the nature of the riverbed and locals advise chest waders for all but a few of the pools. The best fishing runs from late June through July although, unusually, the lower reaches of the river have a run of fresh sea-trout until the close of the season in mid-October. The favoured salmon waters are the Halton beats at higher river levels, with two feet to three feet being the best for spinning. Fly and shrimp come into their own when the water is down to one foot. The lower beat is fly-only but the Toby and Koster are fine in heavy waters. The Garry Dog is popular in the spring and autumn, while the Stoats Tail and Munro Killer are effective in the summer and early autumn. The Mallard and Claret used on the dropper is another first class way of maximising your chances with the sea-trout. Do book up well in advance and hope for a good spate as algae can be a problem.

Cumbrian Waters

Despite the excellence of the river systems in Cumbria, there are a number of excellent fisheries and reservoirs, not to mention numerous tarns, becks and lakes. The border country is particularly well blessed and the countryside is delightfully unspoiled. Fell walking, riding, bird-watching and fishing are just some of the outdoor pursuits to be enjoyed. Border Game Fisheries Ltd are based in Longtown, Cumbria (0228) 791108 and have a number of fishing opportunities including day tickets for fishing on the Esk priced at £12 to £50, as well as a number of other excellent stretches on other northern rivers. The company also has sixty acres of land with two lakes of ten and fifteen acres which make up Oakbank Fisheries. The attractive caravan/camping site by one of the lakes provides a peaceful opportunity for a longer stay. The bird sanctuary, game bird breeding unit and country museum provide additional interests for the family. Oakbank Lake is restricted to fly fishing from the bank but Barn Lake offers some boats and has some limited bait fishing. The waters are regularly stocked with rainbow and some browns and a catch and release policy has resulted in fish up to 8lb.

Some two miles from Hadrian's Wall we find the New Mills Trout Farm, which although dealing essentially with catering and restocking also provides a pleasant excuse for some good fishing in picturesque surroundings. Finally, if you haven't caught anything in years, the Ford Pool is a place to lift the spirits.

Watendlath Fishery (07687) 77293 near Borrowdale is another for the shortlist. It is generally a late starter due to its location but is well stocked with fish, as well as having wild browns. The water is open from Easter to the end of October from 8.00am to dusk and there is a limit of twelve rods per day, so advance booking is essential. The scenery here is magnificent. Outside July and August the waters are often secluded, so the fishing is very peaceful indeed. The water is fly-only and boats are available at a charge of £9 per day and there is a bag limit here of four fish. Alternatively, a half-day ticket is priced at £9 with a bag limit of two fish.

Kentmere Tarn (0539) 822223 is situated on the floor of the Kentmere Valley. Surrounded by hills, this a beautifully secluded spot. Deer and badgers lurk in the nearby woods and the wildfowl add further colour to the scene. The water covers a total of ten acres and is stocked with browns, although wild ones and the odd indigenous salmon can be caught in these twenty-foot depths. The season runs from mid March to the end of September and a charge of £15 a day is levied for the visiting angler. From the banks, anglers may fish with fly or bait and there is a boat for hire for fly fishing only. A similar summary can be applied to Pinfold lake at Raisbeck which once again is rich in flora and fauna. The lake itself is stocked with rainbow and is open all year. The water covers four acres and there is a four rod limit and a four fish limit too. The water may be fished by fly-only and the four fish day ticket is priced at £7 per rod. This lake is particularly convenient for the M6 motorway which is only five minutes' drive away—exit at junction 38. Despite the presence of this major road the area is unspoiled and peaceful. Tickets are obtainable from John Pape (07683) 52148 in the Market place at Appleby-In-Westmoreland.

The Lough Trout Fishery (0228) 576552 is yet another name that should most definitely not be ignored. Thurstonfield Lough is a large and scenic stretch of freshwater in the Northern part of Cumbria, west of Carlisle, and is surrounded by fifty acres of woodland that are designated an area of Special Scientific Interest. The Lough is stream fed and exceptionally well stocked with brown and rainbow trout. Day permits cost £15 and a boat costs a further £5. The fishing is complemented by six Scandinavian pine bungalows available for self catering rent.

The Lakes

Those of you keen to take the family on a sporting holiday should consider the Lake District—it offers some marvellous opportunities. But do not expect a peaceful holiday if you go in season as this is a very popular place for tourists. Bigland Hall Country Sports Ltd. (05395) 31361 offers clay pigeon shooting, archery, windsurfing, a riding centre and, most importantly, sixteen acres of fishing away from the madding crowd. The water is well stocked with rainbows, the record fish being 12lb. The number of rods is strictly controlled and you should endeavour to book well in advance. The day permit costs some £15 with an evening charge of £10.50. If you can't manage to pack your own then rod hire is £8.50 per day.

Esthwaite water is another for the short list. It lies amidst the more gentle hills of the southern lakeland and is unusual in that it is the only major Cumbrian lake commercially stocked with rainbows. The water is controlled by the Hawkshead Trout Farm (05394) 36541 and is popular with locals and visitors. The scenery is once again superb and the fish, often tending to congregate at the end of the lake, are great fighters—this may be due to the fact that the pike, for which this lake is renowned, are monstrously large. The browns, ever keen to avoid these freshwater sharks are both elusive and fight like tigers when hooked. Day tickets are priced at £10 and there is a bag limit of four fish. Hire of a rod for the day can be had for a further £5. Weekly and season tickets are priced at £38 and

£165 respectively. Those anglers may take two fish per visit. There are twelve boats for hire priced at £8 per day. You may fly fish, spin or use bait but no maggots are allowed. The fishery's record for a brown trout is 4lb 4oz and 12lb for a rainbow. The largest pike weighed in at 37lb!

Heading northwards, we arrive at Lamplugh and Cogra Moss (0900) 823638, a fourty-one acre lake which offers fly-fishing for the resident brown trout and stocked rainbows. The water is open daily from sunrise to an hour after sunset and tickets are available from West Lothian in Cockermouth (0900) 822006. Cogra Moss enjoys a perfect setting amidst hills and forests. There are several islands accessible to anglers, except one built by the RSPB for wild fowl and currently inhabited by nesting grebes. Season tickets are £75 with a limit of four fish per day. Day tickets cost £8 with a similar catch restriction.

There are a whole host of delightful small tarns, in fact a number all share the same name which is very confusing! These are often remote and rugged waters but are a delight to fish. Burnmore tarn is a two mile walk from the isolated village of Bouth. The sport, however, can be marvellous not to mention idyllic! Then there are the vast waters of Coniston. Tickets for these waters are available from the Tourist Centre (05394) 41533. Salmon are far from abundant in the water but the brown trout are quite prolific, as is the less common char, a landlocked relative of the salmon. The char generally inhabits deeper sections of the lake, which can be up to 180 feet in places. The popular way of fishing for these super game fish is to trail a small spinner from a light rod—great sport if you find the depth at which they are feeding.

Ullswater is another splendid large lake to fish. Trout here are generally free rising and drifts around Pooley Bridge and Howtown Bay can be especially productive. Night rises can also be excellent, given good weather on such an evening, you will surely be a happy chappie. It is a majestic lake and a splendid scene against the craggy backdrop of Place Fell. Boats are available for hire from Glenridding in the south or Pooley Bridge at the northern end.

Windermere is also good for fishing but it gets horribly crowded in the summer. However, despite all the distractions, brown trout fishing can be good and fish up to 4lb are regularly caught. The lake is effectively divided into two by Belle Isle and the Lake's several large islands are noted spots, indeed boat fishing tends to be favoured. Contact the Tourist Information Centre in Windermere for further details. This is an excellent lake and in the early morning and evening fishing can be memorable. Boats can be hired in Ambleside (05394) 33187 or Bowness on Windermere (09662) 3360.

Lancashire

The River Ribble probably deserves the prize as Lancashire's most prolific fresh water. However, Yorkshire, the county of the white rose, should also receive some acclaim, for the Ribble has its source in the North Riding on Cam Fell, some eight miles north of Settle. There can be no doubt, however, that the principle waters are in red rose country.

The Ribble

The best returns for the game fisherman tend to be upstream of the river's confluence with its two main tributaries the Hodder and the Calder. Few salmon or sea-trout journey beyond Settle and the water tends to be regarded as a good water at the back end of the season, with salmon still swimming upstream in October. The river is tied up with a number of fishing associations and some clubs have a guest day. Only limited water, however, is available to visitors. Some fishing is possible and the Ribble Valley Borough Council have two stretches above the bridge at Brungerley and at Edisford Bridge. Permits are available from Ken Varey (0200) 23267. Fishing costs £4.25 per day and £10 per week and there is a bag limit of three fish. The Mitton Fishery, which is controlled by the NRA, is a fine stretch to note. Tickets are available from Mrs Haynes at Mitton Hall farm (0254) 826281. There are ten permits available for salmon and sea-trout and prices vary between £6 to £11 per day. A brown trout permit will set you back some £3, but only four are available per day and there is a daily bag limit of six. The methods allowed tend to vary with the water level and fly-only fishing is permitted when the level is below the mark stipulated on Mitton Bridge. Fly and spinning are possible when the river rises over the mark. However, from the marker post at Hodder Foot to, and including, the River Calder's confluence spinning, fly and worm fishing can be carried out at all levels. The neighbouring stretch of water is owned by Townson Brothers (0200) 441542 who issue season tickets at £150. This section of the Ribble makes for a delightful scene and is an ideal spot for the fisherman. It runs through lush green pastures and the neighbouring farmland has both dairy and sheep farming—in short a peaceful place to escape to. Great Mitton itself is a charming village, with two friendly ale-houses at which to celebrate or quench your thirst. The Royal Oak, Settle (0729) 822561 is another splendid establishment. On this occasion, a former coaching inn dating from 1684. The hotel sells permits at £11 per day on the Settle Anglers Association stretch which is fly-only water and runs for approximately seven miles, five of which are double-bank fishing.

The Hodder

The River Hodder is a large tributary of the Ribble. The river starts life on Burn Moor, flowing through Stocks Reservoir before joining the Ribble at Great Mitton. The river is largely preserved which is a pity as some great sport is to be found. There are, however, some spots available—for instance a one mile stretch on the Slaidburn

Estate. Permits are available from The Jam Pot in Slaidburn (0200) 446225 and are priced at £7 and £20 for a day and week respectively. This is another delightful spot in which to fish, surrounded by vast expanses of Lancashire moorland. The village pub, the Hark to Bounty is a fine place to whet your whistle. The Hodder Bridge Hotel (0254) 826216 is another hostelry to shortlist. It has a private 600 yard stretch and can organise good and inexpensive fishing on the Rivers Ribble and Hodder. The Inn at Whitewell (0200) 448222 overlooks, and has the rights to, approximately four miles of the Hodder. Costs vary significantly with the season. Day tickets are for residents only and range from £11 to £25. This is a beautiful part of Lancashire and the riverbank setting quite superb.

Lancastrian Waters

Bank House Fishery is situated in the picturesque Lune Valley at the edge of Caton Village, some two miles from the M6 (junction 34). This man-made water has been thoughtfully landscaped of late, with several secluded islands and a number of casting jetties. The water is well stocked with brown and rainbow trout and provides excellent fishing. Some five hundred yards away we find a more illustrious water, the River Lune. Rods are limited here which adds to the feeling of seclusion. The record rainbow weighed in at 13lb— so you can see the inmates are very large. There is a bag limit of four fish per day and two fish for an evening or for a half rod. The season runs from March to the end of October and a day ticket is £17 and £10 for an evening or half rod. You are advised to book in advance and can do so by contacting Bank House (0524) 770412. Stocks Fishery (05242) 61305 is another well run fishery in Clitheroe. Should you need to contact them after the start of the season in March then try the Fishing Lodge (0200) 446602. The fishery has a superb moorland setting in the Hodder Valley, close to the source of this celebrated river and as well as the trout, deer, rabbit and all manner of wildlife inhabit the environs. Bank fishing is permitted from 8.30am until an hour after sunset. Boat fishing is possible from 8.30am until sunset itself. The Lodge is located a mile off the Slaidburn to High Bentham Road. There are numerous charges here, but a day permit costs £10. Rowing boats and outboard motors can also be hired and tackle is available too. One of the delights of Stocks is the abundant wildlife and all visitors to the area are asked to tread with care! This is a well run fishery with an impressive catch rate.

The nearby Trout Fishery at Whalley (0254) 822211 is also worth noting. It is stocked with rainbows and has a number of wild browns. The fishery is open throughout the year for rainbows. Some fifty-five rods per day are available, and fly-fishing only is allowed with barbless hooks. There are some large fish here and a day ticket will cost £15 with a limit of four fish. A six-hour ticket is £9. There are three double boats available for hire at £9 per day and a single boat at £5. The fishery is situated amidst the shadows of Pendle Hill—witches and all—and the scenery is beautiful. The Pennine Trout Fishery (0706) 378325 is another extremely popular fishery with some monstrous fish lurking its thirty-foot depths. There are two lakes with a total surface of five acres. It is close to Greater Manchester but despite this bookings are generally only required for weekends or bank holidays. It is open twenty-four hours with night fishing by floodlight, which should suit all insomniacs. There is little chance of nodding off either—the thought of the 11lb brown or the 24lb rainbow which were taken here should have everyone on their toes. The Top Lake has thirty rods and the Bottom Lake twelve. Four hours here costs £11.00 and eight hours £16.75. There is a two fish limit for the shorter stint and three for the eight hours. If you catch an additional fish you may keep it provided you fork out an extra £3.75. If it's an eleven-pounder then that is good value!

Hurleston Hall (0704) 841064 is another fishery that merits attention. It is situated at Scarisbrick on the A570, Southport Road, a mile or so from Ormskirk. This is a place with a past and there are legends involving ghosts, civil war relics and tunnels for escaping prisoners. This is a haven for spooks and sportsmen alike and the rainbows range from a pound and eight ounces and fifteen pounds. The water is restricted to fly-only, barbless hooks (maximum size 8). A full day's fishing will cost £9, five and three hours are priced at £6 and £4 respectively. There are some good rates for juniors and rods can be hired for £3. All fish taken are costed at £1.70 per pound. Ironically, the water is known as the friendly fishery—one can only assume that the ghosties are similarly inclined!

Preston is well served by trout fisheries and Rawcliffe (0253) 700279 is one suggestion. The fishery lies some six miles from Blackpool and tickets are priced at £7 per half day or £4 for an evening. Barbless hooks are once again required and your prey will be rainbows or wild browns. The lake is small but well worth a peep. The Twin Lakes Trout Fishery (0772) 601093 at Croston is well worth a visit too. It comprises two six-acre lakes and the North Lake is fly-only. Opening hours range from 8.00am to dusk until October and thereafter from 8.00am to 4.30pm. Tickets cost £15.50 per day with a four fish limit and five hours is £9.50 with a two fish limit. Any three hours is £6.00 with a one fish limit. The lake is stocked three times a week with rainbows. The fish are often in double figures in weight and the fishery record currently stands at 15lb 4oz. Tuition is available by arrangement along with rod hire. There are excellent facilities, including a tackle shop and licensed bar—another good excuse for an afternoon's sport here.

What lovelier county could there be than Yorkshire, with its rolling hills, glorious dales and wild moors? As well as its natural beauty, the county also boasts a marvelous selection of stately homes, churches, gardens and famous houses. And here, of course, is some of the finest fishing to be found in England.

The Aire

The River Aire offers trout and grayling fishing in its upper reaches where it is a typical tumbling dales river. Heavy brown trout are recorded downstream of Gargrave and in the Skipton area. Keighley Angling Club has approximately fourteen miles of fishing and day tickets are available from various tackle shops in the area for as little as £2 per day. Willis Walker in Keighley (0535) 602928 and K. Tackle (0756) 794451 handle the permits for Skipton Anglers Association who have three miles of double-bank fishing. Saltaire Anglers Association has a further two miles, again all double-bank, and you should contact the Shipley Angling Centre (0274) 595726 for more information. It is fair to say that the Aire in its lower reaches is polluted, but the game fishing in its upper reaches is well worth sampling and, as you might imagine, the setting is somewhat more attractive in these remote parts too.

The Wharfe

It would not be too outrageous to suggest that fishing in the north and west of Yorkshire is somewhat superior to that in the south of this large county. The River Wharfe is a delightful and extremely popular river. The water has numerous fishing opportunities and the game fisherman will find some fine trout fishing. This is generally in the upper reaches of the river and around Bolton Bridge, Burnsall and Grassington.

The Wharfe rises in Langstrothdale and in its upper reaches the water passes through dramatic upland country. It has fast, rushing waterfalls combined with long, slow glides and an abundance of tree lined banks. After Otley, it becomes an altogether more sedate water and thereafter, coarse fish are increasingly prevalent. The season spans the months of April, through summer to September. Linton, Threshfield and Grassington Angling Club control two miles of water, in the environs of the village of Linton. The Devonshire Arms Hotel, Grassington (0756) 752525 issues day permits at £15 for this fly-only water which is restricted to members only on Sundays. Between Grassington and the village of Barden we find seven miles of single and double-bank fishing. Day tickets are available from the Red Lion at Burnsall (0756) 720204. Fly fishing is permitted and there is a six fish limit. Brown trout costs £16.50 per day.

Another splendid location is on the Duke of Devonshire's Estate at Bolton Abbey (0756) 710227. There are five miles of double-bank fishing here and the charge is £10 per day with a bag limit of four fish. The average weight is one pound but fish of over twenty pounds have been known in recent years. The river at this point is still fast-flowing and strewn with rocks. The Estate have their own hatcheries and as a result the waters are well stocked. Tickets are also available for residents of the splendid Devonshire Arms Hotel (0756) 710441.

The Nidd

Some charming scenery can be found on many stretches of the River Nidd, another tributary of the Ouse System. The river's source is on Great Whernside, from where it flows to Nidderdale, past Pateley Bridge and Knaresborough. Most of the water is controlled by local angling associations but a number of day tickets can be found.

Great Whernside reveals bleak moorland akin to that of the Bronte novels. The river initially feeds two reservoirs and its character is shallow and rocky in its infancy. As the river flows from Gouthwaite Reservoir, it takes on an enlarged character. Here its steep banks are predominantly tree-lined and the scene is a real delight. Nidderdale Angling Club controls seven miles on both banks in the area of Pateley Bridge. Day tickets are available for £7 from the Royal Oak Hotel (0423) 780200 on the village green at Dacre, ten miles from Harrogate on the A59. Theakston's bitter is brewed in nearby Masham and adds further attraction to this delightful area. The York and District Anglers Association waters are not as renowned as those one finds further upstream. Nevertheless, day tickets can be purchased from the tacklist P. H. & J. R. Smith, High Street Knaresborough (0423) 863322, which lies opposite the Little Elephant pub. The staff here are extremely helpful and will advise you on various good waters in the vicinity. Some of the best water is retained by the Harrogate Fly Fishers but, sadly, the water is restricted to members and their guests. Such is life! There is some fine fishing available, a number of outstanding real ales to sample and some really tremendous countryside which the trout, as you will perhaps find out, are far from happy to leave!

The Ure & the Bain

The River Ure holds some good trout and stretches for some forty-five miles from Abbotside Common to its confluence with the Swale at Boroughbridge. Although trout are present throughout the water, they are more prolific in the reaches above Middleham where some 5lb brown trout are taken each year and a couple of 8lb fish have been reported, so be prepared! Wensleydale Anglers Association has some four miles of double-bank fishing on the Ure and day tickets can be obtained from the Rose and Crown Hotel (0969) 50225 on Bainbridge village green. Permits cost £6 a day and £12 a week and fishing can also be enjoyed on the River Bain. This is a delightful little river that provides some fine fishing for browns and grayling. Palmer Flatts Hotel (0969) 663228 some five minutes down from the wild Aysgarth Falls has a small stretch which is free to guests and some £2 a day for non-residents. Further good fishing can be purchased from Lewis Country Wear in Hawes (0969) 667443 who represent the Hawes and High Abbotside Anglers Association. Dry and wet fly as well as worm fishing is allowed from 24th March to October 1st.

The Swale

The River Swale shares many characteristics with its near neighbour the Ure. It provides an ever-changing scene with deep slow-moving bends and contrasting fast-flowing runs. The water is renowned for chub and barbel, but some good trout fishing can also be enjoyed in the upper reaches, particularly above Richmond. The Northallerton Angling Club have some five miles of single-bank available for non-members below Morton Bridge on the Northallerton to Bedale Road. Permits cost £3 per day and a 4lb brown trout was taken here in June 1991. Permits are obtainable from Angling (0609) 779140 in Northallerton. W. Metcalfe, Guns and Tackle, Richmond (0748) 822108 issues permits for the Richmond and District Angling Club for £12 a week and offers approximately eight to nine miles of double-bank fishing between Maske Bridge and Brompton-on-Swale.

The Esk

Despite its rural splendour and its many rivers, Yorkshire only lays claim to one salmon river—the Esk. As you can imagine, the Yorkshire folk are proud of this particular water, but they are not overly possessive and day tickets can be bought. In recent times the river has suffered from low water and some have even written it off as a salmon and sea-trout river. This seems a trifle premature and invariably some good fish are landed; particularly towards the end of the season.

The NRA have embarked upon a smolt re-introduction scheme which is producing good results and which augurs well for the future. As the environment continues to play havoc and the demands on the water supply become ever greater, the situation on the Esk will be fascinating to watch.

The Esk rises on Westerdale Moor and runs into the sea at Whitby. There are fine stocks of brown trout in the many moorland beats which flow into the Esk. The river is largely controlled by the Esk Fishery Association but a number of very attractive stretches are accessible. The Egton Estate (0947) 85466 has a delightful one and a half mile stretch of double-bank fishing which holds three rods. There are some fine holding pools and the brown trout are prolific here. A day's fishing will cost in the region of £15.

Woodlands Hall (0947) 811180, some four miles from Whitby has some superbly scenic waters in the Yorkshire National Park. Permits can be obtained from £10 to £15. Always phone in advance as only two rods per day are permitted. The water includes two salmon pools and three trout runs. John Hobbs will help you with your enquiries here and the nearby Mallyan Spout Hotel (0947) 86206 is one for the notebook.

The North Yorks Steam Railway, which has a delightful journey through the Yorkshire woodlands from Grosmont to Pickering, is a quaint intrusion into a relatively quiet untroubled world. Danby Angling Club has some seven miles of double-bank fishing and the brown trout fishing here is good. Day tickets are available at a cost of £3 from the Duke of Wellington (0287) 660351, which stands proudly in the middle of Danby.

Although much of the fishing is kept on a tight rein and is closely preserved, the Ruswarp Pleasure Boat Company in Ruswarp (0947) 604658 leases one and a half miles from the Esk Fishery Association, from the weir at Ruswarp to Iburndale Beck. This allows some really good value fishing and the possibility that the salmon will return in ever increasing numbers in the years to come. Fingers crossed anyway!

Yorkshire Waters

The Recreational Department of Yorkshire Water have created some fine fishing opportunities in well-stocked reservoirs in the region. But beware. Coin-operated systems are used at many of the waters in the Yorkshire region, so take plenty of change with you.

Not all the fisheries are run by the Authority and the Cleatham Fishery (0724) 855972 is one such example. Although the fishery is a mere four miles from the M18 it is surrounded by agricultural countryside and woodland. The water has a popular catch and release system but four fish can be taken for £10. Heading westwards, we arrive at Hepworth and Heathcote Trout Fishery (0274) 877498. This is a delightful two acre lake set amidst ten acres of woodland. It is stocked with rainbows, brown trout and Arctic char. There is an interesting policy, as any fish over 4lb must be returned. The owner Mr Ted Heathcote-Walker believes that big fish are seldom eaten and often end up in the bin! The policy, therefore, is to leave them and let others enjoy the challenge as they become increasingly weighty. There are several big fish in these waters, one of which was 24lb 8oz. However, it was not a record as it was not killed. Tuition is available and the first lesson is free—an excellent idea. Recently, a blind-person learnt to fish here and caught a twelve-pounder!

The Washburn Valley Fisheries (0943) 880658 are made up of four reservoirs including the excellent Fewston and Swinsty. Each water is in excess of a hundred and fifty acres and all are regularly stocked with brown trout and rainbows. The season can run from mid March until the end of October and the fisheries are open daily from 7.30am. Children under the age of fifteen may fish without a permit if accompanied by an experienced adult who does possess a permit. Fewston is easy to find, on the A59 road between Harrogate and Blubberhouses Moor. Fewston is restricted to fly-only fishing whilst Swinsty allows some bait fishing. The Authority is endeavouring to encourage all manner of recreation on the reservoirs but this will not be allowed to detract from the fishing. Incidentally, Yorkshire Water controls a number of worthy fisheries, among them Thornton Steward reservoir, More Hall, and Scout Dike. Details can be obtained by telephoning (0532) 448201.

Another water which boasts a number of attractions is the Kilnsey Park Water (0756) 752150, which is set in the heart of the delightful Yorkshire dales. This is a relatively friendly introduction to fly fishing but the scenery is beautiful and there is a catch and return policy in operation at the lake. Tickets are available from the farm, shop for a full or half day's fishing. The waters are regularly stocked by the adjoining trout farm which also supplies the shop. As you can see, this will appeal to the casual fisherman. Furthermore, the 'Daleslife' Visitor Centre has a unique aquarium of freshwater fish which are beautifully displayed and labelled. The Fly Fishing in Wharfedale Exhibition provides a visual account of the sport in the area.

Leighton Reservoir (0765) 689224 is another extremely popular fishery, situated on the edge of the windy Masham Moor. The water is controlled by Swainton Estate who have their own hatchery. Browns of 5lb and rainbows of 10lb are commonly caught. Season tickets are available and the fishery is open from late March to the end of November. A four fish day ticket (6.00am to sunset) will cost in the region of £10. There is a coin operated system here too, so take plenty of change.

Northumbria

Northumbria has had a turbulent history, often at the hands of various conquerors, and it has an important place in the history of Christianity. It also includes some of Britain's most spectacular scenery. And fishing!

The Tees

The River Tees has a remote Pennine setting in Cumbria's Cross Fell. The brown trout is the prolific species of game fish to be found on the Tees and the best locations are generally in the upper reaches. The waters between Middleton in Teesdale and a short distance further downstream at Barnard Castle are particularly recommended. The grayling also revel in the faster flowing parts of the upper reaches and Barnard Castle is once again a popular location. Serious pollution in the industrialised areas of Middlesborough have restricted salmon and sea-trout runs, but there is much work being done to try and redress the balance. It will take time, effort and money but let us hope that this once notable salmon river recovers some of its esteem.

The Raby Estate Office (0833) 40209 has some good brown trout fishing on nine miles of the river. The fee is £6.00 per day with a bag limit of four. A week costs £18 and a season £45. The Estate office is located opposite the Teesdale Hotel and tickets can also be obtained from the High Force Hotel (0833) 22264. J Raine & Son (0833) 40406 in Middleton issue day tickets for the Strathore Estate who own the South Bank. The price is £4 for a day, £18 for a week and £45 for the season. The upper reaches are set amidst some delightful scenery and High Force is a celebrated landmark. If there is a good head of water, the falls are truly spectacular and well worth a detour.

The Wear

The River Wear rises on Burnhope Seat to the west of the county, amidst the delightful ragged fells where Cumbria borders Durham. It flows east, a distance of some sixty-five miles through Stanhope, Bishop Auckland and Durham, before it spills into the North Sea at Sunderland. Some serious anti-pollution work and a gradual re-stocking programme have ensured the river's renaissance and the game angler can now enjoy some fine sea-trout fishing. The salmon runs could not be described as substantial but they are progressing, which is tremendous to report. A twenty-two pounder was caught in 1993, and they average at around 12lb.

Bishop Auckland and District Angling Club have approximately twenty miles available for day tickets, which range from £5 to £20 depending on the season. The higher price is naturally charged in the later months when the salmon and sea-trout fishing comes into its own. Assuming a good level of rainfall, the river fishes well, particularly late in the season. Season tickets can be had for £93.50 (plus £23.50 joining fee) from the Secretary, J. Winter (0388) 762538 and day tickets from Windrow Sports in Bishop Auckland (0388) 603759. The Club also have one mile on the River Browney which joins the Wear at Sunderland Bridge; this tributary offers good brown trout fishing.

The Upper Wear behaves more like a spate river, and if there has been sufficient rainfall, sea-trout can be good at the back end of the season and salmon also come up to a mile or so below St John's Chapel, some forty miles from the sea. The Upper Weardale Angling Club has some six miles of water here and day permits can be obtained for £5 from the post office or the Golden Lion (0388) 537231, beside the cattle market. The sea-trout tend to be most prolific in September and October and dependent on summer rainfalls, which sometimes arrive earlier. In other words, keep in tune with the summer weather!

The Tyne

Energetic work in re-stocking and the closure of several collieries, together with an improved attitude to pollution by a number of industries has seen some great improvements to the Wear but it is still shadowed by its more illustrious and much improved sister, the Tyne. This is a tremendous credit to the water companies and all involved.

The North Tyne flows out of the massive Kielder Water and joins the South Tyne near Hexham. Thereafter, the Tyne flows through Corbridge, Prudhoe and Newcastle before arriving at the North Sea at Tynemouth. The river journeys through some delightful Northumberland scenery and there are a number of fishing opportunities for the visiting angler. Falstone Fishing Club have a good two mile stretch of double-bank fishing. Permits are available from the Black Cock Inn (0434) 240200. This charming 380 year old inn sits next to the church and is a fine spot if you happen to like real ale. A seventh-century cross was discovered here in the 1950s, so keep your eyes open for similar relics! Day tickets are £10. The George at Chollerford (0434) 681611 also has water on the North Tyne. The fishing here is excellent value for residents and the setting is absolutely enchanting.

The Northumberland Anglers Federation has three good stretches of approximately five miles which is well stocked with brown trout. Salmon were making a good showing in 1991. The only ticket that is currently available is a fourteen day permit which costs £42 and includes one and a half miles on the River Coquet. Permits are available from the Head Bailiff, Mr Bagnall, at Thirston Mill, West Thirston (0670) 787663. There are a number of opportunities for fishing the Tyne, with a premier beat eight miles east of Hexham. This is a three mile stretch which can be fished from both banks, and there is some first class fishing here. The best months for salmon are from February to May and September to October with sea-trout fishing from May onwards, although September is the best month where both fly and spinning is permitted. Mr A.F. Pollard of Reeltime Fishing Services (0661) 843799 will assist with enquiries. Season rods offer one manned day per week and occasional day rods.

The North and South Tynes are generally fast running rivers which favour dry fly trout fishing. Deep pools near Haltwhistle can be found and trout in the 5lb bracket are lurking—so be prepared! The North Tyne has a number of fine beats: some five miles north of Hexham; Chollerford; up river between Wark and Simonhorn; above Wark, as well as various other beats. Salmon run from March onwards, with March, April and May being good months. September and October are also extremely good and are the two prime months for sea-trout which tend to run from June onwards. The beats are mainly let on a weekly basis and you should contact Mr Gaisford at J. M. Clarke and Partners on (0434) 602301 for all the details. The South Tyne has some quality association waters. The river requires good water and when in spate provides some fine fishing. The salmon run from May with August through to October being the favoured times. Sea-trout will run from June given good water but the best months are again September and October. Weekly permits are available and you are advised to contact Greggs Sports in Haltwhistle (0434) 320255 for further details. Finally, Haydon Bridge Angling Club offers visitors who are staying in the area weekly permits. Details can be obtained from the splendid Langley Castle Hotel (0434) 688888. If you are looking for good fishing in England, the Tyne provides a plethora of good opportunities. Further information on the Tyne, and on all of the region's waters, may be obtained from Northumbrian Water (091) 383 2222.

The River Rede is a tributary of the Tyne that is well worth exploring and two excellent places from which to plan your attack are The Percy Arms (0830) 20261 and The Otterburn Tower (0830) 20620—two extremely pleasant establishments in which to stay.

The Wansbeck

The delightful Northumbrian scenery reveals a number of other splendid rivers for the visiting angler. The River Wansbeck is tied up with private syndicates and clubs but there is a two mile stretch below Morpeth at Wansbeck Riverside Park. It is owned by the council and has produced some good trout in recent years. Day permits can be purchased for £2.70 from the Park Warden in Green Lane, Ashington (0670) 812323.

The Coquet

The River Coquet is a delightful water which rises in the wilds of the Cheviot Hills and flows through Rothbury and, after some forty miles, enters the North Sea at Warkworth. This is a good game fishing river with salmon, sea-trout and brown trout all to be found. The Coquet is generally regarded as a late river with a good run of salmon and sea-trout well into October. The Northumberland Angling Federation lease waters from the Duke of Northumberland and this comprises some eleven miles of fishing, which is spread along the river and includes a variety of waters. Recent reports for the river have looked good, with salmon and brown trout prolific. If you are seeking advice or information on the Coquet contact The Sports Shop in Fawcett's Yard, Morpeth (0670) 514760. For visitors tickets and salmon fishing contact Mr Bagnall at Thirston Mill, Felton (0670) 787663. The Whitton Farmhouse Hotel (0669) 20811, next to Whitton's Riding Stables, also issues fourteen-day trout permits for the NAF. The Angler's Arms Hotel (0665) 570655 at Weldon Bridge also has a small stretch which provides more fine brown trout fishing. Furthermore, in September and October, some great value salmon fishing can be had for £7.50 a day. The Angler's Arms is a classic coaching inn remotely situated beside the bridge where the A697 crosses the Coquet. It is a classic country pub and the nearest neighbours tend to be oyster catchers and goosanders.

Rothbury and Thropton Angling Club have three and a half miles of single-bank fishing. Permits cost in the region of £5 per day and are available from the Thropton Village Shop (0669) 20412, beside The Three Wheat Heads. Night fishing for sea-trout is also permitted here, should you be keen on night fishing, or if you are an insomniac.

Murraysport in Alnwick (0665) 602462 handle a good private beat on the Coquet, The Weldon Water, which offers two miles of mainly double-bank fishing and also has some fine pools. However, rods are limited to only two per day and day tickets cost £11 between February and August and £16 for the months of September and October.

The Aln
The River Aln is comparatively short and flows into the sea at Alnmouth. The Aln Anglers Association, who control a seven mile stretch downstream from Denwick Bridge, is a working trust and all monies are reinvested into the upkeep of the river, which is regularly stocked with one-pound brown trout. This is fly-water and includes some tidal waters where the sea-trout and salmon are most prolific. In 1989, a weighty seventeen-pound sea-trout was caught and four to nine pounders are regularly caught here. Iron Blue Dun is a recommended fly for the brownies and Garry and Viva Green Tail for sea-trout. Fish tend to run in February and March and September and October. The water also provides some fine brown trout sport and comes into its own in the late spring and summer months. There are only weekly or monthly tickets available and the weekly permit will set you back £25. There is no Sunday fishing for visitors. Permits can be obtained from L.K. Jobson (0665) 602135, beside the Hotspur Tower in Alnwick or from Murraysport (0665) 602462.

Northumbria Waters
Lockwood Beck is one of several waters in the Durhsand Cleveland area. It is pleasantly secluded, situated just north of the A171 Guisborough to Whitby Road. A total of five streams and three becks run into the reservoir, which is well-stocked with brown and rainbow trout. The area is set amidst some beautiful woods, and mallards and great crested grebes are among a number of frequent visitors. Curlew and woodcock also abound in the wooded area beyond. The reservoir is limited to fly fishing and is managed by Northumbrian Water Ltd.

One of the delights of reservoir fishing is that it often takes you to some wonderful places and Cow Green (0833) 50204 is no exception. Situated ten miles west of Middleton-in-Teesdale, this reservoir offers tremendous sport on a water that contains one of England's best natural populations of brown trout. A twelve fish bag limit is enforced, with permits available on a self-serve basis from the fishing lodge. This superb wild fishery is complemented by five stocked waters in Lunedale and Baldersdale. For the up to date 'Fisherman's Handbook' of the various options available in the north east you should contact the Northumbrian Water Recreation Department (091) 383 2222.

Tunstall Reservoir (0388) 527293 lies in the valley of Waskerley Beck, three miles north of Wolsingham in Weardale. The water is surrounded by mature woodland and is well stocked with brown and rainbow trout. Boats are available too and day permits can be purchased here. Another fishery which enjoys a Wear Valley setting is the Witton Castle Water which is bounded by the more famous Wear. The water is managed by the Bishop Auckland Angling Club (0388) 762538. The fishery is stocked with rainbow trout between 2lb and 12lb and there are also a number of brown trout, which should be returned if caught. The fishery operates a barbless hook rule. A day permit costs £15, the facilities here are very good and the isolated location ensures a peaceful day out.

Kielder Water is surely the 'Big Daddy' of all Northumbrian waters. The reservoir enjoys a memorable setting and caters for all manner of leisure pursuits. The water is massive and there is plenty of room for all. The fishing comes into its own in the evening and Kielder's wild brown trout are prolific. The reservoir is surrounded by rolling hills and lies in the heart of the Border Forest Park. There are some twenty-seven miles of bank fishing and boats are available for hire and can be reserved in advance by telephoning (0434) 250203. Kielder Water is a splendid place to get away from it all and a little bit of peace and quiet awaits you too!

Our final thought for this area is the Whittle Dene Reservoirs (0661) 853210 where a day's fishing will cost you £12 with a six fish limit. The water lies in close proximity to Hadrian's Wall and other Roman remains, surrounded by woodland and farming—a real delight. Boats can be hired from around £6 per day and permits will cost £8.50. There are a total of four reservoirs here, all well stocked and providing yet another good reason for visiting this part of the country.

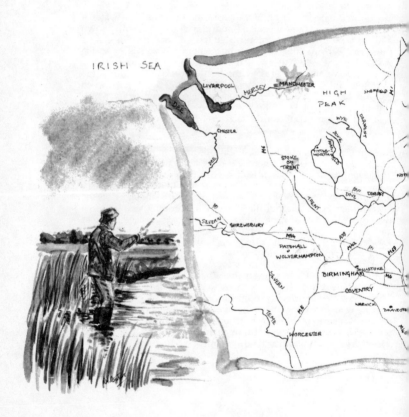

IRISH SEA

LIVERPOOL MERSEY MANCHESTER

HIGH PEAK

SHEFFIELD

DEE

CHESTER

WYE

DOVE

STOKE ON TRENT

TITTES-WORTH

TRENT

DOVE

DERBY

SEVERN

SHREWSBURY

PATSHALL

WOLVERHAMPTON

BIRMINGHAM

SEVERN

COVENTRY

WARWICK

TEME

TEME

WORCESTER

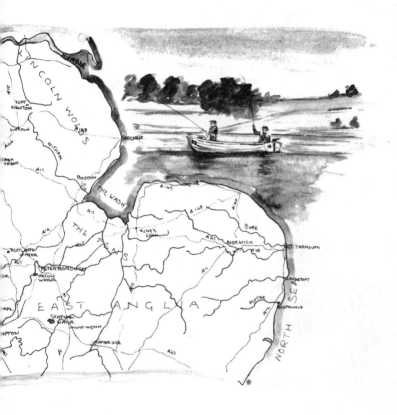

So what constitutes my ideal stillwater? I go fishing for fun and to relax, so it should be in pleasant surroundings. There should be a good amount of weed and bank-side vegetation with woodland nearby, but not so close as to make casting a problem. This will ensure a good range of fly life both in and on the water which, being chalk stream fed, will be gin-clear. The water will be stocked with fish from one to five pounds and, because it is clear, I'll be able to stalk them. The level of stocking will be such that getting in a day's limit will be an achievement, but on the other hand one will not expect to return home empty-handed. The number of rods will be strictly limited so that I'll be free to try different places as I wish and feel that I'm on my own. Finally, the other rods will be kindred spirits so at the end of the day we can all go off and enjoy a drink and a chat in the excellent pub nearby!

Suffolk Waters

One might not think of East Anglia as a game fishing area, but there are good stillwaters and trout streams to be enjoyed here. A short distance off the A12 near Thaxted in Suffolk is the village of Walpole, and Valley Fisheries (098684) 488 have a two and a half acre spring fed lake which is regularly stocked with brownies as well as rainbows. A day ticket here for five fish costs £20. Near Bury St. Edmunds there is the two lake Larkwood Fishery (0284) 728612, while on the Norfolk, Suffolk border off the A143 near Harleston is Mendham Mill Trout Fishery (0379) 852328. Mendham offers four acres of fishing in lakes as well as the River Waveney Mill race and is set in the picturesque Waveney Valley. Locally-tied flies and tuition are available and a four fish day ticket costs £10.

Norfolk Waters

Across the border in Norfolk is the Salmon and Trout Association's stillwater at Lenwade. This is a season ticket water only and you must be a member of the Association. Membership in 1992 cost £12 and can be obtained from Lt Cdr L. D. Temple-Richards (032878) 217. Nearby are the four acre Whinburgh Trout Lakes (0362) 850201 and near Kings Lynn are Narborough Trout Lakes (0760) 338005. These five lakes are well stocked and hold some big fish. North east of Aylesham, just off the B1354 are Bure Valley Lake Fisheries (026387) 666. The fishery's three lakes total ten acres and it has a mile of the River Bure. Salmon were introduced in 1992 and the fishery has been featured on ITV's *Go Fishing.* Downstream at Abbots Hall, Ingworth, members of the STA can enjoy a mile of double-bank fishing on the Bure for £8 a day or £60 a season. There is however, a waiting list for season tickets. Fakenham Angling Club have two miles of the River Wensum. Day tickets are available from Dave's Tackle Shop at No 1, Rear of Norwich Street, Fakenham (0328) 862543. This river does tend to get heavily weeded from mid-summer so it is probably best to inspect the river first.

Cambridgeshire Waters

Close to Peterborough, in Cambridgeshire, is the Orton Water Trout Fishery at Orton Waterville (0733) 239995. Boats are available on this twenty-five acre water, which also holds brook trout and has produced a rainbow of 15lb 10oz and a brown of 7lb 4oz. It is set in the pretty Nene Country Park and is an ideal spot for a family day out, as other attractions include steam trains, horse riding and bird watching. There is an 18 hole golf course very near by, so watch out for sliced shots! A five-fish day ticket costs £10 and a father and son day is £12.50.

Grafham

The county that once bore the name of Huntingdonshire has sadly disappeared from the maps, but of course there is still the former county town of Huntingdon—its name well-known from the legends of Robin Hood. From a fishing point of view its chief glory is Grafham which is now in Cambridgeshire. The county of Rutland has also disappeared from the maps, but the locals strive to keep the name alive and Rutland Water helps to preserve its fame. I cannot help thinking that if the name of this fishery had been changed to something like East Midlands Fishery, it would have lost part of its charm.

The popularity of stillwater game fishing owes much to the celebrated status of Grafham Water (0480) 810531, the reservoir that celebrated its twenty-fifth anniversary in 1991. Grafham is a veritable giant among stillwaters for it covers 1569 acres and holds 13,000 million gallons of water. Over the years it has mellowed and now blends in with the local landscape. This is largely due to the care and conservation policies of Anglian Water. It is a Site of Special Scientific Interest (SSSI), and in recent years, has held nationally important numbers of wintering Great crested grebe, tufted duck and coot, while late summer sees significant numbers of moulting mute swan. There is a wide variety of bank-fishing and boats are available; details of costs etc. may be found from the fishery manager (0480) 810531. The world championships were held here in 1987 and the water has produced a 12lb 6oz brownie. Grafham is the sort of water that can always be relied on to produce good fish and the beginning of May 1991 saw a great bag of three brownies weighing 15lb 12oz, while a week later a magnificent brown of 10lb was recorded. An eight fish day ticket will set you back £11.

Rutland Water

I suppose its original title of Empingham reservoir would have been preferable to East Midlands Fishery, but thank goodness local pressure prevailed and it was called Rutland Water. I am sure the bells of Normanton Church, the well known local landmark, would have rung out in anger at any other name. Although comparatively new, the original detailed landscaping work of Dame Sylvia Crewe has ensured that it now blends in perfectly with the local scenery. Grafham is huge but Rutland is a monster, for it covers over 3000 acres—roughly the same size as Lake Windermere. Peace and quiet are assured here for, although sailing is permitted, intrusive sports such as water-skiing and power boating are banned. An eight-fish day ticket costs £11 and boats are available, further details can be obtained from the fishing lodge (0780) 86770. Part of the western end is a nature reserve and one of the richest reservoir locations for wintering and passage wildfowl in Britain. It is particularly notable for its numbers of mallard, shoveler, gadwell, teal, wigeon, pochard, tufted duck and goldeneye. Rutland co-hosted the 1987 world championship with Grafham and this is not surprising when you consider that over 50,000 anglers fish here every season and the total catch weight is over fifty tons. Both rainbows and browns of over 12lb have been caught as has an eight fish bag totalling 48lb, a record for any European reservoir.

Northamptonshire Waters

North from Kettering on the A6003 is Eyebrook Reservoir at Caldecott (0536) 770264. This 400 acre water is set in a natural valley and has very good weed growth with plenty of snacks; shrimp, sedge, midge and ceria. Not far away is the fifty-acre Elinor Trout Fishery (08015) 786 at Aldwincle near Kettering. Boats are available although the bank fishing is excellent. A few miles north of Northampton are two more well known Anglian Water Reservoirs, Ravensthorpe and Pitsford. Built in 1886, Ravensthorpe is a very mature water and, many would say, the most attractive of the Northamptonshire reservoirs. Further details can be had from the fishing lodge (0604) 770875. Pitsford (0604) 781350 is a 750 acre water whose popularity has increased enormously in recent years due to Anglian Water's hard work in improving stocks and facilities. Unlike many reservoirs, Pitsford trout have a reputation for surface feeding and dry flies are usually very effective. A good range of coarses are on offer here and at Grafham.

Warwickshire Waters

With so many good fisheries in such pleasant surroundings it is hard to remember that the Midlands used to be called 'The Black Country'. However, local industry has seen a lot of changes and coal is no longer king. Many authorities have done a great deal of conservation work. At Bishop's Itchington near Leamington Spa are the Bishop's Bowl Lakes (0926) 613344, which hosted the final of the Troutmasters competition a few years ago. The lakes cover forty acres and are formed from old limestone quarries. The actual rocks are more than 170 million years old and contain a wealth of fossils. Quarrying in 1927 revealed the intact skeleton of a plesiosaur, an aquatic reptile often thought to be the identity of the Loch Ness Monster. This skeleton, which is eighteen feet long, can be seen in the Natural History Museum in London. There are three lakes here. White Bishop Lake is designed to be a 'quick catch' lake and is ideal for the less experienced. The five acre Mitre Pool holds bigger fish, as does Bishop's Bowl which has a great mayfly hatch, and both lakes are designed to appeal to the more experienced rod. A day ticket costs £6 and casting instruction is available.

Less than two miles away at Harbury is Chesterton Mill Pool (0926) 613235. The fishery is set in twenty acres, surrounded by lovely unspoiled countryside and woodland. The water mill, like the windmill, was built in 1620 by Sir Edward Peyto, then Sheriff of the county. The mill was used to grind corn right up to the 1950s when it fell into disuse. By 1976 the lake was so full of silt and overgrown with reeds that the water area was down to half an acre. Restoration work started in 1980 and the lake is now some four and a half acres and has just the right amount of weed and bank-side vegetation to ensure good fly life. A five-fish ticket costs £17.50 and the water is stocked with browns and rainbows. Severn Trent's 600 acre Draycote Water (0788) 812018 is near Rugby and an eight fish day ticket costs £11.40. In 1992 the proposed stocking programme was 49,000 mixed browns and rainbows. The rainbows were mainly around one and a quarter pounds, but there was a significant number of 4lb fish and some over 10lb. At Meriden, near Coventry, is Lord Guernsey's Packington Fishery (0676) 22754. There are three established lakes of twenty-eight, eighteen and six acres which are reserved for members, and three former gravel pits totalling forty-four acres on which day tickets are available. The lakes are stocked with rainbows and the minimum size is 11/4lb. The best rainbow of 1993 weighed in at 12lb 11oz. The fishery also has two miles on the River Blythe. A day ticket costs £14 and that will give you a bag limit of eight fish! The Blythe has rightly been called a sparkling gem as the entire river is an SSSI. The reason for this is that, botanically, the river is one of the richest in lowland England, with some sections containing as many species as the very richest chalk streams. The SSSI system operates in a similar way to the way buildings are listed and can be a bit of a headache for river managers and riparian owners, as any improvements they wish to make must first be agreed by English Nature.

West Midlands Waters

At Coleshill, in the West Midlands, is Shustoke Reservoir, the home of Shustoke Fly Fishers Limited (0675) 481702. The fishery consists of a main reservoir of ninety-two acres and a settling pool which can only be fished by members. Visitors can fish the main water where a five fish day ticket costs £12. An added attraction is the rather good pub within a hundred yards of the main gate. Patshull Hall at Burnhill Green, near Wolverhampton, was once the seat of the Earl of Dartmouth, but now stands empty. Patshull Great Lake, (0902) 700774, is occupied by many splendid hard fighting brownies and rainbows. The Great Lake covers some seventy-five acres and was designed by Capability Brown in the 1740s, the result being one of the most picturesque fisheries in the country. The fishery is particularly keen to support the disabled angler and boats have been specially adapted to take wheelchairs. There is easy access to the bank and there is a very popular annual fishing competition for the disabled. A six-fish day ticket costs £12 and a further £2.20 per fish caught. West of here and some four miles north of Kidderminster on the A442 are Shatterford Lakes (02997) 597. There are four lakes here ranging from half an acre to two acres, and a ten fish day ticket costs £6. The fishery is set in a delightful location on a hillside on the edge of the beautiful Severn Valley and has fine views over the Shropshire Countryside. There are herds of red, fallow and sika deer and a number of peacocks. There is a wealth of bird life including pied flycatchers and wild flowers such as spotted orchids.

The River Teme rises near Newton in Powys and its winding course takes it over the Welsh border into Hereford until it flows south to join the Severn at Worcester. There is an unusual way to fish the upper reaches of this charming little stream—all you have to do is stay in one of the houses in the Knighton area that do bed and breakfast and your fishing is free. Knighton stands half way down Offas Dyke and was described in A. E. Housman's *A Shropshire Lad* as one of the quietest places under the sun. G. H. Medlicott and Son, Solicitors, of Station Road, Knighton, Powys can provide more details about the fishing. The river and its feeders here are pretty small and you won't need anything bigger than an eight-foot rod. Suggested flies include Black Gnat, Black Pennell, Zulu, Red Spinner, Blue Dun, Coachman and Alder. At Lindridge, Mr Ken Powell (058470) 208, has one and a half miles of single and double-bank fishing near Tenbury Wells. This delightful gentleman has been fishing the river for over sixty years and welcomes day visitors to his water. The water was stocked with several thousand trout which have now reached a fair size. There are salmon here, too, and this beat has several pools including one of particular merit. A day in this delightful area can be had for the very modest amount of £2.

The Severn

The headwaters of the Severn are also in Wales and, having a course of over 180 miles on its journey to the Bristol Channel, it is the longest river in England and Wales. The upper reaches offer good trouting and although, in common with most other rivers, the salmon run is not what it was, the Severn is still not bad and produces some good-sized fish. The best part for salmon fishing is the middle reaches since the lower ones are mainly noted for their excellent coarse fishing. If you want to fish the headwaters, the Poachers Pocket Pub at Llanidloes (0686) 688233 issue day tickets which cost £4 for the Dinas Estuary Fishing, which is two and a half miles of well-stocked, double-bank trout water. Llanidloes Angling Association have approximately twelve miles of fishing on the Severn and its tributaries. Salmon are hardly ever seen this far up, except occasionally in a very wet season and afforestation schemes have caused drainage problems here. For a good days trouting, Mr Davis of the Association recommends a visit to Clywedog Reservoir, permits for which can be had from Mrs Gough at the Travellers Rest Restaurant (05512) 2329. Downstream at Caersws, the Maesmawr Hotel (0686) 688255 has one and a half miles of double-bank fishing which is free to residents, while visitors can buy a day ticket for £3.50. This is a beautiful part of the country and there is one particularly good pool on this water. Mike's Tackle Shop at Newtown (0686) 624388 is run by Mike and Carol Barber who can give you comprehensive advice on salmon fishing in the area. This friendly couple are both experienced anglers who welcome phone calls and visitors to the shop and can also introduce you to local fishermen, who will be pleased to show you their favourite waters.

With its medieval church spires, Norman castle, and beautiful Georgian and Tudor black and white houses, Shrewsbury must have one of the richest visible histories of any English town. It also has some good fishing, especially at the Weir and at Monkmoor. Further details can be had from the Council offices (0743) 231456. A must for any fisherman is a visit to Chris Partington's Vintage Tackle shop at 103 Longden Coleham in Shrewsbury (0743) 369373. Chris deals in tackle that spans four centuries and has also set up Britain's Angling Heritage Trust. He is a very experienced fisherman and generous with his advice on tackling both the Severn and the area generally.

Another interesting town lies about fifteen miles downstream. Ironbridge witnessed the birth of the Industrial Revolution, and the eponymous bridge still spans the Severn. A great deal of restoration has been done to the old buildings and factories in the last twenty years and the town now has a wealth of interesting exhibitions. Further downstream, at Stourport on Severn, day tickets can be had from John White's Tackle Shop (02993) 71735. Although salmon are caught here it is predominantly a coarse fishery and the game fisherman would probably prefer to cast his fly elsewhere.

Cheshire Waters

Returning north to Cheshire, Chester, with its half timbered buildings and old shopping area called the Rows, is another attractive town. A short distance away is Mickle Trafford and Meadow Fishery (0244) 300236. This fishery has two lakes of five and two of three quarter acres which are stocked with both brown and rainbow. A four-fish day ticket costs £18 and June 1991 saw a splendid 10lb rainbow, and a bag of twenty-two fish—someone must have been feeling rich!—caught in five hours with a best fish of 5lb 8oz. East of here at Mobberley, which is located between Knutsford and Wilmslow, is the Clay Lane Farm Fishery (056587) 3337. This is a one and a half acre spring fed water where a four-fish day ticket costs £18. Clay Lane has produced a brown of 9lb and a rainbow of 12lb. I am delighted to see that this is a fishery which states that barbless hooks must be used. Other Cheshire stillwaters include Brookside at Crewe (0270) 820528, Marton Heath at Macclesfield (0260) 224221, and Wall Pool Lodge (0260) 223442, also near Macclesfield.

Staffordshire Waters

Across the county border at Meerbrook, near Leek in Staffordshire, is Tittesworth Fly Fishing (0538) 300389. We are on the edge of the Peak District here, and the reservoir has been called the Loch of the Peaks; indeed loch style drifts in a boat with a team of small, wet flies can be very successful. There are five miles of interesting bank fishing here. Lure specialists will enjoy the deep marks at Badger and Scar Hole, while nymph fishermen will have good sport in the shallower waters such as Fosters and Troutsdale. There is also fishing on the Churnet, which is one of the few rivers in the country where rainbow breed naturally. A six-fish day ticket costs £8. Other Staffordshire stillwaters include Gailey Fishery at Penkridge (0785) 715848 and Donkhill Fisheries near Burton-on-Trent (0827) 383296. Also near Burton is Severn Trent Waters Foremark Reservoir, (0283) 701709. A day on this well-stocked water can be had for £9.50.

The Derwent & the Wye

North of here is Derbyshire's Peak District with its heather-clad moss moors and dry stone walls. The source of the River Derwent is High Peak in the north of the county, from where it flows some sixty miles to join the Trent, below Derby. Its lower reaches are monopolised by coarse fish but the upper reaches of the river and its tributary, the Wye, are first class trout and grayling water. The Peacock hotel at Rowsley (0629) 733518 has a small stretch on the Haddon Hall water which holds two rods. The Derwent Hotel (0773) 856616 can offer a day permit for its own small stretch of the water for £2. This lovely virginia-creeper clad hotel is beside the bridge at Whatstandwell and fishing is free for guests. The Duke of Rutland's Haddon Hall Estate has six miles of double-bank fishing on the Wye which is let through the Peacock Hotel at £22 per day. The water is extremely well managed by two keepers who look after approximately twenty-two miles of river. The Head Keeper is committed to restoring the river to as close to a naturally re-generating river as possible, so that fishermen will pay for the good fishing and not for the limit of fish, which sounds highly commendable. Many fish are around a pound and eight ounces but five pounders have been caught in the mayfly season. There is a rather unique stock of natural rainbows. You can't mistake them—full finned, streamlined bodies and beautiful, vivid markings—hence their name! There is of course, a fair number of wild browns and a limited restocking programme. At this stage the Wye can be likened to an old fashioned wild river, meandering through open meadowland and coppice of alder and willow. The Duke of Devonshire's Chatsworth Estate owns six miles of which one mile is available to visitors. Tickets can be had from the Head River Keeper (0629) 87484. The Cavendish Hotel (0246) 582311 has access to the syndicated water owned by the Chatsworth Estate which has three rods on the Wye and three on the Derwent. A day's fishing—for residents only—costs £23.50. Darley Dale Fly Fishing Club (Secretary; Brian Jones (0457) 872967) has four and a half miles of the Derwent, downstream from Chatsworth Park. Darley Dale is a most attractive spot and both the Derwent and the Wye have good natural fly life, such as olives, mayfly and cranefly.

The Dove

For a large part of its course the River Dove forms the boundary line between Staffordshire and Derbyshire. It is also rightly associated with Izaak Walton, but I wonder how many people realise it was his friend Charles Cotton who wrote the part about trout fishing? Among its many fine and interesting possessions the Flyfishers Club in London has got Walton creel and his casting hand. Leek Fishing Association stock and control the whole of the river. The Izaak Walton Hotel (0335) 29555 has a three mile stretch which holds four rods. Another hotel steeped in angling history is the Charles Cotton hotel at Hartington (0298) 84229 which has quarter of a mile, let out for £12 a day. Doveridge Sporting Club (0889) 565986 has one mile of excellent single-bank fishing and also has a well stocked lake. It is set in seventy acres and has a variety of clay pigeon traps. Callow Hall Country Club at Ashbourne (0335) 43164 has a mile of double-bank fishing for guests. The River Manifold is a tributary of the Dove but the only fishing available is a stretch which is owned by the National Trust, who lease it to Mr Grindey of Wetton Mill Farm, of Wetton near Ashbourne (0298) 84341. He allows four rods on his water and the cost of a day is £1.25.

Derbyshire Waters

On the Staffordshire border, near the delightfully named village of Wincle, are Danebridge Fisheries (0260) 227293. The fishery has a two and a half acre lake in the pretty Dane Valley. You may think the lake small but it holds trout of 16lb and is regularly featured in the angling press. At the other end of the county in North Derbyshire, is Ladybower Reservoir (0433) 651254. The cost of a six-fish day ticket for this 504 acre water is £8.70.

Nottinghamshire Water

Residents of the city of Nottingham are fortunate to have Colwick Country Park (0602) 870785. There is a twenty-five acre lake for wind surfing, but the fishing lake is some sixty five acres and is just for fishing. At the end of a successful day you can have a pleasant drink in the Georgian designed Colwick Hall which now acts partly as a restaurant and bar.

Lincolnshire Waters

East of Nottinghamshire is the flat, rich arable land of Lincolnshire. There are not much in the way of trout streams here but there are some nice stillwaters. The River Witham here is good coarse fishing water while, above Grantham, it provides decent trouting. However, most of this is in private hands and the one or two clubs who have game fishing also have long membership lists. Among the stillwaters are Toft Newton at Market Rasen (0603) 7453. The fishery is a privately run reservoir that has been leased from NRA and I am pleased to see it has given up the salmon experiment and now puts brookies in. This forty-acre water is right next door to RAF Scampton. The aeroplanes are not too intrusive but you do get a free Red Arrow display every now and again. The fishery can sell you tackle and gut or smoke your catch. A four-fish day here costs £10.50. Hill View Trout Lake (0754) 72979 is at Hogs Thorpe near Skegness. This two-acre lake is in an attractive woodland setting with lovely views over the Lincolnshire Wolds and is only two miles from the sea. It's mainly stocked with rainbows but there are some browns; the best brown so far has been 6lb 8oz and Hill View has produced a great 12lb 8oz rainbow. Pheasant Tail and Montana Mymphs do well, as do Invictas, Hawthorns and Black and Peacock Spiders. A four-fish day ticket can be had for £10.50. Stemborough Mill Fishery (0455) 209624 is an attractive three and a half acre lake, set in open countryside two miles north of the Roman Centre of England near Lutterworth and £12 buys you a six-fish day ticket. Other good Lincolnshire stillwaters include, Hatton (0673) 858682, Syston Park (0400) 50000, Red House Farm (052 277) 224 and Lakeside Farm (0400) 72758.

The South of England owes much of its prominence in fishing circles to legendary chalk streams such as the Test, the Itchen and the Kennet, together with stillwaters from Bewl Water in Kent to Blagdon and Chew in the west. A day on these gin-clear and beautifully maintained waters is a unique experience. One of the delights of fishing a chalk stream is the abundance of fly life. Many a fisherman's preferred natural fly is the mayfly, for this is the trout's favourite delicacy to which he rises without thought or care. The mayfly hatch is around the first two weeks in May and is often referred to as 'duffer's delight', because the trout rise so freely that beginners will strike lucky. Old fishing books are full of stories about the excitement the news of a hatch brought.

The Houghton

Before the improvements to the A303 I always used to take the A30, for not far from the M3 motorway the road winds down a hill to the small town of Stockbridge. At the Grosvenor Hotel here is that most exclusive of fishing clubs, the Houghton, which has been so ably served by three generations of the Lunn family. Looking over the bridge to the far end of the town, one can see the clear water with its inviting patches of weedy shelter and the trout swimming lazily against the current. Several of the houses have little feeder streams running past their gardens and here, where only two or three feet separate the banks, there can be trout of up to two pounds, fat on tit-bits from their human neighbours.

The Kennet

Another good place for trout watching is Hungerford, which is not far beyond Newbury and is a few miles away from the M4. This small town is the antiques capital of the area; there is a large range of shops from an indoor antique market to the most exclusive, dealing in top quality Georgian furniture. At the bottom of the town there is a bridge under which flows that delightful stream, the Kennet and close by is the recently restored Kennet and Avon canal. Walking though the meadows alongside the river one can see trout lying in wait for those appetizing morsels that the river brings to their larder. You can fish the Kennet for free as some of the old buildings have fishing rights and shooting rights on the common.

The Frome

Dorset is a sportsman's paradise. While the hunting may not be as good as Leicestershire, the shooting as good as Norfolk nor the fishing as good as Hampshire, few other counties can boast such a good overall standard of all these sports. The best known river in Dorset is the Frome whose source is near Evershot. This river has been described as a miniature Test, with chalk hills on either side and rich meadows in between which the river meanders over its gravel bed on its way through Dorchester to Wareham and Poole Harbour. The upper reaches are good for trouting while below Dorchester it used to be regarded as one of the best little salmon rivers in the south of England, at the turn of the century regularly producing forty-pounders! I have heard of salmon as far up as Maiden Newton where the river is no more than a few feet across, but it holds some nice wild trout.

Downstream at Frampton, there used to be marvellous trout fishing in the days of the Great Edwardian sportsman, Squire Brinsley Sheridan—a descendant of the famous playwright. In 1907 the Vicar, the Rev. Filleul, hooked a notable trout just above Dorchester. Having played his fish he eventually bought it to the bank but it was too big for his net. Luckily a servant was passing on her way to the Manor and she was asked to bring him a washing basket! The fish was successfully landed in the basket and found to weigh 12¾lb. The Frome holds the record for a sea-trout caught in the British Isles at 24lb. The salmon fishing suffered a setback about thirty years ago when the army dumped a large quantity of lead-based paint in the river. However, the Frome has recovered well and has produced a forty-two pounder in the last decade, while fish of between fifteen and eighteen pounds are not uncommon.

The Piddle

The other main river is the Piddle which is mentioned in the Domesday Book and whose name is of Saxon origin. From its source near Alton Pancras to its mouth at Poole Harbour, near that of the Frome, the river is some twenty two miles long. The names of some of the villages through which it flows were bowdlerized by the Victorians, who felt that Piddle offended their sensibilities for, after flowing through Piddletrenthide and Piddlehinton, the pre-fix changes to puddle and the river reaches Puddletown and then on to Tolpuddle of 'Martyrs' fame. The river is smaller than the Frome and produces only the occasional salmon and sea-trout, but these can be big fish. A salmon of 34lb and a sea-trout of 14lb have been caught within the last fifteen years. The Piddle and its feeders offer good trout fishing with fish weighing up to 3lb.

Nearly all the fishing on the rivers is privately owned and difficult to get on, but help is at hand from Richard Slocock's Wessex Fly Fishing at Tolpuddle (0305) 848460. First class tuition is available here as are bed and breakfast and self-catering cottages. There is a comprehensive tackle shop and a wide range of courses from one hour casting lessons to four day courses. Fishing for guests can be arranged on both the Frome and the Piddle, with day tickets available to non-residents. The fishing on the Piddle is on a catch and release basis with barbless hooks and a maximum of ten fish may be caught in a day.

Wessex Waters

Wessex also has lakes stocked with brownies and rainbows up to 10lb. Mr Harry Maddocks of Wool Bridge Manor (0929) 462313 has one and a quarter miles of single-bank fishing below East Burton on the Frome. Salmon here are around 16lb and the grilse run between July and September and are between 7lb and 10lb. Nineteen ninety saw 28 fish caught on this water and in 1991, eleven had been caught by July. This beat has two rods and a day permit costs £25.

Another good stillwater fishery is Flowers Farm (0300) 341351. This fishery is not far from the village of Cerne Abbas with its famous prehistoric giant cut into the chalk hillside and is situated on the edge of Batcombe Down, with views over Blackmore Vale. There are five spring-fed lakes here, all of a smallish size. A four-fish ticket will cost £16 per day. Half day and evening tickets are available too. Day tickets start at 5.30am. Completely different in character is Wessex Water's 142 acre reservoir at Sutton Bingham. This is just off the A37 Dorchester to Yeovil road on the Dorset Somerset border. It is a very attractive situation and much work has been done recently to remove the silt from the southern arm of the reservoir, which should also improve the fishing both in that area and generally. The lodge is designed to cater for the disabled fisherman and boats can be hired from the Ranger, Ivan Tinsley (0935) 872389.

The Avon

Any county would consider itself fortunate to have one river as famous as the Test, or the Itchen or the Avon. Hampshire has all three! The Avon rises near Devizes in the Vale of Pewsey and its course runs close to Stonehenge. At Salisbury it is greatly enlarged by its tributaries, of which the Wylye and the Nadder offer the best trout fishing. From Salisbury the river runs due south to enter the sea at Christchurch in Dorset. The Avon used to be one of the most famous mixed fisheries in England; the Upper Avon is a typical chalk stream and offers first class trouting for those lucky enough to fish it. The middle Avon has salmon, trout and coarse fish, while its lower reaches offer salmon, trout and superb sea-trout fishing. The river has good weed growth throughout its length which makes for good insect life and, while it may not be a prolific salmon river, its deep pools are renowned for producing heavy fish. Once again, however, this is another water that is little more than a shadow (or puddle?) of its former self; several of its tributaries above Salisbury are dry and the wet winters relied upon by the water boards are, at present, failing to materialise. Salisbury and District Angling Club has some excellent varied chalk stream fishing. Their twelve miles of the Avon is prime trout and grayling water and some of the lower stretches offer the chance of salmon. The Club's fishing stretches from Durnford, two miles north of Salisbury down to Burgate and also includes some fishing on the Bourne and three quarters of a mile on the Wylye. The Club has a relatively open membership and your first annual subscription will cost £47 plus a registration fee of £15. Further details are available from John Eadies, 20 Catherine Street, Salisbury (0722) 328535.

A few miles south on the B3347 is the village of Winkton and the Winkton Fishery, whose two and a half miles of double-water fishing is divided into two beats. In the old days this used to be a spring fishery but the season now extends until the end of July. Day rods are occasionally available and if you are interested in fishing either this water or the Bisterne Fishery you should write to Major J. M. Mills of Bisterne Manor, Ringwood, Hampshire. Alternatively, for Bisterne you could try the Tyrrells Ford Hotel (0425) 72646 or the Fisherman's Haunt (0202) 484071 for Winkton. This used to be a favourite pub for fishermen but in the opinion of the keeper now caters more for the yuppie crowd!

At Christchurch is the famous Royalty Fishery which has two miles of water. Bridge Pool is particularly good for sea-trout and June 1991 saw a fine fish of 14lb caught here. Fishing starts at 6.00am and most rods start the day with a fly, before changing to bait during the day and returning to fly in the evening. Only two rods are allowed and the price for them, including a punt, varies between £60 and £75 according to the season. Rather less expensive is the stretch of river above Bridge Pool where a day's salmon fishing costs £24 and sea-trout between £7 and £11. The Compound at the top weir tends to only fish well in good water levels, while the holding pool, Parlour, does well in low water conditions. Two rods can fish the pool for between £46 and £64 a day. Further details may be had from the owner, Lt Col Ransley of West Hampshire Water Company, Water Mill Road, Christchurch. Day tickets are also available from Davis Tackle Shop (0202) 485169 at 75 Bargate, which is almost opposite the Royalty Inn (used to be the Red Lion), known locally by some as the 'spud pub' for its large variety of baked potatoes.

The Wylye & the Nadder

The Wylye and the Nadder are both first class chalk streams. The Marquess of Bath's Estate at Longleat has the uppermost two and a half miles of the Wylye dry fly water. Season tickets only are available at a cost of £450 plus VAT and can be obtained from T. R. W. Moore Esq. of the Longleat Estate (0985) 844400. Day tickets can, however, be bought for the Sutton Veny Estates water (0985) 40682 which is the next main fishery downstream, at a cost £25 per week day or £30 at weekends. Tuition and tackle can be arranged for guests but prior notice is required. The estate has three and a half miles of double-water fishing and the average brownie on this stocked water is 1³/₄lb. Both the Wylye and the Nadder flow through Wilton Park. Wilton House is famous for its cube and double cube rooms designed by Inigo Jones and there is a delightful Palladian Bridge over the Nadder. Tisbury Angling Club has a good stretch of approximately four miles on the Nadder. This water has a good stock of wild brown trout who average around 1¼lb. The Club is keen on its grayling fishing and has many imports from other clubs anxious to limit their numbers of this prolific breeding fish. Membership costs £20 a year with a £4 joining fee and further details are available from the Secretary, Mr H. J. Haskell of The Forge, Fovant, Nr Salisbury (0722) 714203.

The Test & the Itchen

The Test is probably the most famous chalkstream in the world. Talk to fishermen as far apart as the Shores of Lake Taupo in New Zealand or on the banks of a trout stream in Montana and the Test is the English trout stream. Although fishing books have spread its fame, its glories have been known to fishermen for hundreds of years. Many famous fishermen have stalked its banks and peered into a pool or a likely lie. Here, at Longparish, that veteran of Wellington's Peninsular Campaigns, Colonel Peter Hawker, killed forty trout in three hours and over twelve thousand trout in fifty years. I purposely used the word 'killed' as this great sportsman only killed fish of over 3³/₄lb and returned far more than he took. In Stockbridge is the Grosvenor and, above its portico, is the Houghton Club, founded in 1822 and the most famous fishing club in the world. Here is Compton, the home of the late Sir Thomas Sopwith, the designer of the pioneer fighter plane, the Sopwith Camel, who would not allow his guests to fish in the evening and who, with his wife, killed twenty-one salmon in a day in 1954. Broadlands used to belong to Lord Mount Temple and here is Lady Mount Temple, fishing the special place where monster trout lurk. In the morning she has seen a large fish and determines to try for him in the evening. She hooks him and brings him safely to the net but he is not the one she spotted earlier on so he is returned although he weighed 11lb. The pool is rested and she tries again with a special lure, for these trout are more accustomed to dining on exotic morsels such as liver rather than flies! There is a fierce tug. It's the fish, and after a gallant fight he is landed and found to weigh 13lb. Many famous fly-tiers have walked these banks and observed the hatches and the trouts' ensuing banquets. Here are Francis Halford and George Marryat of the Houghton Club who helped to pioneer dry-fly fishing and G.E.M. Skues who tied many a fly but is probably best known for his pheasant-tail nymph which also works so well in stillwaters.

The twenty-five mile course of the Itchen which Skues knew so well, offers superb trout fishing along its length, from its source near New Alresford down to Southampton. Like the Test, it has an abundant weed growth and hence a wide and varied insect life with prolific hatches of mayflies, olives, hawthorn, damselfly and sedges. Similar to its famous sister, salmon and sea-trout are caught on its lower reaches. The Test may be better known but I know several friends who would prefer to fish the Itchen, just as the many excellent small streams like the Meon are overshadowed by the better known waters. Fishing on the Test and the Itchen is very sought after to say the least! As a result, they are difficult to get on and very expensive when you do! Mrs Howlett of the Rod Box in King's Worthy, Winchester (0962) 883600 may be able to help you as the company rents, or acts as agent, for approximately forty miles of fishing on the two rivers. Prices start at £65 per day on the Itchen, and £200 for a two-rod day on the Test. Bookings can be made on a seasonal basis on a named day of the week either as a full or half rod, the latter being one day a fortnight. There is a waiting list. The Greyhound Hotel at Stockbridge (0264) 810833 has a third of a mile single-bank fishing on the Test, which is adjacent to the hotel and just downstream from the Houghton Club's Grosvenor Hotel. This beat holds two rods and, although hotel guests have priority, day tickets are sometimes available and cost between £40 and £50.

Mr Robin Gow of Orvis at Nether Wallop (0264) 781212 can arrange a day for you on the Itchen near Abbots Worthy. This half mile beat is mainly stocked and dry fly and upstream nymphing are the permitted methods. The trout average 2½lb and the cost of a day is £270 for three rods and includes a ghillie. Mr Gow also has access to beats on the Test such as Timsbury 5 and 6 which are below Kimbridge and the famous Ginger Beer Beat at Kimbridge, four miles upstream from Romsey. This prime beat comprises half a mile of shallow pools and deep runs. It has four rods and costs £375 per day. At Broadlands, the home of the late Lord Mountbatten, there is over two miles of the Test which is divided into three beats. A season's salmon fishing for two rods on a named day costs £780 while half a rod is one day a fortnight and costs £395. The comparative costs for trout fishing are £950 for a full rod and £500 for a half. Day tickets are available at between £355 and £75 per day with further information obtainable from the Estate Office (0703) 732354 and the indefatigable head river keeper, Bernard Aldrich. Roxton Sporting Agency (0488) 683222 let days on the Compton Manor Estate water, which comprises some six miles of prime fishing on the Test divided into ten beats. Two of these beats will be let by the day at a fixed cost of £1000, plus agency commission. This price includes fishing for four rods, lunch and the services of a ghillie.

Hampshire Waters

For those of us with more modest means, there is excellent stillwater fishing to be had in Hampshire. Avington Trout Fishing (0962) 779312 is near Itchen Abbas and offers fishing on three lakes, which are stocked on a daily basis, and a chalk stream feeder of the Itchen. The fishery is open all year, including Christmas Day and New Year's Day, and is renowned for its big rainbows. Several 14lb to 20lb fish have been caught here and the record is a superb fish of 23lb 10oz. A day here costs £35. At Sandleheath, near Fordingbridge, there is the Rockbourne Trout Fishery (0725) 3603. The fishery has six spring-fed lakes which have good hatches of fly and three beats on the Sweatford water which is a tributary of the Avon. The lakes are stocked on a daily basis with rainbows which average 2lb 8oz and a five-fish day ticket costs £28.00. A comprehensive range of flies and tackle is available from the fishery office. In 1990, ten percent of the fish caught here were over 4lb, the best rainbow was 13lb 12oz and best brownie 6lb 14oz. An added attraction is that the fishery has a licensed bar with meals and snacks.

There are two good stillwaters in the Andover area, Rooksbury Mill and Dever Springs. Rooksbury Mill (0264) 352921 is set in sixteen acres on the outskirts of Andover and has two lakes of six and a half acres and two and a half acres as well as one mile on the river Anton, which is a tributary of the Test. The fishery shop has a comprehensive range of tackle including its own range of carbon rods. Expert tuition is available as is a smoking service. The fishery can also organise corporate days for parties of more than twenty rods and will prepare breakfast and lunch. A five fish day ticket costs £25.

Wiltshire Waters

If it's big fish you're after then I suggest you visit Dever Springs (0264) 72592 at Barton Stacey, which is just off the A303 some six miles east of Andover. The fishery has two lakes totalling six acres and a half mile stretch of the Dever, a tributary of the Test. The minimum stocking size is 3lb and the average is 4lb 8oz. Double figure fish are taken most days on this water which has excellent fly life including an abundant mayfly hatch. Casts with a breaking strain of under 6lb are prohibited which is not surprising since the Dever has produced a rainbow of 22lb 15oz and a brown trout of 18lb 2oz. The chance of catching one of these big fish on a four-fish day ticket costs £45. Among other good stillwater fisheries in Wiltshire is Avon Springs (0980) 53557. This fishery is at Durrington on the A345 and just a few miles north of Amesbury. There are two spring-fed lakes of two acres and five acres which have excellent mayfly, sedge and olive hatches. The water is stocked on a daily basis with fish from 2lb upwards. The fishery also has a stretch of the Avon which is dry-fly and upstream nymphing water and only barbless hooks are permitted. A four fish day ticket on the lakes costs £28. The 1993 season saw a best bag of 32lb 10oz and a best fish of 15lb 6oz. Perhaps more significant is the high average weight of 3lb 2oz and the rod average of 3.4 fish. Some ten miles further west on the A303 is the junction with the A36 and less than two miles south on this road is the village of Steeple Langford and Langford Fisheries (0722) 790770. The fifteen-acres lake has excellent insect life and in particular has spectacular evening rises to hatching buzzers. The average fish is around 2lb 4oz, while the record rainbow is 17lb and brownie is 8lb 5oz. A five fish day ticket will cost you £23. The fishery can also arrange corporate days when tuition by well known experts can be arranged. It is in the beautiful Wylye Valley and is unique in that it is also an officially recognised nature reserve. Zeals is the most westerly Wiltshire village on the A303 and here, Zeals Fish Farm (0747) 840573 has a two acre lake stocked with rainbows of up to 14lb. The record is 16lb 8oz. A day ticket costs £20 for four fish and it is nice to see that barbless hooks are preferred.

Bristol Waters

West of here are the well known Bristol Waters Fisheries of Chew, Blagdon and Barrow. Blagdon was the first reservoir to be opened to the public for trout fishing. In 1904 this was regarded as a daring venture, but soon gained popularity. The precedent has been followed by many other reservoirs. Over the years, the fishery has mellowed and now has all the appearance of a natural lake with varied marsh vegetation, wild-flowers, rich meadows and mixed conifer and broad-leafed woodlands. Twelve rowing boats, including one adapted for the disabled, are available on this 440 acre water. Chew is nearly three times the size of Blagdon and is surrounded by unspoiled meadows and woods. There are some seven miles of bank fishing and twenty six motorboats are available. John Horsey, the resident professional here, is on record as having said he takes around eighty per cent of his fish uing a dry fly! Something of a revelation, and you might like to bear this in mind. Barrow consists of three small reservoirs of sixty, forty and twenty-five acres and the average fish is around a pound and ten ounces, slightly less than Blagdon and Chew where the average is two pounds. The total yearly catch on these waters is over 50,000 and there are many better fish of 4lb and over. The company is actively concerned with conservation. There is a nature reserve at Herriotts Pool on Chew where of islands have been created to encourage nesting ducks, and in the twenty acres of parkland which are managed by the Nature Conservancy Council, there are green winged orchids. A day costs £11 and permits can be obtained from the lodges which also sell tackle and flies. There is a wide range of help on offer to beginners. There are free casting lessons or you can pay for more comprehensive tuition given by NAC qualified instructors. For under eighteens, there is a special £1 permit for the first five visits if accompanied by an experienced fisherman. Also on offer are special beginner's days when experienced local anglers will help you to have a go at trout or bank fishing. Further details can be had from the company's Woodford Lodge Office (0275) 332339 and from Veals Tackle Shop, 61 Old Market Street, Bristol (0272) 260790.

Gloucestershire Waters

There are several stillwater fisheries in the disused gravel pits around Cirencester in Gloucestershire. They tend to be quite deep and having only recently been converted, lack the maturity of Blagdon and Chew. North of here at Upper Swell near Stow-on-the-Wold is Donnington Fish Farm (0451) 30873. The lake is stocked with browns and rainbows and an unusual feature is that two fish are guaranteed on a day ticket. The shop sells both hot and cold smoked trout and a very good smoked trout pate.

The Coln

The River Coln is a typical Cotswold chalk stream and has long been prized for the availability of its trout fishing. The Bull Hotel at Fairford (0285) 712535 has one and a half miles of single-bank fishing which takes six rods. Hotel residents pay £9.50 for a two fish day ticket and the charge for non-residents is £15. The water is stocked with browns and rainbows which average around 1¹/₂lb. At picturesque Bibury, the Bibury Court Hotel (0285) 740337 has got just under a quarter of a mile of river which is available to guests only and costs £10 per day. Also at Bibury is the recently refurbished Swan Hotel (0285) 740204 whose six hundred yards hold three rods. There is a three fish limit and in 1988 an 11lb fish was taken here. This part of the river is a popular tourist attraction and although requested not to, people often throw bread for the trout. However, they will take a fly and early morning and evening are the best times.

The Lambourn & the Kennet

East of here are the Lambourn and the Kennet. The Lambourn is a delightful little chalk stream with a good stock of brownies and a two-pounder on this small water is a good fish. The course of the Kennet covers some forty-four miles from its source near Marlborough Downs to where it joins the Thames above Reading. The lower reaches are a combination of river and canal and are not of interest to us, but the stretch from above Marlborough to the Hungerford area has long been famous as some of the finest chalk stream fishing in the country. The Town and Manor of Hungerford bought their fishing from King James I in 1617 and, as a result, enjoy fishing on two miles of the Kennet, half a mile of one of the carries and a mile on the Dunn. A full time keeper is employed on the water which has both brownies and rainbows. Two-pounders are caught regularly and there are fish of up to five pounds. Season tickets only are available and cost £957. Further details may be obtained from Colonel Macey (0488) 682770.

Some of the best small stream fishing you could wish for can be found at the Denford Fisheries (0488) 684179 which has two and a half miles of carriers and a short stretch on the Kennet itself. In 1990 there were 1100 rainbows and 110 brownies caught here and of the rainbows 98 were over 2lb, 53 over 3lb. Dry-fly only is the rule until the end of June, after which upstream nymphing is permitted. The water holds six rods and a day's fishing costs £32.50, except in June when it is £35.00. The reason for this is that early June sees a fine Mayfly hatch.

At Kintbury is Mr Edward Hill's Barton Court Fishery (0488) 58226 which has three miles of double-water fishing on the three main streams and some carriers. This area of the Kennet used to be marshland until it was drained by French prisoners of war in Napoleonic times and now offers many types of water. A four fish day ticket on this brown trout water costs £25, with a season weighing in at £600. It is regularly stocked and the stocking size is a pound to a pound and eight ounces. The best fish here was seven pounds and July 1991 produced one of five pounds ten ounces. Downstream at Newbury, the Millwaters Hotel (0635) 528838 has half a mile of fishing and a stocked lake which is available to residents only. This though, is on the Lambourn which, like the Kennet, flows through the hotel's gardens.

Oxon Water

North of here, at Abingdon, near Oxford is Millet's Farm Trout Fishery (0865) 391394. The fishery has two spring-fed lakes on limestone which total seven acres. There is an abundance of natural water life such as nymphs, shrimp and corixa. Flies and refreshments can be obtained from the lodge and professional tuition is available. The water is stocked with the powerful fighting shasta strain of rainbows which average 2¼lb. A five- fish day ticket costs £20 to £50 and half days and evening tickets are also available.

Capital Waters

There is a wealth of trout fishing within easy reach of London. Church Hill Farm (0296) 720524 at Mursley, near Winslow in Buckinghamshire is only fifty miles away. The two spring-fed lakes total ten acres and both are alkaline and very productive of natural lifeforms. The water is regularly stocked with brownies and rainbows of between 1½lb and 12lb. The fishery has a particularly fine clubhouse which is a converted eighteenth- century barn. Nymphs such as damsel, mayfly and montana are particularly successful and the best fish caught here was 17lb ½oz. The price for a four-fish day ticket is £23.

Also in Buckinghamshire are the Latimer Park Lakes (0494) 762396 which are sited in the Chess Valley on the south eastern side of the Chilterns. The lakes, which are eight acres and four acres, are well over two hundred years old and the fishery can also offer chalk stream fishing on the river Chess. The lakes are chalk stream fed which ensures a prolific food supply and are restocked on a daily basis with rainbow and brown trout that are reared on the premises. Around 10,000 fish are caught here every season and over half of them are larger than 2lb. A four fish day ticket will set you back £23, with a complimentary evening ticket given to anyone who has failed to catch a fish during the day. At Slough, is the Queen Mother Fly Fishery (0753) 683605. A day ticket on this 475 acre water costs £10. There have recently been improvements here, including thirty-three new boats and ninety-six casting platforms and the water is now stocked with brookies as well as browns and rainbows. The Chess, sad to report, has almost disappeared in places, with other stretches of one of the country's best chalk streams reduced to stagnant pools. The stretch of the river that runs through Chesam is worst affected, with fish moving downstream, and the NRA are praying for substantial rainfall to restore both water levels and the chalk bed itself.

If you live in East London or Essex, a wide range of stillwater fishing is available. Near Chelmsford, is the Essex Water Company's Hanningfield Reservoir (0268) 710101. Boats are available on this six hundred acre water which is stocked with 65-70,000 of the company's home-reared rainbows every season. The fish average between 1¼lb and 2½lb and a six-fish day ticket costs £13.50. The whole area of the reservoir is a wild bird sanctuary which adds to the tranquillity of an excellent day's fishing. Near Colchester is the well known Ardleigh Reservoir (0206) 230642 which in 1991 hosted the European International Trout Fishing Competition. The average weight is just under 1¼lb and the record is 4lb while the best brown is 9lb 12oz. An eight fish day ticket is priced at £13.30. Expert tuition is available as are locally tied flies and bed and breakfast can be arranged. Among the good, privately-owned waters are Aveley Trout Lakes (0708) 868245, Chelmer's Fisheries at Thaxted (0371) 3595, Chigboro at Maldon (0621) 57368 and Cooks Farm at Brentwood (0277) 72265.

South of the Thames, there is the excellent stillwater and river fishing in Surrey, Kent and Sussex. In the Tillingbourne Valley, near Guildford in Surrey are the Duke of Northumberland's Albury Estate Fisheries (0486) 412323. They are set in a 3,000 acre estate which has pleasure grounds and terraces laid out by the seventeenth-century diarist John Evelyn and offer a wide range of fishing. The Park Fishery has two lakes and three beats on the river Tillingbourne which is predominantly chalk water, and can be fished on a season ticket basis only. The Powder Mills Fishery is a lake of nearly four acres and is designed to appeal to the experienced fisherman. The water provides excellent buzzer fishing and is stocked with rainbows. A less experienced fisherman might prefer the Weston Fishery which has wide banks and easy casting. The main lake is some four acres and there is a smaller one which is ideal for dry fly. A four fish day ticket for either Weston or Powder Mills costs £20. One of my favourite fisheries is Willinghurst (0483) 275048 which is just off the A281 Guildford to Horsham Road. There are two main lakes and four smaller ones which are set in woodland. It is a delightful country setting with not a house in sight. Other good Surrey stillwaters include Crosswater Mill at Churt (0251) 254321, Enton Lakes at Godalming (0428) 792620, and Gatton Manor at Dorking (0306) 79555.

At Lamberhurst, Kent, is Bewl Water Reservoir (0892) 890352 which attracts over 20,000 fishermen a year. Six fish, brace and evening tickets are available. Boats and tackle can be hired and there is a tackle shop at the Lodge. A range of courses are designed to cater for the beginner as well as the more experienced fisherman. Nearby, is the excellent sixteen acre Bayham Lake Trout Fishery (0892) 890276. This lake is one of the most prolific trout fisheries in the country; it is stocked with rainbows averaging 2½lb and running up to 12lb and more. The fishery includes double-water fishing on the River Teise which has a series of beautiful and very prolific waterfalls and pools downstream from the lake. Instructors are on hand to help and advise if required and you can also try your hand at clay pigeon shooting in the nearby woodland. Bayham can also provide superb lunches, which are served in the former boathouse which has a promenade deck overlooking the lake. A six fish day ticket costs £28. The River Teise rises near Tunbridge Wells and covers some twenty miles on its journey to join the Medway near Yalding. The upper reaches are well stocked with brown and rainbow trout and offer good dry-fly fishing. Just below Bayhams water, is the Hoathly Fishery which has 1½ miles of the Teise and a similar amount on Bartley Mill. A day here is priced at a modest £3 and tickets are available from Bassett's Garage in the village. Other stillwaters include Chequertree at Ashford (0233) 820383 and Tenterden Trout Waters at Tenterden (0580) 763201. Tenterden has three lakes totalling five acres of water and is situated at Coombe Farm which is about a mile outside the town. One lake is for dry fly and nymphing only and the water is regularly stocked with brownies and rainbows of between 1½lb and 10lb. The fishery has a unique basket system which allows continuous fishing with no restriction on the number of fish caught, though fish not required must be returned at the end of the day. A three fish day ticket costs £15.

The Rivers of Sussex are best known for their coarse fishing but the lower reaches of the Arun, Western and Eastern Rother, Ouse and Adur all have runs of sea-trout which are generally larger than in Hampshire. There are a number of good stillwaters in the county too. At Burwash, near Heathfield, is Lakedown Trout Fishery (0435) 883449. This is owned by Roger Daltrey of The Who fame. Game fishing is popular in the music business and Eric Clapton is also a very keen fisherman. The fishery is set in a delightful valley and has four lakes and a well equipped lodge. North of here, just off the A267, is the Yew Tree Trout Fishery at Rotherfield (0892) 852529. The fishery consists of three beautiful lakes surrounded by fields and woodland. The price of a four fish day ticket is £16 and tuition is available. At Flimwell, on the A2115, the Spring Wood Trout Farm (0580) 87525 consists of three lakes totalling more than five acres and is set on the peak of a hill overlooking Bewl Water. Two lakes are dry fly and nymph only and the water is stocked with brownies and rainbows. Bed and Breakfast is available at the farm house and a four fish day ticket costs £20 with reductions for morning and evening only tickets. Corporate Fishing Days can also be arranged.

West of here on the A24 London to Worthing Road some ten miles south of Horsham is Ashington Trout Farm (0903) 893066. This is a new fishery set under the famous Chanctonbury Ring at the base of the South Downs. The water is fed by chalk streams and stocked with rainbows and, consequently, has some double figure fish. Overnight accommodation is available and a four fish day ticket costs £16. Another newish fishery, not far from West Meon on the A32, is Meon Springs trout Fishery (073087) 249. Although only one and a half acres, the fishery occupies an attractive location and is well stocked with rainbows and brownies. Further west at Arundel, on the Duke of Norfolk's Estate, is the delightful Chalk Springs Fishery (0903) 883742. The four spring fed lakes total five acres and a four fish ticket costs £24.50. The water is very clear and gives you the opportunity to stalk rainbows and brown trout which run into double figures in weight.

The Hastings Flyfishers' Club (0580) 880407 was formed as a limited company in 1932. The club has the fishing on two reservoirs; Darwell which is 165 acres and Powdermill at 54 acres. Southern Water have plans to extend the former, to cater for increased water demand, and details of trout fishing on both reservoirs can be obtained from Mr D.E. Tack on (0424) 33957. Rowing boats are available on both waters which are very attractive and well established. Powdermill is so named because it used to drive the waterwheel of a gunpowder works which blew up! The waters are well stocked, mainly with rainbows, but there are some natural and stocked browns. A six fish day ticket costs £12.50 and the average size is around 1¼lb but fish of up to 6lb and more can be expected. Southern Water also manage the Weirwood reservoir (0342) 822731 in Forest Row, the only mixed reservoir fishery in the area, which incidentally is also an SSSI. A final suggestion is Colin Godman's Trouting (0825 74) 322 near Uckfield in East Sussex. This private syndicate has three lakes covering seven acres in attractive scenery and is well stocked with rainbows and natural brownies. A few rods are occasionally available at £370 or £210 for a half rod.

For all the trials and tribulations that can be attributed to the advent of motorway driving it has to be said that it makes getting to places like the South West much easier, providing of course there are no road works to hold things up! It is perfectly possible for anyone living in London or the Midlands to be on Exmoor in three and a half hours or less. After leaving the M5 at Junction 27 one can afford to drive at a more leisurely pace and take the A396, which follows the course of the Exe and then north of Bampton a left turn on to the B3222 will take you to Dulverton and on to the heart of Exmoor.

The Exe & the Barle

Serious fishing on the Exe begins at Dulverton. In recent times it has become rather a summer and autumn river with September being the best month. The Exe has become predominantly a spate river and summer fishing especially this far up depends on rain but can be very good, with grilse averaging around 5lb and salmon between 8lb and 12lb. Flies such as the Black Great, Tupps, Greenwells Clergy and Blue Nun are popular choices.

The Carnarvon Arms Hotel (0398) 23302 has five miles of fishing on the Exe and its main tributary, the Barle. It has been a sporting hotel for many years and looking at an advertisement in the Anglers Diary for 1928, little seems to have changed apart from the telephone number which in those days was Dulverton 2! It still has a billiard room and livery stables as it had then. These days it can also offer guests a day's shooting and the West Somerset Polo Club plays on the hotel meadows. Set in the midst of Negley Farson country, both the Exe and the Barle are typically moorland rivers with clear and bright shallow runs between the pools. The wild brownies are usually excellent fighters and average two or three to the pound. Salmon range in size from 3lb grilse, to the 8lb-12lb summer and autumn fish. Fished on a strict rota system, the different beats offer a wide variety of fishing to suit all age groups and abilities. Salmon fishing on the Exe costs from between £12 and £25 per day and £100-£130 per week for residents of the hotel. Non-residents can get permits but the prices are doubled. Whilst the droughts of the last three years have affected catches, last year's numbers represented a slight improvement on the previous year. Trout fishing on both the Exe and the Barle costs between £7 and £12 per day, with any fishing beyond four days provided free. Non-residents can fish for £20 a day. Popular flies include Black Gnat, Pheasant Tail and Kite's Imperial.

The Barle is the most important tributary of the Exe and flows through the heart of Exmoor Forest. The Exmoor Forest Hotel at Simonsbath (064383) 341 can offer guests fishing on eight and a half miles of the Barle and a small stretch of the Bray. Fishing for non-residents costs £8 a day. Some of the fishing takes some getting to and it is rather rocky in places so good boots or stout shoes are essential. However, like all things that require an effort, it is well worthwhile. South Molton AC also has water on the Bray with a day's fishing costing £5.

Downstream just above Hawkridge are the picturesque Tarr Steps which appear on so many calendars and boxes of chocolates, but this is not surprising for they capture the spirit of English countryside at its best. The Tarr Steps Hotel at Hawkridge (0643) 85293 has three miles of fishing, most of which is double-banked and free to guests. It is good to hear that salmon catches are on the increase and 1992 the best recent year, saw ninety-three fish grassed from this water. The proprietor, Mr D. Keane, can also arrange fishing on the Exe and shooting for guests. The Fishing Tackle shop in Dulverton's High street can steer the under sixteens towards some free water exclusively for them. An NRA licence is required but no grown-ups is the rule and that includes Peter Pans! John Sharpe of J.S. Sporting has seven miles of fishing on the Exe and the Haddeo and a nice one and three quarter acre lake stocked with rainbows. The Haddeo is the small river that drains Wimbleball Reservoir and compensation flows help to keep a reasonable water level. The cost of fishing on this stretch of the Middle Exe is £10 for trout and between £18 and £25 for salmon according to season, with tuition also available.

By the time the Exe reaches Tiverton the valley has widened out and from here to the sea the river, which is the longest in the area, strolls through rich and fertile parkland until it flows into the estuary near Exeter and finally into the sea between Exmouth and Dawlish Warren. The Tiverton Fly Fishing Club owns half a mile of the Exe and leases a further half-mile from the NRA where the cost is £330 a day, with August being the best month for salmon. The club also has three and a half miles of fly-only trout fishing on the Knightshayes Estate Water. This concession was granted by the late Sir John Amory to residents within Tiverton Borough. The estate however retains the salmon rights.

Five miles or so south of Tiverton is the village of Bickleigh where the Fishermans Cot (0884) 855289 has a quarter of a mile for guests. The NRA own three miles of the Exe and the Exeter Angling Centre (0392) 436404 will be able to give you further information about this water. Exeter City Council also own some water but it has to be said that it is not of the very highest quality, besides with so much fishing in lovely countryside being readily available, I would rather fish there than near a town.

The Teign

The Teign begins its life as the North and South Teign high up on Dartmoor. These small streams join forces just west of Chagford and between there and Steps Bridge the river tumbles through a wooded gorge. Fingle Bridge is a popular beauty spot and vantage point from which to see the river. Down to just south of Mortonhampstead the river is referred to as the Upper Teign and from there down to Newton Abbot is the Lower Teign. It is not a big river and so easy to cover and is also one which will delight the spring fisherman for at that time of the year the banks are thick with daffodils particularly around Clifford Bridge. There is good brown trout, sea-trout and salmon fishing to be had here. Permits for the Upper Teign Fishing Association's water may be had from the Anglers Rest at Finglebridge (0647) 21287 or James Bowden and Son of Chagford (0647) 433271. Chagford Weir provides a good holding pool and it is essential to book as only two permits a day are issued. A combined salmon and sea-trout ticket costs £12 and a permit for brown trout costs only £3 a day. Sea-trout offer particularly good sport here and many fishermen mark the fish in daylight and return to stalk them at night.

The Mill End Hotel at Chagford (0647) 432282 has just under half a mile, which is free to guests and fishing can also be arranged on six miles of the Upper Teign Fishing Association Water. The Great Tree Hotel (0647) 432491 have access to a two and a half mile stretch of the Teign for two to four rods. This stretch is excellent for sea-trout, and the hotel has a 'REFIS' indtructor for beginners and advanced! Mrs C. Thatcher (0647) 52805 at the Ryecroft Fishery issues evening, day, weekly and season permits. This one mile stretch of double-bank fishing is first class and it is advisable to book as it is very popular. A day's permit for the Lower Teign Fishing Association's water can be had for £10 (£5 juniors) from the secretary, Mr P. Knibbs of Shaldon (0626) 873612 and from Drum Sports in Courtenay Street, Newton (0626) 65333. The Salmon season runs from 1st February to 30th September and the Seatrout season from 15th March to 30th September.

The West Dart

The West Dart's source is on the moor above the famous prison at Princetown. It joins the East Dart at Dartmoor and much of the river is owned by the Duchy of Cornwall. Below Dartmoor the river tumbles down a wooded valley and leaves the moor at Buckfastleigh to flow to its estuary at Totnes and the sea at Dartmouth, under the guard of the famous naval academy. This is good fly water and its tributaries also fish well. There is a delightful reach on the Blackbrook, a tributary of the West Dart which can produce pre-life hatches of duns where you can have the fun of fishing to rising trout, though success, of course, depends on whether you can match the hatch. The Prince Hall Hotel (0822) 89403 issues permits for the West Dart as does the Two Bridges Hotel (0822) 89581 where the river runs through the hotel grounds.

Below Dartmeet at Holne, the Church House Inn (03643) 208 issue NRA licences and Duchy permits and make a point of putting visitors in touch with experienced locals. This is particularly helpful as there is a lot of water and advice on likely spots and flies will save you a long walk and a boring day. Just downstream at Ashburton the Holne Chase Hotel (0364) 3471 has a nice stretch of just over a mile of single-bank fishing upstream from Holne Bridge, which has five pools and is free to hotel guests. This is fast flowing water which fishes best on the fall after a spate. This fishing is in a wooded valley and the ability to spey or roll cast will save you a lot of time from trying to retrieve flies from trees.

The Dart

There are many, especially those who live in the area, who consider the Dart to be the most beautiful river in the South West. It is a spate river whose occasional floods can scour the banks of vegetation, but this of course is on the upper reaches and below Dartington Hall the river is much more sedate. This is another river which alas suffered the ravages of UDN and the spring run is sadly now almost non-existent and July onwards is the best time. It is particularly good sea-trout water however. The Dart Angling Association has five and a half miles of good sea-trout water. A day's salmon fishing costs £12 and sea-trout £10 while the charge for brown trout is £8. Weir Pool is a local favourite and in 1992 permits were available from C. Harris of Prismatic in Totnes (0803) 867154, though it is worth checking with the Totnes Information Centre (0803) 863168 as permit issuers do change. From a family point of view, there is the added attraction of a ride on a steam train for the Dart Valley Railway runs close to the river between Totnes and Buckfastleigh.

The Avon

West of here, entering the sea at Thurlestone, is the Avon, one of the better, what I would term 'minor league', rivers in the area. It is the sort of water that produces fifty or more salmon and around two hundred sea-trout a year. The Erme produces a handful of migrating fish but the Plym and Tavy are another matter. The Tavy rises in Cranmere Pool, that strange spot which also sees the start of the Dart and that good tributary of the Torridge, the Okement. The Plym produces under fifty salmon a year but it averages over three hundred sea-trout a season and some years have yielded double this amount. The Tavy is slightly better averaging around four hundred sea-trout and over a hundred salmon. All these rivers are very good dry fly waters.

Fishing for sea-trout on these rivers is great fun. The water is crystal clear and requires a very careful approach, as it is very easy to put them down. A thorough reconnaissance during the day is essential and with polaroids and a stealthy approach you can see the fish and mark the lies. It also gives you the opportunity to work out how you are going to fish the water at night. Casting at night confuses many a fisherman as it is impossible to see what is going on! There is a natural tendency to bring the tip of the rod back too far which can lead to lost flies. To cast too quickly will cause the line to land in a heap and make for wind knots in the cast. Night fishing is no different from day fishing in that to be successful the fly has got to be presented in the right manner and the best thing to do is to practice away from where you will be fishing.

Once you have mastered the art, the memory of a successful night's sea-trout or peal fishing as they are locally known will cheer many a winter's evening. Numerous tacklists in the area can be of help and supply day permits for the Tavy; for example, Barkells in Tavistock (082261) 2198. The cost for the fisherman is £10 per day and trout fishing is £3 per day.

The East Lyn

On the north coast of Devon is a small river of just some six miles in length that fishes very well and is inexpensive whilst set in beautiful countryside. What more could you want apart from knowing its name! It is the East Lyn and until recently seems to have been a well kept local secret. The river is formed by several small Exmoor streams. Weir Water and Chalk Water continue to form Oare water which is joined by Badgworthy Water at Malmsmead and this is the start of the East Lyn. It is very much a spate river which drops and clears very rapidly after rain and as with any river of a similar character it is all a matter of hitting it at the right time. From Brendon Bridge down to Rockford through a deep wooded gorge, which, though a local beauty spot, is no place to wander about at night and for sea-trout it is advisable to pick a good pool before the light goes and stay there. This part is the Glenthorne Fishery while below Rockford down to Lynmouth is the Watersmeet Fishery which has the best salmon fishing. This belongs to the National Trust and like Glenthorne is administered by the NRA. This white water tumbles from pool to pool, some of which are quite large and others pocket handkerchief size. The spinner and worm are the most successful methods and the fly only really works on the large slower pools. There is a daily limit of two salmon and six sea-trout and permits can be had from the Brendon House Hotel at Brendon (05987) 206.

The Taw

Driving south west from Lynmouth on the A39, is the road to Barnstaple and the much better known Taw. This river which rises on Dartmoor is, at fifty miles, one of the longer ones in the region. It and the neighbouring Torridge have long been regarded as the most important Devon salmon rivers. Indeed they are recorded in the Domesday Book where they were valued at 25 shillings a year. In the 1950s, rods were accustomed to taking 2000 salmon a year while a further 3000 were netted. Sadly, catches have declined since then but they are both good salmon and sea-trout waters as is the Taw's main tributary, the Mole at Eggesford near Chumleigh. The Fox and Hounds (0769) 80345 has seven miles of fishing on the Taw and also has some water on the Little Dart. The cost of a day's salmon, brown-trout and sea-trout fishing is £18.50. To help get beginners started the hotel has a three quarter of an acre novice pond which is well stocked.

Downstream at Umberleigh there is the well known Rising Sun (0769) 60447 which has been looking after anglers for many a year. Its three and a half miles are divided into seven beats which produce good numbers of summer sea-trout and autumn salmon and a fair few fish in spring, although the spring run is not what it was. Day tickets for residents are priced at £17.50 and for non-residents £25. The West of England Centre of Angling (0805) 23256 also has water on the Taw, upstream of Umberleigh at £25-£30 for a daily ticket. Lower down is the Barnstaple and District Angling Associations water which extends to some two miles and it also has trout fishing on the Yeo. Four permits are issued a day but not for weekends or Bank Holidays and they can be obtained from the Secretary, Mr A.J. Penny (0271) 73241, or the Devon Angling Centre in Barnstaple (0271) 45191.

The Torridge

The source of the Torridge is not far from the picturesque seaside town of Clovelly near the border with Cornwall. After a tortuous course, full of bends and loops, the river doubles back on itself and flows into the Taw estuary at Bideford. Throughout its length it flows through rock rolling farmland and in spring its banks abound with daffodils and primroses. This river also has a famous sporting hotel at Sheepwash, the Half Moon Inn (040923) 376, which has twelve miles of very good fishing. Spinning is allowed in spring—which has seen fish of up to 19lb but fly only is the rule after May 1st. It is not a large river and an eleven-foot rod will enable you to cover the water. Popular salmon flies are the Yellow Torrisch, Silver Doctor and Thunder and Lightening while the Silver Butcher, Peter Ross and Connemara Black are favourite choices for sea-trout. The fishing is easy to get at as the banks have been cleared on all beats. It also offers excellent trout fishing and its waters are stocked with good brownies of around the one pound mark.

Group Captain P. Norten-Smith (08053) 317 owns the Little Warham Fishery at Beaford. This one and a half mile stretch of single-bank fishing is divided into four beats and there are four named pools on each beat. This, like the Half Moon's stretch, is prime water. However, for those wishing to fish the upper reaches both the Devil's Stone Inn at Shebbear (040928) 210 and the Woodford Bridge Hotel at Milton Damerel (040926) 481 have their own water. Simon Gawesworth (0805) 23256 provides tuition and expert advice in conjunction with the hotel, which has some fishing rights on the hotel. A few miles south of Beaford on the B3220, is Winkleigh and the Stafford Moor Fishery (08054) 360. This well known stillwater consists of two lakes of fourteen acres and eight acres and produces some very big rainbows. A stillwater of a larger size at forty-one acres is Wistlandpound Reservoir (03987) 372 which is north east of Barnstaple, and a day costs £5.50.

The Tamar

The A30 is the main road to Cornwall and its sandy beaches and sailing creeks. Just east of Launceston this road passes through the village of Lifton. To the casual driver there is nothing remarkable about it, houses line the road on both sides and on one side is a pleasant looking hotel. This ivy-clad building is the Arundell Arms (0566) 84666, which is known to fishermen around the world as a hotel for fishermen run by fishermen. Anne Voss Bark has fished the hotels waters for many years. Expert tuition is on hand and the hotel runs many courses. There are courses for beginners, advanced salmon and trout casting, fly fishing and refreshers to brush up your technique. In winter, the hotel can arrange a day's shooting, including driven snipe.

The Arundell Arms has twenty miles of fishing on the Tamar and its tributaries, the Lyd, Carey, Wolf and Thrushel. The salmon that run up the hotel's water on the Tamar and the Lyd average 10lb but there is always the chance of a twenty-pounder, while the average sea-trout is between ¾lb and 1lb 8oz, but there are a number of larger fish up to 6lb. There is very good trout fishing to be had here and dry fly works particularly well. The trout average two or three to the pound but are genuinely wild and are prime fighters. When the rivers are in spate, excellent sport can be had on the hotel's Twynhay Lake. This three acre water is just down the road from the hotel and is stocked with rainbows and some browns up to 9lb. The water is clear and quite deep and nymphing with a long leader is often a productive method.

The beautiful Endsleigh House at Milton Abbot (0822) 87248 is set in seventy acres and is owned by a syndicate; the Endsleigh Fishing Club. For most of the year it is run as a hotel and guests can fish the hotels nine miles of double-bank on the Lower Tamar. The cost of a day varies between £20 and £42 and fly is the most successful method. The seven year average for this water is two hundred and twenty-eight fish.

The Lamerhooe Lodge Fishings on the Lower Tamar have recently been bought by the River Beauly Fishings Company Ltd. (0463) 782215. This delightful beat is set in a beautiful wooded valley and consists of one and three quarter miles of double-bank fishing with eighteen named pools. It has been in private hands, with only three owners since the sixteenth century and the fishing has always been retained for them and their guests. The Beauly team have made substantial improvements to the river and the pools and fly only is the rule. The fishing is now available to let to four rods who can stay at the company's Lammerhooe Lodge which has five double bedrooms and is set in sixty acres. A ghillie is on hand to help guests.

The Bude Angling Association has trout fishing on the upper reaches of the Tamar and the River Claw. Permits cost £3 a day and can be had from Bude Sports (0288) 352943. The Tamar is a small river this far up as it runs through rolling farmland and produces fine trout of about ten or eleven ounces and the odd grayling in winter. Nearby, for those who enjoy stillwater fishing, is Upper Tamar lake. This is a natural stocked fishery and provides fine fishing and excellent value for money.

The Fowey

The best sea-trout water in the area, and indeed in the South West, is the Fowey. Although like every river the last year or so has been disappointing, in the past it has yielded between 1500 and 2000 or more fish in a good year, including around 300 salmon. On this small river, which has few pools and tumbles down wooded valleys, fly fishing can be difficult, though a flashy fly which resembles a small fish such as the Silver Invicta may be very successful. Most rods however, will be spinning and Rapallas are a popular choice.

The river flows through the ground of the National Trust's beautiful property, Lanhydrock House and permits for here cost £5 a day or £15 a week and can be had from the Trust's regional office or Lanhydrock (0208) 74281. Slightly more expensive at £7 a day or £25 a week is the water belonging to the Liskeard and District Angling Association, but they do have six miles of it. Indeed, the Association has some twenty five miles of fishing in all, including stretches of the Camel, Lynhea, Inny, Looe and Seaton. Permits for here and the two miles controlled by the Lostwithiel Fishing Association can be had from Ken Raymond's Fishing Tackle in Liskeard (0579) 47324. The Fowey produces big sea-trout that can be up to 8lb, while its average salmon is between 8lb and 12lb, although in 1990 a thirty-eight pounder was found dead, beached on a bank.

At Bolventor is the Jamaica Inn of Du Maurier fame and from Fowey West we are in the romantic hidden creeks of Cornwall, which the author also immortalised. It is an area which abounds in picturesque place names like St Just in Roseland, Praze-an-beeble, Nancegollan, Mevagissey and Indian Queens, so called because the tragic Red Indian Princess Pocahontas, stayed there.

On the north coast is the River Camel, which hit the headlines after aluminium sulphate was inadvertently released into the domestic water system and then flushed out into the river. As a result, a large proportion, 60,000 was the estimated figure, of the young fish stock were killed. Time will tell how badly this has affected the river. Accidents by their nature are chance happenings, but like the 1991 spillage of 25,000 gallons of slurry into the Tamar, a very short time can undo many years' work. In 1990 the level of rod caught salmon was relatively normal and saw three fish of over 20lb. This river is the converse of the Fowey for it is a better salmon water than it is sea-trout, though those that are caught are large fish.

The Camel
The Camel rises near the Fowey and this clear, fast-flowing river has a course of some twenty-five miles before reaching the estuary at Padstow. The best fishing is from Trecarne down to the tide and there are about a hundred and fifty pools in this stretch. This is a river for winter fishing with a good salmon run from October through to December. Wadebridge and District Angling Association has four and a half miles which is best suited to spinning. Mepps always do well, as do a local creation called Muppets. Permits can be had from North Cornwall Angling Centre in Wadebridge. Bodmin Angling Association (0208) 75513 has eleven miles of the Camel and a short stretch of the Fowey. The scenic Camel Trail runs beside the river for several miles from Padstow to Wenford. This smooth sand-ed path is the track of the former Bodmin to Adebridge railway line. Further down the coast at St Mawgan, which is just above Newquay trout fishing can be had on the River Menalhyl.

Smaller Rivers
To the east of here are several good small rivers. The Lynher rises on Bodmin Moor and joins the Tamar estuary opposite Plymouth. The twin rivers, East and West Looe, have their sources near Liskeard and join shortly before reaching the sea at Looe. Still small-er is the Tiddy which enters the sea near Devonport. These rivers produce the occasional salmon and good brownies, but their main claim to fame is that they are excellent sea-trout fisheries so don't ignore them! The Tavy is one of the several rivers that have their source in Cranmere Pool on Dartmoor and flows through Tavistock on its way to Plymouth, where in the estuary it meets up with the Tamar. It is an excellent salmon and sea-trout water.

South West Waters

Just the other side of the A396 from Dulverton is Wimbleball Lake. This is the third largest reservoir in the area and is administered by South West Water, whose dedicated team of rangers do a great job running all the company's fisheries. They have a busy life, as several of their waters have over 100,000 visitors a year, drawn by the nature reserves and sailing as well as fishing. Wimbleball is fairly new, having opened for fishing in 1980, but has built up an impressive reputation and the Benson and Hedges competition heats are held here. Near the dam wall it is 160 feet deep, but the best fishing is to be held at the shallower northern end and Cow Moor is a favourite spot. Boats are available and there is one which is specially equipped for handicapped anglers. The lake's 374 acres have a natural stock of brownies which run up to 4lb and are regularly stocked with rainbows, for which the current record is 10lb 4oz. Before setting out it is worth calling Bob Lunk, the ranger, to ensure that it is not a competition day. Nearby is the Exe Valley Fisheries (0398) 23328 which has been a trout hatchery and rearing farm since 1885. This is a put-and-take water which is just the place for a beginner. The cost of a five-fish day is £5.50 plus £1.30 per pound of fish caught and they will clean, smoke and freeze your fish if you want.

The village of Oakford is not far from Bampton and is just off the main road to Barnstaple and here you will find Bellbrook Valley Trout Fishery (03985) 292. Peter Swaby's fishery is as pleasant a stillwater as you could wish to find. Its three lakes and two pools are in a beautiful valley and the old Iron Mill Stream and adjacent woodland supply an abundance of natural feed for the fish. Professional tuition is available as is bed and breakfast accommodation at the fishery farmhouse. The cost of a day on this noted Troutmaster Water is £20 with a four fish limit. Half-day tickets are available, or you can pay less and then pay £1.50 per pound of fish caught. One lake is for large fish only, the minimum weight is 3lb and you can have a half day for £17 with a two fish limit, or a full three fish day for £25, or a four fish limit day for £30. These big fish are fine fighters and not like the underweight submarines found on some fisheries. To give you some idea of what may be in store, Bellbrook holds the South West record with a superb 17lb 12oz fish taken in 1988.

A fifteen minute drive south west of Chagford will take you into the heart of Dartmoor and Fernworthy Reservoir. This is a beautiful away from it all spot where you will only meet fellow fishermen or ramblers. The seventy-six acre water is very established, having been created fifty years ago and with its moorland setting will remind many of a Scottish loch. It is stocked on a regular basis with brown trout which go up to 4lb and may succumb to the allure of a Hawthorne early in the season, while Daddies, Black Marilous and Sedge Patterns work well later on. The cost of a day with a four fish limit is £13 and if you want to book a boat it is advisable to ring the ranger, Mr John Baker (0647) 432440, in advance.

Approximately ten miles east of Fernworthy and a quarter of an hours drive north of Bovey Tracey, are Kennick and Tottiford Reservoirs where £11 buys you a six-fish day ticket. This is another beautiful but remote water and is regularly stocked with rainbows and has a stock of native brownies. The best rainbow to date is 5lb 14oz and there are rumours of brown trout of just under double figures. Hawthorns and Daddies do well here as do Montanas and Vivas. This water is only twenty-three feet at its deepest/widest point so it is possible to fish all of it.

If you prefer big fish on a smaller and more private water you should try John Hern's Watercress Farm Trout Fishery at Chudleigh (0626) 852168 which is about seven miles north of Newton Abbot. The three gin clear lakes are fed by springs and stocked on a daily basis with rainbows of between 1¼lb and 15lb. Day tickets are available but booking is essential as the number of rods is limited. A day's fishing will cost either £18.50 with a five fish limit or £6.50 plus £1.55 per pound with a six fish limit. Other prices and variations are also offered.

Among other stillwaters in this area are the Avon Dam and Meldon reservoirs, where fishing is free to NRA licence holders—although I can't help feeling that this reflects the quality of the fishing. If you enjoy reservoir fishing the 150 acre Burrator Reservoir near Yelverton is likely to be more productive, and a day ticket costs a modest £3.50.

With over 730 acres of water, Roadford Lake is set to become one of the country's leading brown trout fisheries. This magnificent, meandering stretch of water has been stocked with fingerlings which have grown on to become as near to wild fish as is possible. Brownies in excess of 3lb have regularly been recorded and are all perfectly proportioned. The vast reaches of shallow water will offer the cream of this crop, and with over half the fishable bank side consisting of such water the challenge for the sports fisherman is obvious. The A30 passes within half a mile of the lake. The season here is from 14th April to 12th October, fishing is fly only and there is a bag limit of four fish over ten inches. Any smaller fish must be returned. A day here will cost £12.50.

Heading west from Launceston the A30 takes you through the heart of Bodmin Moor. Just before you reach Bolventor there is a small turning on the left which will take you to Liskeard. This minor road follows the upper reaches of the Fowey over Smallacombe Downs and Siblyback Reservoir is close at hand. This 140 acre water is widely considered the second best of South West Waters' first class stocked rainbow fisheries. Every year sees some good trout caught here and the current record is 13lb 2oz. There is a natural head of brownies and permits can be had from the Ranger, Reg England (0579) 342366, who can also advise you on flies and where the fish are! Reg also looks after neighbouring Colliford which is brown trout only and has many pleasant bays.

Porth is a thirty-eight acre stocked lake near Newquay. Not far off the A394, south of Penryn, is Stithians Reservoir. Permits cost £5.50 and can be had from the water sports centre or the shop in Stithians village.

Wales is a land of vivid contrasts—spectacular scenery and a rich industrial heritage. It is also a country which boasts several fine rivers weaving intricately through largely unspoiled mountainside and wooded countryside. It may not be a game fishing mecca but it has a number of excellent salmon rivers, as well as some engaging streams where the brown trout fight like demons.

Sewin (Welsh for sea-trout) fishing is, like rugby, a passion amongst the Welsh. Sea-trout are prolific here and tend to move in pairs or threes, often reaching 8lb to 10lb. Sewin fishing is a real game fisherman's delight and only starts properly at twilight when the world around is quiet. Make no mistake, these fish fight and good judgement and planning are essential if you are to have any chance of success. Unlike brown trout, the sewin will journey within the river system, so the visiting angler must, therefore, endeavour to track them down before embarking on an evening that can hold its own alongside game fishing to be found almost anywhere. One tip here, it is always worth visiting the local hostelry in search of some essential tips for the battle ahead. The locals will tell you that colour and depth of presentation are two major keys to your success. Fishing a good pool will achieve little if you are unable to offer your fly on a plate, so to speak. Mind you, when you feel that monumental tug, prepare for chaos. The sewin plunges to the depths and occasionally, unbowed, he will leap skyward. This is a celebrated fish and, pound for pound, it will give you a fight equal to the wildest salmon.

As in many places, the salmon fishing is not as good as it once was. Salmon fishing can nevertheless still be found in all rivers although the runs do vary radically from year to year. The River Wye is particularly excellent. Autumn runs tend to be more productive than those in the spring when the salmon dart up the river in good numbers. This is the sport at its best. Brown trout fishing is also good in Wales and this crafty fish will test all your skills.

The River Wye

The River Wye is probably the best known river in Wales and one of the most famous of Britain's salmon rivers. It crosses the border between England and Wales and is often referred to as England's best salmon river! The Wye rises on the south side of Plynlimon and rushes as a boulder-strewn stream down river—a delight for brown trout. As the river grows, so the trout gain stature. Around Rhayader a number of important tributaries join the Wye, including the Irfon of which we will have more anon. Through careful conservation and control of nets the salmon catch is impressive. Although much of the river is privately owned there are several hotels and associations with rights to the water. Many people who fish the Wye will take advantage of some of the splendid opportunities afforded by Harris and Stokes (0432) 354455 who have reminded me of a

Scottish fishing custom. On the first day of the season, a half bottle of whisky should be poured into the water to bless, and, hopefully, intoxicate the fish. You must be sure to keep a half bottle nearby, not only to celebrate your catch but also to keep you warm. It can be very cold on the Wye as the last two seasons have proved. Demand remains high for the prime beats and lettings are far from cheap, but some lesser known beats are good value and the fishing is still very good.

Another point that Roger Stokes makes is that the economic recession is effecting the take-up of certain beats and, if you haven't been too badly effected yourself, then you might just be able to acquire some rods here. Harris and Stokes have in excess of 400 salmon rods to let each year, principally on the Wye and the Usk, but can also arrange fishing in the smaller rivers.

The Wye from Chepstow to Builth Wells is made up of large bends and loops and the water glides in leisurely fashion, in striking contrast to its infant pace. There is some one and three quarter miles of fishing, some double-bank, such as at Lydbrook five miles below Ross-On-Wye, with season tickets still available. Ross itself has some town water available to visiting anglers and G. & R. Sports (0989) 63723 will provide you with all the details.

It is also worth mentioning that trout streams abound here; the Monnow, Lugg and Garron are particularly good and landowners sometimes do consent to fishing them. The Birmingham Anglers Association have a number of excellent opportunities here as well as on other waters in Wales. Hattons (0432) 272317, who are based at St Owen Street in Hereford, also issue day licences and permits.

The visiting fisherman may often be referred to the splendid Red Lion Hotel (0981) 500303 at Bredwardine, who own eight miles of the Wye and assuming the water is good, provide excellent fishing. The water is made up of nine beats which run consecutively and hold two rods per beat. The fishing has been much improved in recent years and the brown trout have been much in evidence. The hotel sells and lends tackle to residents and day tickets can be purchased for £28. Permits and tackle, along with some good fishing, can be obtained from H. R. Grant (0497) 820309 in Castle Street, Hay-On-Wye. As well as issuing permits for town waters they have one mile of their own single-bank fishing.

The Swan Hotel (0497) 821188 also offers some good water. The Swan is a member of a syndicate which owns a four and a half mile stretch of single-bank fishing on the Wye. There is excellent salmon fishing here. The Old Black Lion in Hay (0497) 820841 does not have its own water but has good local contacts who can provide fishing on one and a half miles of single-bank and about eight good pools. This water is understandably available to residents only, who must bring their own tackle. Two weeks notice is also required. This is a very friendly place to stay and if you are seeking a bit of local advice then a ghillie can be hired at a cost of £25 per day.

The Irfon

The Wye has numerous tributaries and one of the most celebrated is the River Irfon, in which good trout and salmon fishing can be enjoyed. The Grove Park and Irfon Angling Club have water available on both the Wye and the Irfon, as well as Caer Beris Stillwater Fishery. Tickets are available from Mrs Morgan (0982) 552759. Caer Beris Manor (0982) 552601 at Builth Wells have some thousand yards of the Irfon with access to some excellent fishing on the Wye and some lake fishing at Caer Beris. The brown trout on the Irfon are fighting fit and provide tremendous sport. They usually weigh in at under a pound but there are a few wily fish who are considerably larger. The salmon fishing can also be good and 38lb 8oz record fish is a testimony to this. The hotel offers a package which includes dinner, bed and breakfast and free fishing for two nights for £95 per person—excellent stuff!

The Lake Country House Hotel (05912) 202 also has private fishing on the Irfon available to guests. This spans four and a half miles of single-bank fishing. The hotel is situated at Llangammarch Wells and you have to inspect your map closely to find it at all. The river is a typical Welsh stream, which runs over a hard stone bed of layered rock, resulting in some delightful pools. In other locations the river is wide and shallow, but always take care when wading as it is easy to slip over here. The wild trout are supplemented by the Lake Hotel (05912) 202 and its charming companion the Cammarch Arms Hotel (05912) 205, also in Llangammarch Wells. The proprietor of this establishment, Mr Alan Tansley has made a considerable effort to keep these waters and his care has most definitely reaped dividends. Incidentally, in the vicinity lies the only barium spring in Britain, considered to be a cure for gout, heart disease and rheumatism. Any afflicted anglers will therefore have a second good reason to make a trip here.

The Cammarch Arms' water is divided into three sections spanning three and a half miles of single-bank fishing, available to non-residents as well as guests. The hotel also has a mile of the Wye and three and a half miles of the Cammarch and Upper Dulas. Further upstream, we find real 'trout country'. In Rhayader, you will find the newsagents have excellent value day tickets and licences, sold on behalf of the Elan Angling Club, who own a one mile stretch of double-bank fishing. This is the place where a 10lb trout was caught—that should give you food for thought. There have been a number of efforts made to stock this part of the river but the fishing is likely to take some time to regenerate itself, despite all efforts made. Indeed, the water bailiffs believe it may be as long as five years before the likes of Llangurig see fish of any consequence again.

The Usk

The River Usk is regarded as one of the finest fisheries in the United Kingdom and it is certainly one of the finest trout rivers in the principality. It is also a fine salmon water. The river affords some spectacular scenery and the wild native brownies offer a challenging duel. The best fishing is in April and May, during the prolific fly hatches.

The water starts its journey some 2400 feet above sea level from Carmarthen Fan and travels through limestone and sandstone outcrops. Much of this water is preserved, but the visitor can still fish on the town water and Jean Williams at Sweets Fishing Tackle (02913) 2552 is perhaps the best person to talk to. Tickets are £7 a day and a licence can also be obtained here. The Bridge Inn (0873) 853045 is situated on the river and on occasion, when the river floods and breaks its banks the hotel is in the river! The water is particularly good and comprises calm stretches which break into rapids and changes again into deep pools. Trout tickets are available from The Bridge at a price of £6 per day or £15.50 per week. Salmon fishing will cost you £11.70 per day and £32.50 per week. One of the best spots from which to enjoy the Usk is from Gliffaes Country House Hotel (0874) 730371 who hold two attractive stretches. Gliffaes owns a mile of water and has two thirds of a mile double-bank fishing a few miles upstream.

The Usk is extremely susceptible to changes in the water level. However, when the waters are up the river is a delight to fish. The Usk is renowned for its early start and fine sport can be had in March and April. The hatches tend to occur in the morning during March and the rise gradually occurs later through April and May until the evening hatch in June. Traditional wet flies work well and this is also good dry fly water. Naturally, each individual has their own preferred methods and the Gliffaes offers local advice on the most successful methods and flies. Beats are rotated each day. In recent years salmon catches have dwindled significantly due to a number of factors. There is some reason for optimism, as sea nets are being restricted in Ireland and the estuary nets are also being more stringently controlled. The average size of the salmon tends to be about 10lb to 12lb but there are some bigger fish to be taken and the largest caught at Gliffaes was 35lb. Gliffaes offer trout fishing at £11 per day and salmon at £16 per day. Non-residents are welcome but guests do have preference.

The Vine Tree Inn (0873) 810514 at Llangattock issues tickets on behalf of the Crickhowell and District Anglers Association waters, which comprise three separate stretches. One is a mere 100 yards from the inn which is great value at £2 per day. The other stretches are a little further away and consist of three quarters of a mile of double-bank water and one and a half miles of single-bank fishing. Trout fishing is priced at £12 per day and salmon fishing at £17. The fishing is good provided the water is not too low. Returning downstream, The Bell Hotel (0873) 810247 at Glangrwyney has a few hundred yards of single-bank, predominately trout water, which is priced at £5 per day. At Abergavenny, permits for the Town Water, at £6 for a day's trouting, can be obtained from PM Fishing Tackle (0873) 853175.

Talybont on the Usk offers a variety of waters and one of the most accessible to the visiting angler is the three quarters of a mile stretch of single-bank fishing available at the Usk Hotel (0874) 87251. This water includes four good salmon pools and is also some of the best brown trout fishing in the vicinity. Fishing is available for residents only. The hotel has a number of shooting opportunities available too, including grouse, pheasant, partridge and duck.

South Wales Waters

There are a large number of stillwaters in south east Wales and the angler who crosses the Severn in the hope of a good catch will surely not be disappointed. Lladegfedd (04957) 55122 covers a huge area and is located in the lowlands among wooded, rolling hills between the Usk and the valleys of South Wales. The water is restricted to fly-only and there are numerous opportunities available to the visiting angler. Day tickets are priced at around £9 and season tickets £250. The season runs from mid-March to mid-October. The fishery opens at 10.00am and boats may be rented from 8.00am onwards. Closing times vary from month to month in accordance with the daylight hours. There is a six fish limit per day and if you wish to explore the water to its full extent, then a motor boat will set you back £15 and a rowing boat £6. They can be reserved in advance by telephoning the fishery. In the closed season, the water is a haven for wintering wildfowl.

Two fisheries to the south of here are Llanishen and Lisvane (0222) 618919 which are joined by a central embankment and cover some eighty acres in total. They are situated a short distance outside Cardiff on the southern tip of the Welsh Hills in attractively wooded and open countryside. Lisvane is another reservoir which is popular with wintering wildfowl as well as local fishermen. The reservoir is stocked with rainbows and browns. Day tickets are priced at £10 and the waters are open from sunrise to an hour after sunset.

There is some fine sewin fishing in South and West Wales. The stillwaters are also useful when other waters are out of condition. Before we examine the delights of the major rivers, a glance at one or two less well known ones is well worthwhile.

The Ogmore

The River Ogmore has fishing opportunities for trout, sewin and salmon and the Ogmore Anglers Association which has just celebrated its centenary year, owns eighteen miles of double-bank fishing of this good water. Weekly tickets are available at £25 which represents good value for money. The Association bye-laws stipulate that you may only fish if you are introduced by a member of the club. In reality, the extremely friendly Mr Protheroe, Secretary, (0656) 861139 will merely sound you out on the telephone.

The Tawe

The River Tawe flows through some superb scenery in its upper reaches and the sewin and salmon fishing is very much improved, although some parts of the river still suffer from pollution. Mainwarings in Dillwyn Road, Sketty (0792) 202245 sell licences and permits for the Pontardawe Angling Club who own eight miles of double-bank fishing between Pontardawe and Morriston. Assuming conditions are in our favour, the fishermen can enjoy some fine sport and day tickets can be purchased for £8.

The Towy & The Cothi

The River Towy (or Tywi) rises in the Cambrian Mountains and flows thence from the Brianne Reservoir to Carmarthen and the Bristol Channel. Although the reservoir has been blamed for many ills in the water, it does act as a potential safety fuse for surges of water and consequent flooding. This generally ensures some good, easy fishing. It is excellent sewin water and the fish generally run from the first day of the season in March. The association waters are available but some of the water is understandably retained for private use. However, the Land and Leisure Group (0874) 623181, a subsidiary of Welsh Water, have a large amount of opportunities for sewin and to a lesser extent salmon. The Group also have some water on the River Cothi, a rocky stream which can prove quite difficult to fish. This tributary of the Towy has some excellent sewin fishing from June onwards. Prices are available on application.

The Forest Arms (0267) 202339 in Brechta also have a mile on the Cothi. The locals are generally delighted to share their expertise and permits are available for £8 and £5. The Forest Arms also doubles as a good value bed and breakfast for people who wish to stay a day or two. The Tackle Shop at Felingwm Uchaf (0267) 290207 sells permits and can also arrange fishing on the Treflyn Estate some distance away near Tregaron. This comprises some six and a half miles of double and single-bank fishing on what is delightful water. The Estate also rents cottages by the week, which may appeal to the many fishermen who enjoy the freedom of self-catering.

Returning southwards we arrive at Llandovery. Mrs Thomas at Tonn Farm has a short half a mile stretch which is good for trout fishing enthusiasts. Mrs Barbara Leech, who runs the antique shop (0550) 20602 sells tackle as well as licences for Llandovery Anglers Association who have a good stretch on the Towy. Permits cost £7.50 for a day and £20 per week for the lower water, and £15 and £70 respectively for the upper water. The proprietor is most helpful and will be delighted to assist you. Llandovery AA also have three miles of the River Bran, an excellent trout stream. Although much of the water is in the hands of Land and Leisure, The Golden Grove Arms Hotel (0558) 668551 has a three quarter mile stretch of single-bank which is excellent for sewin and salmon. The hotel bar is well frequented by locals who are happy to offer good advice on the area, especially if you are buying.

Carmarthen and District Anglers Club (0267) 231945 is currently in the care of Mr Evans. The Club has six miles of mixed bank fishing on the Towy as well as a stretch of the Cothi. Permits on most waters are £12 a day. Lyric Sports, King Street in Carmarthen (0267) 237166, will supply tickets for these waters and also for the Carmarthen Anglers Association waters. These comprise some six and a half miles of predominantly double-bank fishing on the Towy and two and a half miles on the Cothi. The Club Secretary (0267) 237362 is also extremely helpful and you should note that a £50 season ticket will allow you to fish any of the Club's waters, which also includes stretches on the Gwili and Taf.

The better salmon fishing tends to take place toward the end of the season and the sewin will provide some thrilling sport earlier in the year. There will be few fishermen who will not delight in the varied opportunities that are afforded by the River Towy.

The Cleddau

The River Cleddau has two limbs, one which stretches east and the other west. Both then journey north through parts of unspoiled Wales. The Pembrokeshire Anglers Association have fifteen miles of fishing, much of which is double-bank. Salmon tend to run from March to the end of June and sewin from mid-June onwards. In league with the NRA, the Association have also an extensive cleaning operation underway to improve the banks and habitat of the Western Cleddau, creating some five or six new pools to add to the many already existing. County Sports in Haverfordwest (0437) 763740 issue permits, and licences at £6 per day or £32 a week, together with an extensive range of tackle. Maps are issued with the permits which is often the case in Wales—just as well as some of the pools are in remarkably remote settings. The Chairman, Mr Tony Summers (0437) 763216 is extremely helpful and is happy to advise you on currently favoured flies and the better times to fish. This is a common trait amongst the Welsh fishing fraternity who could not be kinder, but obviously visitors should be respectful of privacy.

The Eastern Cleddau is mostly taken up by private syndicates, but the Slebech Estates (0834) 860905 have one and a half miles of double-bank fishing which offers good opportunities for salmon, sewin and trout fishing. The water is restricted to fly-only, a twenty-four hour permit will cost you £17, and a day pass in the order of £12. The Estate also rents riverside cottages to visiting anglers, which sounds very promising. Try and contact Jim Brown around meal times!

Those anglers fishing in south west waters should make a note of Llys-y-Fran (0437) 532273 which is an attractive reservoir on the edge of the Preseli Hills and provides bank and boat fishing. Fishing takes place from 8.00am to half an hour after sunset. The reservoir which is situated near to Haverfordwest, has good quality fishing for rainbow and brown trout. If you are looking for a family day out this is a good place as there are picnic tables, walks and nature trails. The price of a day ticket is £8 and there is a six fish bag limit. Boats may be hired for £15 per day and a superb wheelie boat is available for disabled anglers free of charge. Another fishery which also provides additional activities is located at Mynyddcerrig near Pontyberem. The Granffrwd Trout Fishery (0269) 870539 provides riding and shooting as well as some fine fishing that has been acclaimed by the angling press. Day tickets are £18, there is a four fish limit and if you don't manage to catch anything you can have your money back! The fishery enjoys a wonderful setting just nine miles from Camarthen. Canadian Pine Cabins with bathroom and kitchen make for an ideal family holiday.

Teifi to the Dee

Whether you are fishing at nightfall or early in the morning in hopeful anticipation of your lunch, you will find a wealth of good sport in Wales. In this age of pollution, grinding mechanisation and awesome technology you will find places where seemingly time has stood still. These are charming villages in idyllic surroundings, providing a perfect excuse for a timely excursion into some of Britain's most remote and unspoiled reaches. Here, you can pause from fishing as otters plunder the waters. Here, you are accompanied by birds of prey and many wildfowl. The Welsh Water Authorities are doing a tremendous job promoting these waters without sacrificing their intrinsic charms. If you are keen on fly fishing then a journey to all corners of Wales must be high on your list of forays.

The Teifi

The River Teifi rises in Lyn Teifi near Strata Florida in the Cambrian Hills not far from the source of the Towy. The river is often titled the Queen of Welsh Rivers and this is hardly surprising when one reflects on the sport available. The river flows south west and then westwards, entering Cardigan Bay south of the town. There are a number of opportunities for the visiting fisherman and fishing is at a premium for sewin in July and August, particularly from dusk until dawn. The Cenarth area holds good salmon and at Cilgerran one can see historic Coracles. The river runs through enchanting scenery including the Caron Bog, a renowned nature reserve. Salmon and sewin tend to dominate in the lower reaches while trout naturally tend to predominate in the upper reaches and the tributaries.

The Teifi concludes its journey a little south of Cardigan. Mr Cliff Jones (0239) 710405 is Secretary of the Teifi Trout Association and is something of a Welsh wizard on the area when it comes to fishing. The association has some fifteen miles of the Lower Teifi. One bank offers continuous fishing, the other has four beats in and around Newcastle Emlyn and permits can be obtained at £10 a day or £35 a week from Andrew Sports in the town (0239) 710349. Cenarth Falls is the last site of historical coracle fishing for salmon. The Castle Malgwyn Hotel (023987) 644 in Llechryd have a mile of fishing which is available to guests as do the Llwyndywys Mansion Hotel (023987) 263. These waters both have trout, salmon and sewin fishing.

The Llandysul Anglers Association has some twenty-two miles of the middle waters of the Teifi and this is an extremely popular stretch of the river. Salmon run in the spring months and again from August through September, while sewin are prolific from July onwards. Mr Artie Jones (0559) 362317 is the secretary and permits are available from Alma Stores in Llandysul (0559) 363322, just beyond Barclays Bank.

The Llanbydder Anglers Association has some five miles on the Teifi and Bill Wilkins (0570) 480038 is the man at the reel, so to speak. Tickets are available direct from him or David Morgan, Siop-y-Bont, Llanybdder (0570) 480980.

The Tregaron Anglers Association controls several miles of the Upper Teifi and Mr D.L. Evans (0974) 298304 is the Association's Honourary Secretary. There is some fine brown trout fishing available on these stretches. Wet fly fishing tends to be the most favoured in March and April with dry fly coming into its own in early May. Salmon will run up this far if the water conditions are favourable, particularly later in the season. Permits can be purchased from the newsagents in Tregaron or from the post office in Pontrhydfendigaid (try asking for directions to this village!) There are also good value day tickets available here for trout fishing only. The Talbot Hotel (0974) 298208 have good contacts with the local association and are delighted to arrange fishing for their guests. The water bailiff is also a helpful chap as are so many of the association officials. This may be a queen of rivers but it is one of the most accessible as well as one of the most beautiful in the area.

Finally, if you are endeavouring to fish the seven mile stretch of Llyn Gynon you will find the Visitors Centre in Glan Village (0597) 810880 a mine of useful information. Permits are also available from the centre. Access to this water is difficult but well worth making an effort for. The wild brown trout fight like tigers. Day tickets are priced at a reasonable £3. If you happen to be sitting at home with little to do, reflect on the River Teifi. Imagine, if you will, the morning quiet or the evening solace, the flow and the ripple.

The Aeron

There are many reasons for going fishing; the solitude, the scenery and the challenge. The River Aeron is a relatively small but still attractive river with an excellent run of sewin from June onwards. The lower reaches are generally the most productive and are controlled by the Aberaeron Angling Club. Permits are available from Cei Lee Sports in Bridge Street, Arberaeron (0545) 571123. Local residents are given priority and pensioners and juniors even better treatment. Visitors who live two or more miles away from Aberaeron are required to pay £60 for a year's fishing. Please contact Geoff Parry, West Winds, Wellington Street, Aberaeron for further details. Night fishing for sewin in this area is often excellent. Upriver the water flows through farmland but the waters are still often fishable by virtue of the local farmers who allow fishermen onto their land. The Post Office in Abraeron generally has a list of farmers who are welcoming. The banks are often overgrown here, but in the later weeks of the season the sewin fishing is phenomenal. The Butcher and the Silver March Brown are two popular flies used locally.

The Rheidol

There are numerous streams in Dyfed and the Rheidol is one that is well worth your attention. The sewin that run up-river in May are of top quality and the middle reaches, which have long glides suit wet fly fishing for sewin. The level of water often fluctuates dramatically by virtue of the fact that the Nant-y-Moch and Dinas Reservoirs are used for hydro-electric power generation. Although the increased levels may aid fishing, the changes in water temperature make it doubly difficult to tempt the devious sewin which are so prolific in these waters. The Aberystwyth Anglers Association own all the water and some eight lakes in the district. Permits can be obtained from the Aberystwyth Tackle Shop (0970) 611200 and prices are in the region of £12 per day or £55 per week. There are some excellent sewin lurking, which will give you some great sport should you be lucky enough to catch one. It is a good idea to use both a floating and a sinking line to counteract the changes in temperature that follow any fluctuation in the water level. Equipped with wet fly you should be fortunate to have a lot of fun amid the pools and deep glides of the River Rheidol.

The Dovey

The Dovey is one of the finest waters in Britain and its sewin fishing is outstanding. The thirty or so miles of water starts amidst mountainous terrain and hereafter the waters wind their way in a south westerly direction to Aberdovey. This spate river also has some three hundred and fifty miles of feeder tributaries which offer some fine trout fishing. The New Aberdovey Fishery Association (0654) 702721 controls twenty-eight miles of river and as you may imagine, rods are somewhat hard to come by. Indeed, no day tickets are available to visitors, although weekly permits at £80 are available. The lower beats are almost impossible to get on and you must book well in advance to stand any chance here. The upper beats are less popular and you may well be able to purchase a weekly ticket from the post office in Cemmaes. The sea-trout tend to range from 2lb to 8lb and salmon from 8lb to 10lb. In June 1991, a 30lb fish was taken—the largest since 1930. There are numerous pools of note; Rhiwlas, Tank, Glandwr and Cottage are some of the most celebrated. Equally notable is the Haslan Fly which has made a reputation for itself on this water. The Brigands Inn (0650) 531208 is an historic establishment in which to stay. It dates from the eighteenth century and has welcomed anglers to the area for a hundred years. The inn owns two miles of predominantly double-bank fishing on the Dovey which is almost entirely reserved for residents. Eight rods are allowed per day and these are priced at £17. The hotel arranges special fishing breaks and you should contact them for further details. We have received very positive reports on the sea-trout fishing in this stretch and in 1990 a 24lb fish topped the scales here. Salmon are also reported to be on the increase. This is a first class river and if you are able to fish it you are extremely fortunate

The Vyrnwy & the Tanat

The River Vyrnwy runs from the lake of the same name to the north of Powys and offers some fine trout and salmon fishing as well as some good coarse fishing. The Vyrnwy is a tributary of the Severn and whilst it is not a classic salmon river, it has given up some 30lb fish in recent seasons and is well located for the many anglers of the Midlands who are not so spoilt in their choice of good game fishing rivers. The sport has been restricted of late by low water levels here, but when the river rises the clear waters are a delight to fish. A mere £8 covers the cost of a season ticket here—

tremendous value. Tickets are available from Sundore Fishing Tackle and Leisure in Shrewsbury (0743) 361804 or direct from Oswestry and District Angling Society (0691) 772045. This is a wonderfully unspoiled area and awaits your attention.

The River Tanat is a tributary of the Vyrnwy and is a good trout river which will appeal to those living on the border. Much of the water is owned by syndicates but two inns offer good value fishing and provide an excellent base for exploring this delightful countryside. Llan-y-Blodwel finds the Horseshoe Inn (0691) 828227 which has three rods available per day for fly fishing only. The Green Inn in Llangedwyn (0691) 828234 has three quarters of a mile of single-bank fishing, again with three rods available (the other bank is too steep to fish from).

The Mawddach & The Wnion

The River Mawddach rises on a remote hillside between Bala and Trawsfyndd Lake, holds salmon, trout and to a lesser extent, sea-trout. Although much of the water is preserved, there are two excellent hotels from which to enjoy the fishing. The Tyn y Groes Hotel, Granllwyd (034140) 275 has a mile and a half of single-bank fishing available for guests. This is predominantly salmon water and licences can be obtained from the nearby post office. Permits are available at the hotel and are priced at £10 per day. The proprietor, Barry Rithwell, has access to other rivers as well as a splendid knowledge of the Mawddach. The delightful Dolmelynllyn Hall (034140) 273 is a true haven and the hotel can provide guests with some twelve miles of fishing on the Mawddach and its best known tributary the River Wnion. This is a tumbling, often turbulent water. Guests can enjoy the fine fishing here for free. Permits are available to non-residents for £15 although they should always enquire in advance as to availability. Licences can be purchased in the local village. An encouraging thought for the younger, aspiring anglers is that in 1992 the first salmon, a seven-pounder, was caught on this stretch of water by a fourteen year old boy.

Further information is also obtainable from Dolgellau Angling Club (0341) 422906 who control much of the association waters. They are particularly well organised and have in the region of twelve miles of salmon and sea-trout fishing on the Mawddach and Wnion at Dolgellau in addition to the recently acquired Storehouse waters. Both rivers are stocked with salmon and sea-trout from the Mawddach Hatchery. Weekly permits are well priced at £26 and day permits are £9 (river and lake combined). Tickets can be purchased from the Seafarer (0341) 280978, a tackle shop in Barmouth.

The Dysynni

Journeying westwards, we find the River Dysynni which rises in Llyn Cau on the towering Cader Idris. The water falls rapidly via Dol-y-Cau and into the picturesque Tal-y-Llyn. Emerging from the lake it flows westwards as a small upland river but grows ever deeper as it carves its way through the valley to enter the sea at Cardigan Bay, a mile or so to the north of Tywyn. The river offers interesting trout and sewin fishing and in the late summer the occasional salmon will be encountered. The Estimaner Angling

Association owns three miles of the lower river and seven miles of its upper reaches and the Peniarth Estate has a further four miles. This is one of the most picturesque rivers you are ever likely to fish and permits are available from Abergynolwyn Post Office (0654) 782635 in the Square, opposite the Railway Hotel. Day tickets cost £9, weekly tickets £12. The Sports Shop in Tywyn (0654) 710772 also has permits for sale. If you are looking for an escape in superb scenery then this fishing is first rate.

Central Wales Waters

Central Wales reveals some interesting lake fishing, all of which offers good daily forays for brown trout and rainbows. Bag limits are usually around six fish per day and tickets start at £6 for a full day's fishing. Dinas and Nant-y-Moch Reservoirs are both under the ownership of Powergen (097084) 667 and are part of the Rheidol Hydro-Electric Power Scheme. They are both very popular and the fisherman landing the largest fish wins a season ticket for the following year. If you happen to be fishing the Rhayader, then surely a visit to Elan Valley Fisheries is in order. In fact, it is a good idea even if you're not in the area. The interlinked reservoirs of Caban Coch, Garreg Ddu, Graig Goch and Pen-y-Garreg are controlled by Elan Trout Fisheries and provide 850 acres of excellent trout fishing in a beautiful setting. Permits can be bought from the Elan Valley Visitors Centre (0597) 810898, take the B4518 from Rhayader.

One of the most renowned stillwater lakes in Britain is Lake Vyrnwy. It spans 1100 acres and is 800 feet above sea level. The rights to this water are owned by the Lake Vyrnwy Hotel (069173) 692, a delightful place to stay. The lake is surrounded by moorland, meadow, mountain and forest, which all provide a stunning backdrop for the casting fisherman. The lake is restricted to fly fishing only from the hotels boats which are available with or without engines. Tackle can be hired and licences can also be purchased from the hotel. Late in the season when the water level drops, bank fishing is also possible.

The lake is well stocked throughout the season with brown, rainbow and American brook trout to complement the indigenous population of brownies. For groups, tuition is available and the services of a ghillie can be arranged. The price of day tickets is in the region of £6, with boat hire costing £10.50. An engine will cost a further £9.50 and there is ample room for two people in a boat. There are a whole host of other permits obtainable from the hotel and this is an ideal place to stay and enjoy some good fishing in a superb natural environment.

Gwynedd offers a number of fishing opportunities. The Lakes of Blaenau Ffestiniog number twenty and offer some first class fishing for wild trout. Here, the fishing is managed by the local angling association and if you like being well away from the crowds then these lakes are for you. The Dolgellau Angling Association (0341) 422706 control the waters of Llyn Cynwch as well as first class river fishing. The lake is situated near the renowned Precipice Walk and all around are stunning views of Cader Idris and the Mawddach Estuary. The lake is stocked every three weeks with brown and rainbow trout and has natural brown trout too. The record fish is an impressive 10lb. The northern section of the lake is fly-only but the remainder is open fishing. Tickets for the lake are priced at £7 and for the views that come with it, that seems like good value!

South of Dolgellau we find another hotel which provides superb lakeside fishing. The Tynycornel at Talyllyn (0654) 782282 provides fishing on one of the most beautiful waters in the principality. The management also control the fishing on Bugeilyn, a truly remarkable setting in the hills above Llanbrynmair, where boat fishing for the wild brown trout will provide a feast of memories.

Snowdonia not only has wonderful scenery but some delightfully unspoiled mountain lakes too, gouged out by glaciers many thousands of years ago. One such lake is Llyn Crafnant (0492) 640818. Formerly the exclusive territory of the wild brown trout, these wild fish now share their home with rainbows which are stocked weekly, including a former record fish of some 17lb. The lake is signposted from Trefriw on the B5106 which is in the Conway Valley some five miles north of Betws-y-Coed. Day tickets are priced at £10 and can be purchased from the Lakeside Office. There is also some cottage accommodation available.

The Dwyfawr & the Glaslyn

Venturing ever northwards, one has a choice between the wilds of Snowdonia or the coastline, dotted with small fishing villages and larger resort towns. There are numerous streams in Gwynedd and the Dwyfawr, Glaslyn and Erch are three which flow from the Lleyn Peninsula and attract quality fish. The locals love their fishing here and when the sewin are running everyone knows! However, in recent years numbers have been substantially reduced. This is an area of quite stunning scenery, much of which can be enjoyed with fishing rod in hand. Most of the Dwyfawr is in the hands of Criccieth, Llanystumdwy and District Anglers Association and permits, licences and tackle can be purchased from Pritchards (0766) 522116. Mr Goodman Jones is a member of the Club and is very helpful. Permits are priced at approximately £75 for a season or £30 for a week. A day's fishing will cost you £10. There had been a decline in sea-trout here in recent years, but reports for 1993 were actually very encouraging. Salmon, moreover, have increased in number.

The Glaslyn which rises in Llyn Conwy and runs along the valley floor to Portmadog is another sewin river although the Glaslyn Anglers Association owns much of the river. Monday to Friday tickets are £10 and are available from the Angling and Gun Centre (0766) 512464. If you wish to fish at the weekend you must hold a season ticket which is priced at £50. Once again, the surroundings are perfect and the river is well known for its early run of Sewin.

The Conway

The River Conway (Conwy) rises in Migneint and flows through the Carnarvonshire countryside, through Betws-y-Coed and Llanrwst and into Conway Bay. The upper part of the Conway Valley takes in some celebrated unspoiled countryside and much of the land is in the care of the National Trust. Permits are available for a number of stretches of the river between Conway Falls Bridge and Rhydlanfair. In total, the National Trust (0492) 860123 handle four beats and weekly tickets are available at £10 or £3 per day. Although the trout are small, they fight well and the scenery is quite breathtaking. Tickets are also available from Bob Ellis (0690) 710567 and from The Old Library Newsagent and Tackle Shop (0492) 641 477 in Llanrwst at £45 for a weekly permit. It is also worth considering the National Trust on a number of other fishing opportunities, and also Conway Valley Fisheries (0492) 650063, who have day and season tickets available on a two acre spring fed lake.

It is difficult to consider such beauty and at the same time pay sufficient attention to the worries over pollution and acid rain, but the Conway is susceptible to both these problems. As a result, trout fishing was in trouble here a couple of years ago. Since then, however, things have taken a definite turn for the better. Salmon still run the river and average between 9lb and 12lb. The Betws-y-Coed Angling Association (0690) 710618 has some four and a half miles of mixed bank fishing as well as three lakes on the river. The Committee have passed a ruling that no day or weekly tickets are to be issued after August each year but prior to that, day fishing is available at £15 and weekly tickets at £40 (Monday to Friday). A season ticket is priced at £105. Mr Melvin Hughes, the Membership Secretary, is happy to hear from prospective members (after 6.00pm please). Permits and maps are obtainable from Gareth Parry at the Tan Ian Restaurant, Betws-y-Coed (0690) 710232.

Those wishing to fish later in the season might be advised to stay at one of the nearby hotels. The Maenen Abbey (049269) 230 have one mile of single-bank fishing available to guests and there are a number of locals who frequent the bar with useful knowledge and advice! The Gwydyr Hotel (0690) 710777, Betws-y-Coed has about six miles of double-bank fishing. Tackle is also available for hire, but only guests can fish for salmon at £55 per day or £140 per week between March and May, and £235 per week for the latter part of the season. Night fishing for sea-trout is possible at a price of £18.50 or £110 for a weekly permit (residents only). Two of the Conway's chief tributaries are the Lledr and the Llugwy. Betws-y-Coed Anglers Club has permits for the latter, whilst Dolwyddelan FA has one and a half miles double-bank fishing on the Lledr. Daily tickets, costing £20 a week for trout and salmon, are available from Dolwyddelan Post Office (0690) 6201 if you are staying in the village.

The Clwyd

The Clwyd, which meets the sea at Rhyl, is predominantly controlled by clubs and associations which restrict the waters to members only. However the St Asaph Angling Association have two beats available to day visitors from Monday to Friday. The fishing, which includes salmon in the summer and autumn is priced at £5 per day. The Club also has two miles of excellent trout fishing on the River Elwy. Permits are £3 per day—great value indeed! Foxon's Tackle (0745) 583583 in St Asaphs sells permits for the waters and will help with any information. The water is good below Ruthin and the Ruthin Castle Hotel (08242) 2664 has rights to the water which is free to guests. It is fly-only and guests may fish for salmon, brown and sea-trout.

The Dee

Unlike the Clwyd, the River Dee is far easier to fish and the visitor will not only find good value but also a delightful setting. In an age when the price of a beat is extremely high and fish harder to find, the Dee is a real treat. It is well cared for by the associations that own much of this water. The nature of the valley is varied, sometimes deep, and on other sections bordered by meadows. As you will appreciate, access is not always possible. The River Dee rises in the Cambrian Mountains and threads its way to Chester, flowing through Bala, Corwen, Llangollen and Overton. The river holds trout, salmon, sewin and grayling. The grayling in particular are top quality and offer good sport when other game fish are out of season. The insect life is staggering and your fly box will have to be well filled to compete. Membership of the principal clubs such as the Corwen and Llangollen is excellent value. The Llangollen Angling Association has some six and a half miles of double-bank fly fishing and recently hosted the 10th World Fly Fishing Championships. D.M. Southern in Chapel Street, (0978) 860155 Llangollen sells permits at £3 a day for trout and £10 for salmon. Weekly permits are priced at £15 and £30 respectively. Mr Southern can also sell permits for Midland Fly Fishers Syndicate who have three miles of double-bank fly-only water, priced at £4 for trout and grayling fishing.

The Bryn Howel Hotel (0978) 860331 has access to the Llangollen Anglers Association waters and issue permits for trout at £3 per day, and salmon at £10 a day. As we head towards the Corwen Anglers Association waters we should pencil in a visit to the Berwyn Arms Hotel at Glyndyfrdwy (0490) 83210 which has two miles of single-bank fishing. There is a tackle shop at the hotel and the owner, Mr Gallagher, fishes regularly. Permits for trout and grayling cost £5 and salmon is priced at £12 per day. The trout fishing is fly-only. Corwen and District Angling Club controls most of the trout and grayling fishing on the Rhug Estate. Permits are available from local tacklists and a visit is thoroughly recommended. Pale Hall at Llandderfel (06783) 285 have bought some ten rods on the Dee, using Bala Association water and covering several sections of the Dee, Towyn and a mountain lake. There is some good salmon fishing here and tackle is available should you wish it. Fishing is reserved for guests only and is free. A licence can also be purchased at the hotel, should this be required. In Bala itself, Siop Yr Eryr, Sports and Tackle (0678) 520370 has an excellent range of tackle and the proprietor, Mr Evans, is a member of the local association and, as something of an expert, he is also generous with his advice. Mr Evans is a specialist in fly-tying and has some good examples of old eighteenth and nineteenth century Welsh patterns.

North Wales Waters

North Wales has a number of stillwaters rich in fish. Llyn Brenig (049082) 463 is situated high on Denbigh Moors and offers fly fishing for rainbow and brown trout. It is particularly notable as a boat fishery and hosted the World Championship in 1990. Day permits are £9 and boats can be hired for £15. Fishing takes place from mid-March to the end of October and between 8.00am until an hour after sunset. The water is located off the B4501 and is well worth a visit. Other waters to note include Felin-y-Gors (0745) 584044, which offers ten acres of fly fishing and four spring fed lakes in secluded surroundings. The fishery which opens from 9.00am to 10.00pm hires out tackle and also has some pleasant self-catering accommodation for people wishing to stay in the area. The cost of fishing varies with the duration of your stay and the longer you are here the more fish you may keep. Four hours will cost £8, maximum two fish, whilst a day ticket costs £22.50 with a six fish limit.

Journeying to the Moelfre Hills, we find the Tan-y-Mynydd Trout Lake (0745) 823691 on the B5381, St Asaph to Conway Road, just three miles outside Abergele and three and a half miles from the coast. There are ten self-catering cottages on site and a licenced bar and restaurant too. The tariffs and bag limits vary according to the number of hours you wish to spend here. There are a total of five small lakes which cover three and a half acres and each lake is stocked with rainbows, American brook trout and brown trout.

N59
L. CORRIB N17
COSTELLOE GALWAY
N6
GALWAY BAY
N18
NOUGHSHANNA
ENNIS
KILLALOE
N4
N9
LIMER
GO
FEALE
GALEY
N20
N23
N22
BLACKWATER
MALLOW
N72
KILLARNEY
LOUGH
CARAGH
GLENCAR
INNY
ROUGHTY
LEE
CO
BRIDE
LOUGH
CURRANE
KENMARE
WATER-
VILLE
BANDON
BANTRY
DUNMANWAY
BANDON

ATLANTIC OCEAN

MIZEN
HEAD

N55
ATHLONE
N62
TULLAMORE
N6
N4
N3
N2
N1
DUBLIN
LIFFEY
PROSPEROUS
N7
NAAS
BANAGHER
BARROW
N7
N9
WICKLOW MOUNTAINS
PORTLAOISE
N81
NORE
N8
CARLOW
N11
ST GEORGES CHANNEL
N10
N80
BARROW
N9
N10
N76
NORE
SUIR
N24
CARRICK ON SUIR
PILTOWN
CLONMEL
N9
N25
WEXFORD
HARBOUR
N25
N25
BALLYDUFF
CAPPOQUIN

Dublin City, its environs and the Counties Wicklow, Meath, Kildare and Louth make up the naturally beautiful Eastern Seaboard. Dublin Bay makes a glorious sweep northwards to Howth Head Peninsula, where there are spectacular views across the bay from the cliff walks, and southwards to the picturesque Dalkey, and its island with Benedictine ruins, then on to Killiney, where it is said that the view south compares with that over Naples. The Georgian city of Dublin was the European City of Culture in 1991 and its heritage trail around the old medieval parts of the city allows the visitor an insight into the nature of the Irish and also gives them the opportunity to sample some of Ireland's more modern culture—in the pub! The Irish are world renowned for their hospitality and in Dublin you will not be disappointed. There is no such thing as a quiet pint in Ireland, as you will inevitably be drawn into conversation by the locals.

The Boyne

With early Christian monuments scattered around the Boyne Valley to the north, the Newgrange burial chamber dating from 3000 B.C., some fine stately homes and gardens at Kilruddery and Mount Usher to the south, there is much to see and do. To the west of the city is the mecca for Ireland's other great passion—horseracing. Here, on the flat open plains of County Kildare, some of the best racehorses in the world are bred, trained and raced at the nearby Curragh. The River Boyne rises near Edenderry and flows for about seventy miles through County Meath to enter the sea near Drogheda, north of Dublin. Leave Dublin to the north-west, on the N2, where the imposing Slane Castle dates from 1785—the road from Dublin to the castle was supposedly straightened to hasten George IV's visits to his mistress! Here we find the fine limestone fishery with good runs and some deep pools. Unfortunately, due to low water levels, in recent years fewer fish have been taken, but some large salmon have been caught and this fishery really deserves a better reputation. Once a river of note for salmon, the arterial drainage scheme has lowered the water table and this has affected the runs up river. Brown trout are prolific in certain areas and come to wet and dry flies as well as spinners and worms. However, the river does tend to weed up from late July onwards. Sea-trout on the lower reaches are good in the autumn but generally the river is better known for its brownies. Local knowledge is absolutely essential and can be gleaned from any of the fourteen angling clubs or landowners who control the water.

The Trim, Athloy and District Angling Association (046) 31487 have a beat on the Boyne, and Gerard Lee wil be happy arrange a day's fishing on their behalf for IR5. This is fly-only water, and there is a bag limit of nine fish. A 5lb trout was caught here in 1993. Among the better flies for this stretch of the river are March Brown, Greenwells Glory, Sherry Spinner and Black Midge. In recent years, some of the best fishing has been between Navan and Drogheda, with the lower stretches having good runs of grilse and sea-trout. The Kells Blackwater and Lough Ramor have also produced some good trout, averaging 2lb, especially during the mayfly hatch and in the evenings. The season runs from 1st February to 1st September for salmon and 1st March to 14th September for trout with permits priced at around IR10 per day.

The Navan Anglers' Association, Abbey Road, Navan, has fourteen miles of mixed bank fishing with excellent wild brown trout, and both wet and dry fly fishing is permitted. Michael Connor (046) 29007 is the man to contact. Permits for the Navan Club Waters only are available from the Sports Den (046) 21130 in Tringate Street, Navan.

Drogheda and District Anglers control one mile of the tidal section near the town which is good for sea-trout, and three miles up river which is particularly good for brownies around mayfly time. Salmon can be caught here too depending on the height of the river. In addition, the Club controls the rights to two reservoirs at Killineer (fly-only) and Bernattin, where you can use any method. Both are put and take reservoirs and are stocked with brownies and rainbows. The club also has the rights for the nine mile long River Nanny nearby, well stocked with brown trout.

Sean Keenan, The Military Connections (army surplus and tackle shop) (041) 34371, 8 Lawrence Street, Drogheda, sells permits for the Drogheda Angling Waters and Shane and Rosslin Anglers' Association, who have stretches of mixed bank fishing on the Boyne totalling two miles. These adjacent waters have a good mixture of deep pools and fast flowing waters with a couple of weirs. Sean Keenan will be happy to advise you as he fishes these waters himself.

The Liffey

The source of the River Liffey is around thirteen miles southwest of Dublin in the Wicklow mountains, but it winds its way through Poulaphouca, Golden Falls and Leixlip Reservoirs before reaching the sea eighty miles away at Islandbridge. It is essential to check the river before beginning to fish, as artificial floods do affect fly fishing and there are few salmon above Leixlip Bridge. The lower stretches are much better.

The Liffey is controlled by the Federation of Liffey Angling Clubs, (045) 33068 which co-ordinates all the clubs' fishing. The river is either club or privately owned with no free fishing anywhere on the eighty mile stretch. The season here runs from February to September, with the best salmon fishing from February to April, and sea-trout and grilse from July to September. The first hatches of dark olives begin in late March, the hawthorn and iron blue dun in early May, mayfly in May and June and various sedges throughout the summer. The Clubs welcome visitors and the cost of a day's fishing should be around IR5.

Dublin and District Anglers' Association; Pat O'Molloy (01) 6558594 at 16 Whitehall Crescent, Terenure, controls fisheries at St Raphaels, Celbridge, Avondale and Islandbridge. Rory at Rory's Tackle Shop

(01) 6772351, 17a Temple Bar, Dublin 2, fishes all over Ireland and is also a member of the North Kildare Trout and Salmon Association. He is happy to advise on the Liffey and elsewhere. The North Kildare Association has around thirty miles of mainly double-bank fishing stretching from Millicent Bridge to Kilcullen, with good salmon in September and an excellent stretch for trout near Millicent Bridge. Tom Walshe, also a member of North Kildare, can be contacted at John Cahill & Sons (045) 79655, and is happy to offer advice on all matters.

Dublin Trout Anglers' Association have fisheries at Clane and Straffan and contact should be made with Mr J.R. Miley (01) 6902163. Michael Casey of the Clane Trout and Salmon Anglers Association (045) 68995 can arrange day permits for approximately four miles of the Liffey for IR5. Dry-fly is the most productive method here. Worm and spinning for trout is allowed but not encouraged. Salmon are taken either spinning or with worm. (You should note that white maggots are banned on all salmonid rivers in Eire). This stretch of the middle Liffey runs slow and rich and has all of the flies familiar to chalkstream anglers. Early season sees falls of hawthorn flies and hatches of spring olives. The most important fly, the grey flag, appears in mid-May and can provide exceptional sport although it has declined in recent years. There is good evening sedge fishing and an abundance of blue-winged olives which provoke consistent rises to the sherry spinner in the evening and into the dark. There is a good mayfly hatch in late May. It should be noted that there is an electricity power plant on the lake at the top of the river and heavy floods occur. These can be dangerous to an unwary angler as they can appear at any time with no warning although they are fairly infrequent in the peak angling season. Dan O'Brien, New Road, Blackhall and Sye Gallagher, Reeves, Straffan—both County Kildare—can provide you with day permits. Tom Deegan (01) 6980222, of the Ballymore Estate Anglers' Association also controls some stretches in this area. Leixlip Anglers have a good salmon pool but it tends to be very heavily fished. Garnetts and Keegans in Dublin can supply you with all the necessary tackle.

The Sunny South East

Four picturesque river valleys wind their way to the Irish Sea; the Suir, the Barrow and the Nore at Waterford and the Slaney at Wexford. This is the sunny south east corner of Ireland with long stretches of sandy beaches along the south coast. It is the home of the world famous Waterford crystal and is one of the most beautiful areas of the country. Of great historical importance, the National Heritage Park at Wexford traces the history of man and here we find the medieval Kilkenny, with the imposing castle on the bank of the Nore.

The Suir

The Suir has some of the finest trout fishing in the country for virtually its entire 130 mile length, from its source on Devils Bit Mountain near the border of County Tipperary and County Offally to Carrick-on-Suir where it meets tidal waters. A 57lb salmon was taken here in 1874, but today (unfortunately) the average weight for fish taken here is around 7lb and trout are far more abundant than salmon. The season runs from March to September with fine fly-fishing in May, June and September. The Suir is a rich limestone river with several shallow and deep glides, only occasionally interspersed with shallow riffles. At Templemore, where the river is about fifteen feet wide, many trout are taken at around the 2lb mark.

Downstream from Thurles, the River Drish joins the Suir near Turtulla Bridge, where Michael Mockler (0504) 22493 is Secretary of the Thurles, Holycross and Ballycamas Anglers' Association. There is some free fishing on this stretch where good trout are taken and further information on the best water can be gleaned from the locals here, who are only too happy to offer help and advice. Further downstream, Ardmayle House (0504) 42399 is four miles west of Cashel on the L185 and has one mile of double-bank fishing which is free to guests staying at this comfortable hotel. The water is quite slow in parts here, and deep, but good for brownies. The owners can also organise fishing on other stretches both up and downstream.

At Camas Bridge, the river becomes wide and shallow, with some spring salmon. The grilse run is in July and August. The Cashel Golden and Tipperary Anglers Club control both banks up to the delightful Suir Castle and share the west bank to New Bridge with the Cahir and District Anglers' Association. Permits are available to fish this peaceful and secluded stretch, set in beautiful rolling green countryside, from Breeda Morissey at Morissey's Bar (052) 41516 for IR5 a day. Permits can also be obtained from Breeda for the Ara and Aherlow tributaries. The bar is a favourite haunt for many fishermen and is an excellent place to pick up good local tips as well as to hear some very entertaining stories.

Downstream from Cahir, fly fishing only is the rule. The waters here are shallow and free flowing as they glide under the walls of the beautiful Cahir Castle, standing on the banks of the River Suir.

Good stocks of trout are found in this pretty stretch of water. Kilcoran Lodge (052) 41288, set in twenty acres of landscaped gardens on the slopes of the Galtee Mountains, has a nine mile stretch of the Suir and eight miles on the Aherlow.

The Tar
In the beautiful Knockmealdown Mountains, the Shanbally and Duag join forces to form the River Tar, with good-sized trout found in the deeper pools. The Tar enters the Suir upstream from Newcastle, but for much of its length the fishing is free and also readily accessible, as the river runs close to the main road to the west of Newcastle. The Ardfinnan Anglers Club do control some of the Suir around this area and contact should be made with John Maher (052) 66242, the Club Secretary, Green View, Ardfinnan (the corner house beside Maher's Foodstore).

The Nire
The bubbling, fast-flowing River Nire winds its way from the Nire lakes through tree-lined glens and enters the Suir downstream from the town of Newcastle. The river varies in width from between fifteen to fifty feet and contains a good stock of brown trout. All legitimate methods of fishing are allowed here. As the Nire enters the Suir it widens to forty yards and comprises fast flowing shallows interspersed with long glides. Frans Beckers (052) 36433 and Eileen Ryan (052) 36141 control a four mile stretch of water on the Suir and seven miles on the Nire. Fishing here is fly-only and the cost for a day ticket is IR5. Salmon fishing here has seen a downturn of late. Nevertheless, as if proof were needed that this glorious part of Ireland was attractive to overseas visitors, Jean Loup Trautner of the Marlfield Fisheries (052) 25234 has an answering message in French!

Downstream from Clonmel, the Rivers Anner, Clashawley and Moyle meander peacefully through the Tipperary countryside past Anner Castle, to enter the Suir upstream from Kilsheelin. The Glencastle Fishery's water (052) 33287 is one and a half miles long and is very well stocked to provide some of the best fishing on the Suir, with deep pools and gentle glides, although it is barely two miles upstream from tidal waters. Fly fishing only is the rule and day tickets can be purchased for IR5. Mrs Long organises self-catering accommodation right on the river—perfect for a fishing holiday.

At Carrick-on-Suir, in a spectacular setting lodged between the Slievenamon Hills and the rolling slopes of the Comeraghs with their small mountain loughs, there is good salmon and trouting on what has become a splendid stretch from the Devils Bit Mountain.

The Nore
The Nore lies between the Barrow and the Suir and runs into the same estuary towards Waterford. Trout are regularly restocked and the sport is excellent. Mountrath and District Anglers Club (0502) 32540 offer day permits for IR1, a week for IR2. A season's fishing can be had for IR4. Four boats are available for hire. Thomas Watkins is the Honorary Secretary of the Association, and recommended flies are Red Butcher, Green Olive, Black Midge and May Fly. The association recommends that all unwanted fish are

returned. Thomastown Anglers Association (056) 24363/24378 have eight miles on the Nore. A twenty-pound salmon was caught here in 1993 and a day permit will cost IR8, or IR3 for trout. No prawns or shrimps are allowed and flies and worms only for trout.

The Munster Blackwater

From its source in the Killarney Mountains near the Cork border with County Kerry, the Munster Blackwater (sometimes referred to as the Irish Rhine) meanders slowly eastwards through the scenic Blackwater Valley, before turning sharply south at Cappoquin to enter the sea at Youghal Bay through an estuary which stretches for fifteen miles. This is probably the most famous salmon river in Ireland and consistently provides fishermen with excellent sport and excitement. This great river has to be fished—even if it is the last thing you do.

The salmon and sea-trout season begins on 1st February and brown trout on 15th February and runs until 18th September. Sea-trout tend not to go up the main river but rather swim up the River North Bride, although they may occasionally be caught in the tidal section of the Blackwater River. The river runs through some twenty-five miles of the most beautiful countryside from its source, to be joined by the Rivers Dalau and Allow at Kanturk. Salmon predominate these waters with good brown trout in the tributaries and permits are available from John O'Sullivan (029)50257 at the Tackle Shop in Kanturk. The Assolas Country House (029) 50015 is an elegant manor house set on the banks of the river. This family-run establishment, near to Kanturk, has a well known restaurant where the Bourkes use freshly prepared local produce. The hotel can organise fishing for their guests on the nearby Blackwater and you should contact Mr Bourke for further information. Downstream, there are more good stretches of salmon fishing, some of which is free, but details on the waters are available from Dick Willis (022) 21057 at the Bridge House Bar in Mallow. Day tickets for this six mile stretch are priced at IR5 for brown trout and IR10 for salmon if the water level is high enough, and are available form the tackle shop in Mallow (022) 20121.

Blackwater Castle (022) 26333 is an imposing twelfth-century fort, built to protect the Holy St Patrick's Well which stands high above the Awbeg River at Castletownroche in County Cork. It provides excellent accommodation and has a fine gourmet restaurant. The Castle can also offer guests fishing on the Awbeg in one of the most scenic parts of the Blackwater Valley.

The Careysville Fishery, three miles downstream from Fermoy, consists of two miles of double-bank fishing with good pools and provides some of the most productive beats in Ireland. There is an excellent run at the start of the season below the Weir, with good salmon fishing throughout the fishery until May. June sees the grilse run, with good catches taken downstream peaking in July. The fishing remains good throughout the latter part of the season. The average weight in recent years for salmon has been 10lb with some rare fish weighing as much as 50lb. Details for the fishery can be obtained from the Estate Office, Lismore Castle, County Waterford

(058) 544244, who also sell sea-trout and brown trout permits. The Ballymaquirk Fishery run by Julie O'Conner at Greybrook House, Waterfall, County Cork, has a good stretch of water upstream from Mallow. Peter Dempster Ltd. (058) 56248 in Conna has approximately nine miles of fishing for clients at IR30 per rod per day. Tackle and tuition are also available. Ballyduff Trout Fly Angling Association (058) 60201 have five miles of the Blackwater. The Secretary is Eamon Bolger, the brown trout avcerage around 8oz and a week's permit is available for £6.

The Blackwater Lodge Fishery (058) 60235 at Upper Ballyduff is a high-yielding stretch with fifteen miles divided into seventeen beats downstream from Ballygarrett near Mallow. Again, there is a good spring run of salmon in February and March and the grilse run starts in May and peaks in July. The autumn run in late August and September generally sees some heavier fish. In recent years 1500 fish have been taken in a season, up to 25lb in weight. The most popular methods have proved to be spinning and worms. In 1993 permits were available for between IR28 and IR35 per day and ghillies can also be arranged through the lodge. The Blackwater Lodge is owned and run by Ian Powell who is happy to advise all his guests on one topic—fishing! The lodge stands on the south bank of the Blackwater in an ideal location for the fisherman. The Cappoquin Salmon and Trout Anglers Club (058) 54317 have five beats on the Blackwater. All methods are allowed and a day permit can be had for IR12.

The Gulf Stream Coast

Counties Cork, Limerick and Kerry, with their warm gulf breezes, provide a conducive climate for exotic and sub-tropical species of plants and vegetation. To the west of the area lie picturesque river valleys contrasting with the mountain ranges, deep loughs and rugged coastline. In Cork itself, lies the famous Blarney Castle and Stone. One kiss and you're immediately bestowed with the Irish gift of the gab!

The Lee

The River Lee drains Gouganebarra Lake and flows fifty-three miles to Cork Harbour through rugged mountains and rolling moorland, through two large dams used to create hydro-electric power. There is a feeling amongst the locals that the introduction of the dams has had a detrimental effect on the fishing here, but not everyone shares this view. However, game fishing on the Lee now seems to be concentrated on the seven miles or so between the dams and the city of Cork. The salmon season runs from February to the end of September. Mid March is the best time for spring fish and September fishing is also good, if the water levels are right. The trout season runs from 15th February to 12th October and licences are not required. Although more noted for its salmon, the Lee is also a first class trout stream. Anglers should contact the local angling clubs as there are voluntary restrictions operating with regard to the minimum length (seven inches) and size of catch.

The South Western Regional Fisheries Board (026) 41221 in County Cork can advise you on where to fish and will also issue you with some useful local maps. Immediately below the dam is the Inniscarra Fishery, controlled by the Board, which consists of three quarters of a mile of double-bank fishing, noted for its spring fishing and grilse run in June and July. Both spinning (Yellow Belly or Toby) and fly fishing (Hairy Mary or Shrimp) have proved very successful in recent years. The Board's fisheries are manned by keepers and bailiffs and permits can be obtained from the fishery. However, advance booking is strongly advised. The Lee Salmon Anglers (021) 342511 (Brendon O'Flaherty) have about three miles of the lower River Lee, below the dam, and sell daily and weekly tickets at IR10 and IR40 respectively. The Cork Salmon Anglers (021) 872137 (John Buckley) also have about three miles of mixed bank fishing here, with several salmon pools on their stretch. Day tickets can be obtained from the very helpful Mr Buckley at T.W. Murray and Co. (021) 271089 in Cork. There is also free fishing from the footpaths along the river above Waterworks Weir.

Downstream, the Lower Lee Fishery at Thomas Davis Bridge (also a Fisheries Board stretch) is one and a half miles of water with a fine, deep pool which is best fished around high tide with shrimp or prawn. The Tackle Shop, Lavitts Quay (021) 272842 will take bookings and give advice on all other matters regarding the fishing here.

The Bandon

Rising some fifty miles to the west, the River Bandon flows through this beautiful part of County Cork to enter the sea at Kinsale. The season for salmon and trout on the Bandon runs from 15th February to 30th September. February through to May are considered the best months for salmon, especially if it rains, and there are reasonable runs in August and September. Sea-trout and grilse run in June and brown trout fishing is good all season.

From just below Cork, down to the coast, the river becomes tidal and so the fishing is largely free. However, it is advisable to check locally beforehand. Mr Lee (023) 41178 at the Saddlers and Tacklist in Cork regularly fishes the river and is very happy to advise you on the appropriate flies to use. Michael O'Regan, 21 Oliver Plunkett Street, Bandon (023) 41674 of Bandon Anglers' Association controls eight miles of double-bank fishing on the Lee. Salmon fishing costs between IR10 and IR15 a day and IR50 a week. Trout fishing costs IR5 a day or IR25 a week. Contact him directly for further information. David Lamb (023) 47279 at Kilcoleman Fishery in Enniskeane can arrange self-catering accommodation in a lodge or part of a larger house, with one rod included in the accommodation fee. The brownies here are excellent. Accommodation is also available at Blandfield House (021) 885167 which has access to a mile of single-bank fishing on the Bandon, with good salmon in February and August. The Innishannon Hotel (021) 775121 owns eight miles of the tidal Bandon and fishing is free for guests and within the hotel's own grounds. The hotel also has access to five miles of water controlled by Bandon Anglers Club. Trout is fly-only and fishing here is best from June to the end of the season. Any legal method is permitted for salmon.

Smaller Rivers

Argideen Anglers control the best three miles of sea-trout fishing on the Argideen, which enters the sea at Tinoleague. Visitors tickets are available for night fishing from the Fishery Office at Inchy Bridge. Peter Wolstenholme (023) 46239 may be able to help you here.

Several small salmon rivers, principally the Roughty and the Sheen, discharge into the Kenmare river and its deep lough, where the spectacular coastline and picturesque valleys are a delight. March is the best time for spring salmon, with grilse starting their run in July and August.The Sheen Falls Lodge (064) 41600 in Kenmare is situated on the River Sheen and the hotel enjoys seventeen and a half miles of water which is reserved for residents only and the fishing is free. The fishing is limited to fifteen rods per day with ghillies also available from the hotel. The two mile stretch immediately adjacent to the hotel is the best stretch for salmon. Mr Jan O'Hare (064) 41499 runs an electrical shop in Kenmares Main Street but he is more than willing to give interested parties a guided tour of the local fishing—by phone! He also sells tackle, licences and permits for a one and a half mile stretch of the River Roughty belonging to Artully Castle Salmon Fishery (064) 41447 run by Michael Harrington, just five miles outside Kenmare on the Code Road. The river is about fourteen miles long and the stretch owned by the Artully Club has some fabulous holding pools. Much of the river runs through open farmland and permission must be obtained from the local farmer or landowner. There is also some good sea-trout here, but few brown trout in the Roughty or the Sheen. There are a number of small loughs in this area, and the Kenmare Trout Anglers Club, Secretary John Dewey (064) 41676 offers day permits for IR3.

Lough Currane

Lough Currane in County Kerry, often referred to as Waterville Lake, is linked to the sea by the short Waterville river. The lake is generally considered to be one of the best game fishing loughs in the country. Near to the village of Waterville, it yields more sea-trout than any other fishery in the country, usually over three thousand each year, with some of the fish weighing over 10lb. A few years ago sea-trout numbers were down. The Waterville Anglers' Association began some extensive work cleaning up spawning grounds, putting new gravel down and, with the new salmon hatchery up and running, there is much less pressure on the sea-trout for spawning beds. The best fishing is from May to the end of the season in mid-October. In addition to the sea-trout, however, there is excellent spring salmon from January through until June and the average weight is 10lb.

The grisle run in the lough is best in July and August. It is an excellent water for the beginner and expert alike and the fishing is free except for the cost of your state licence. Boats may be hired through the Waterville Anglers' Association. Michael O'Sullivan (0667) 4255 is more than happy to offer advice on the waters in the area and he can be found at The Lobster Bar and Restaurant in the centre of Waterville. There is also a Waterville Hotel (0667) 4310, now owned by Club Med, which testifies to the area's popularity with European visitors. Possibly one of the best known hotels in Ireland, the Butler Arms Hotel (0667) 4156 looks out over the Atlantic. The Huggards provide a warm welcome to all guests and keen anglers are able to make use of the hotel's four privately owned lakes, set high in the mountains, where boats and fishing are free to guests. The hotel will also arrange ghillies on request. Non-residents are charged IR15 per day for fishing which includes a boat. The hotel will also be happy to arrange a day's salmon fishing on the River Inny at a cost of IR10.

Lough Namona

Lough Namona, connected to the Currane by the Cummeragh River, holds a good stock of brownies but is fished for the large sea-trout, as is Cloonaghlin Lough. Also part of this system is Derriana Lough, set high amidst the most spectacular scenery and fishes well for salmon, sea-trout and brown trout which are taken from the bank. Towards the end of the season, you must try the Coppal Lough which drains into the Currane at the east shore via the Coppal river. If you are not staying at the Butler Arms permission will be required for these four loughs.

Glencar Lake & the Caragh

Driving north-east across country from Waterville will bring the intrepid fisherman to another great Irish lough—Caragh. Set at the mouth of the magnificent Glencar Valley, Caragh is often called Glencar Lake and is noted for its spring salmon and grilse. For some unexplained reason the fly is not a method often used and most salmon are caught towards the southern end of the lough on the troll or by spinning. Sea-trout are caught from July and, historically, the best area has been around the mouth of the outflowing Lower Caragh. Brownies are small but on light tackle the sport is very thrilling. Fishing is free and for boats and boatmen contact the Glencar Hotel (066) 60102 which owns Loughs Acoose, Cloon and Reagh. Acoose will provide a great day for the trout fisherman who might find himself battling it out with a small salmon. The trout are small but quite free rising and many a local lad has been broken-in on this water.

The River Caragh completes the system flowing north into Dingle Bay. Mr Pat O'Grady (066) 68228 has been fishing this corner of Ireland for years and is very happy to advise newcomers to the area. He also issues permits for two miles of double-bank fishing on the Lower River Caragh, some private boats on the nearby River Laune, and day tickets for some rainbow stocked lakes. Mr O'Grady lives six hundred yards outside Glenbeigh on the Killarney road. His house is called Ferndale Heights.

The Glencar Hotel (066) 60102 has a good seven miles of double-bank fishing on the Upper Caragh costing around IR200 per week. After July 1st, day tickets are available for IR30. The hotel is owned by a Swiss-German partnership and bookings made during the season are handled by Mrs Doppler in Kssnacht, Switzerland (01- 910) 3662. Bookings made out of peak season are done directly through the hotel. Salmon are from 1st February to mid-July.

The Shannon & Lough Derg

Wild brown trout, sea-trout and Atlantic salmon lie in the rivers and lakes of the Shannon region, which comprises the Counties of Clare, Tipperary, West and South-west Offaly, Limerick and North Kerry. The Shannon is the largest, longest river in Ireland and Great Britain. It stretches from its source three miles south of Blacklion, running for two hundred and twenty miles through central Ireland, entering the Atlantic via a long estuary. Mainly a slow-running, limestone river with an abundance of weed and insect life, the active fishery management have, to a large degree, rescued the river from the devastating effects of an hydro-electric scheme introduced in the 1940s.

South of the Shannon estuary and Limerick lies County Limerick and North Kerry. Numerous rivers and loughs enter the estuary with the productive River Feale often yielding over three thousand fish each season. The Loobagh and Camogue join the River Maigue, which enters the estuary west of Limerick, with good stocks of brown trout. Bunratty Castle stands on the banks of the Bunratty River at the river's estuary and there is some easy fishing from the river banks with sea-trout best in June and July.

Chris Meehan (061) 361555 at Shannon Development, Shannon Town Centre, County Clare, controls the fishing in the Shannon region and is very helpful with up to the minute information about the state of the river and the best stretches to fish.

At twenty-two miles long, Lough Dergh is the largest lake on the Shannon, with the best trout fishing during the mayfly season, which can start as early as the end of April. Dapping is popular here. Artificial flies such as the Spent Gnat and Grey Wolff are popular, with trout averaging 2lb although much larger fish are regularly caught. Historically, Derg was one of the great trout fisheries but has not lived up to its reputation of late. However, many anglers still

make the pilgrimage during the mayfly season. This is a large lough and a boat is something of a necessity. There are boats available from points all around the lough and Chris Meehan will be able to give you a contact for wherever you wish to fish.

South Offaly and North Tipperary stretches from the River Brosna, with its small run of spring salmon and good grilse in early July, to Limerick in the south. Contact Jim Robinson (061) 414900/377666 at his shop in Limerick or Castleconnell for licences, permits, ghillies and boat hire. The best salmon fishing is on the Lower Shannon at Plassy. You will also find good salmon on the Mulcair, a twenty mile spate tributary at Castleconnell, where the salmon are fabulous and the season extends from March 1st to the end of September.

Elsewhere on the Shannon, the season starts on February 1st for salmon and February 15th for trout, ending on September 30th. Jim Robinson can also arrange private beats at Castleconnell for IR25 a day and boats on his own trout fishery—stocked with browns and rainbows at the fifty-five acre Lough Bleach.

The Fisheries Office, E.S.B. Hydro Group, Ardnacrusha, near Limerick (061) 345588 and The Limerick Sports Store, 10 William Street (061) 345647 can make all the necessary arrangements for anglers around Parteen, Plassey, Castleconnell and the Mulcair. Good trout fishing is possible at Killaloe, especially during May and in the autumn. This is where Lough Derg drains into the Shannon and the people to contact are McKeoghs in Ballina (061) 376249.

Shannon Region Fisheries restock Pallas lake, eighteen miles east of the river, with rainbow and brown trout. Here, the season starts late on 1st May and runs until 12th October, with good bank fishing. Further information is available from Jim Robinson.

Lough Ree at Athlone, is stocked with trout by the local angling association and good fishing is available here in June. Through County Roscommon, Longford and Leitrim is Lough Allen, the most northerly lake on the Shannon, where large trout and pike are often taken. This is a reservoir supplying Limerick's power station and the water levels rise and fall, leaving dangerous rocks exposed.

The Shannon Regional Fisheries Angling Centre (049) 36144 overlooks Chambers Bay on Lough Sheelin. Reached by heading north east from Granard on the M55 and following the small signpost. Take the turning off to the right towards the lake shore, which serves Mullaghboy Guest House, Kilnahard Boat Quay and the angling information centre. Sheelin is one of the great Irish limestone loughs with a high-pH, ensuring a rich stock of natural food for the sizeable and excellent quality trout. In fact, fishery scientists have estimated that the lake has the greatest trout carrying capacity in Ireland and supports approximately 100,000 trout! Crover House (049) 40206 sits on the northern shore, providing fine views down the lough and has excellent accommodation. This two hundred year old manor house is run by the friendly O'Reilly family. Set in ninety acres, this hotel has its own airstrip and a boat pier with fifteen boats and ghillies available. A permit costs just IR2 for a day from the angling information centre and the fishery officers can give you all sorts of useful advice. Please ring first before you go.

The Western Fishery Region comprises almost all of County Galway and part of County Mayo, stretching from Hog's Head in Galway Bay to Pidgeon Point in Westport Bay and taking in the great limestone loughs of Corrib, Mask and Cara.

The Corrib

Only 4½ miles long and 150 yards wide, the River Corrib runs through the city of Galway into Galway Bay, draining the vast 41,000 acre Lough Corrib—the Republic's largest lough. About two and a half miles of the river is suitable for salmon and sea-trout fishing, depending on the time of year. Don't forget your state licence as no local permits are required. Licences, tackle and advice are all available from Freeney's in Galway's High Street (091) 68794. It is the only tackle shop I know of that has a bar right next door (with the same name and owner), providing a ready-made audience for those tall fishing tales! Another rich vein of local information, offering all manner of advice and assistance for the visiting angler, is Gillie Angling (092) 48165.

Lough Corrib, or 'The Corrib' as it is generally known, stretches some thirty miles north from Galway to Maum Bridge. With its numerous tiny islands, bays and inlets it is perfectly suited for good brown trout—the larger fish tend to be taken in the southern part of the lough, although salmon have also been taken here. February 15th signals the start of the salmon season with trolling particularly popular at this time of year. Flies are also quite successful, even this early in the season. Mid-March sees hatches of chironomids, whilst olive hatches are best in April, May and September. From around the second or third week in May, the mayfly season allows you to fish for trout by dapping the natural mayfly, using both wet and dry flies. Some five thousand trout are usually caught in this period which lasts for approximately four weeks. Right up to the end of the season, daddy-longlegs and grasshoppers can be dapped and wet fly fishing is also successful. As no permit is required, fishing is free on this vast expanse of water. Recently, good catches have been taken in the Cornamona, Greenfields and Cong areas, generally using dapped mayfly or wet flies, the best being Hackled and Winged Mayflies, Green Peter, Olives and Bibio.

Detailed maps and information on fishing, boats, accommodation and other necessities are available from the Angling Officer of the Western Regional Fisheries Board at Weir Lodge, Earl's Island, Galway (091) 63118 for the southern end of the lough. For information on the northern end, contact the office at Cushlough (092) 41562. Currarevagh House, Oughterard (091) 82313 is a splendid Victorian manor set in 150 acres of park and woodland overlooking Lough Corrib and will provide boat, gillies and tackle for hire at around IR40 per day.

Lough Mask

The mysterious Lough Mask has several underground outflows where you can hear the water leaving. There is also a canal which has been constructed connecting Loughs Mask and Corrib, which only flows in times of high water in the winter months. The water levels between summer and winter can vary here between seven or eight feet. This 20,000 acre limestone lake holds large brown trout, with the larger fish normally caught by trolling. Rapallas are always popular but there are many excellent lures to use and if you have success with one—the advice is to stick to it! Traditional wet flies that do well are Connemara Black, Invicta and Olives.

The Mask has a similar season to the Corrib and anglers are free to use their own boats, although it is possible to fish from the lough shore. The annual World Cup Wet Fly Angling Competition is held here. Open to everyone, it normally attracts around four hundred entrants, including some of the sport's more famous names. Sponsored by Guinness, the first prize is a boat and outboard motor. Further information on the competition is available from the Western Regional Fisheries Board Information Centre, Cushlough, Ballinrobe (092) 41562 and the Fishery Board Officer, Joe Cusack (092) 41180, will also be willing to help. The information centre is a new bungalow-type building on Lough Mask's shore in Cushlough which can be reached from a tiny, dead-end track from Ballinrobe. The centre is open from 8.30am until 5.00pm but it is best to try to get there between 8.30am and 9.30am. There are numerous public access areas but anglers are asked to be cautious, due to the dangerous shallows.

Lough Carra lies in the shadow of Lough Mask (it shares the same information centre) and covers an area of over 4,000 acres. Tiny in comparison to Lough Mask, this limestone lake is one of the most picturesque in the country; with perfectly clear water over a white marl bottom the trout are easily seen when rising to take the fly.

The season here lasts from March to September and the lough is stocked with brownies each year by the Fisheries Board in order to supplement the native wild brown trout. An 18lb trout has been taken in the past but the average is nearer 1¼lb. The mayfly season can produce good catches by dry fly, wet fly and dapping. Although standard patterns, including Green Drakes, are popular it is the Spent Gnat dry fly that produces the best results at all times of the day. In the summer and autumn, lake olives, murroughs and small sedges are the main fly hatches, with artificial flies such as Claret, Murrough, Invicta and Bibio being the most popular. A boat is essential for fishing Lough Carra and hire can be arranged through the Western Regional Fisheries Board at Cushlough (092) 41562 and other local outlets.

Western Region Waters

The Lough Inagh Fishery is set in a beautiful valley between the Twelve Bens to the west and the Maumturk Mountains to the east. Lough Inagh and Derryclare Lake combine to make up the Lough Inagh Fishery. The N59 and N344 run along the east side of the fishery and enquiries should be made to the Fishery Manager (095)

34670 at the Lough Inagh Fishery, County Galway. At four miles long and up to three quarters of a mile wide, Lough Inagh offers quite splendid fishing.

Fine sea-trout fishing is available at Corloo, where the outflow from the Inagh tumbles through the Trout Pool. There is excellent fishing for sea-trout at night at the Derryclare Butts, where the river enters the lake. Glendollogh Butts, on the south east of Derryclare Lake provides good fishing, with the well known Pine Island a favourite spot for salmon and sea-trout. At the outfall from the lake, the angler can take both salmon and sea-trout from an area known as Green Point. April and May are the best months for salmon here, with fish averaging 10lb. June and September are generally the most productive times for grilse, whilst sea-trout are traditionally summer sport. However, last year saw a very slow start to the sea-trout season. Wet fly and dapping are both successful with Blue Badger, the Shrimp and Red Daddy flies best for salmon; Bibio, Delphi, Silver and Green Peter recommended for sea-trout. Boats and tackle are available at the fishery office, with ghillies normally required to be booked in advance. The clarity of the waters and the clean, crisp air, together with the number and size of fish make this a veritable haven for the fisherman.

Another fishery worthy of serious consideration is Galway Salmon Fishery (091) 62388, where a full day ticket ranges from IR12 to IR25, depending on the season. This unique fishery is situated on the river Corrib, practically in the centre of Galway. The season usually opens in February and closes in September.

The Delphi Fishery is situated in south County Mayo, on the R335 Leenane to Louisburgh road. The Delphi Estate is idyllic, set in a lovely valley with a magnificent mountain backdrop. The crystal clear waters afford the most perfect and tranquil setting for the fishing. The one and a half mile long Bundorragha River drains three main loughs and four main rivers to the sea at Killary Harbour.

From high in the beautiful hills at Lough Cunnel, where brown trout thrive, the Glencullin River tumbles into the lough of the same name, one of the most peaceful in the country, with steep mountains rising from the shore. Here at Glencullin Lough, is a boat to cover the half mile of lough, with good sea-trout taken on the fly from July onwards. With three boats, nearby Doolough is well known for exceptionally large sea-trout and some salmon. Fly-only is the rule here, although some trolling for salmon may be possible in the early part of the season.

The Delphi Lodge and cottages overlook Finlough, where two boats cover the shallow picturesque water with its fine stock of salmon, grilse and sea-trout. Just a couple of miles east of the Delphi system is Tawnyard lough, the beautiful principal lough on the Erriff System, famous for salmon and sea-trout taken on the fly. Please note in particular the Erriff Fishery (095) 42252, which offers salmon and sea-trout fishing on the Erriff, one of the major salmon fishing rivers in Ireland, and on Tawnyard Lough. Derrintin Lough, a small hill lough, is also worth a visit, and sea angling is available in Killary

Harbour, aboard the 'Aasleagh Lady'. However, possibly the best river in the west of the country, with plenty of white water and nineteen pools, is the Bundorragha River, which is semi-spate and is most productive after heavy rain. Again, fly fishing only here, with salmon taken throughout the season and sea-trout from June to August. All enquiries regarding accommodation, boats, ghillies and state licences should be made to Peter Mantle (095) 42213. A daily permit for the Delphi Fishery costs between IR40 and IR50, with cottages available at peak season for IR300 per week.

Recommended flies here include the Delphi Silver and Badger, Green Peter and Hairy Mary but again, it is worth spending some time chatting to Mr Mantle who is full of useful tips on the local waters. The long season, the variety of fishing, the perfect setting and the water's excellent record, averaging 100 salmon and 1000 sea-trout annually, make the Delphi Estate the ideal location for the keen fisherman.

It must be said that Delphi, like most of Ireland and the British Isles, has experienced the depressing disappearance of the sea-trout. In fact, the renowned Zetland Fishery closed in 1991, but the lovely Zetland House Hotel (095) 31111 is still thriving as there is much to do in this part of Connemara. Fishermen in the area could, of course, cast a fly on nearby Lough Shannaghcloontippen (nineteen letters, to save you counting!).

The North Western Fisheries Region is made up of the majority of County Mayo and parts of County Sligo, County Leitrim and County Roscommon. From Pidgeon Point, County Mayo, around the coastline to Mullaghnmore Head, County Sligo, the area encompasses all the rivers and loughs which flow into the sea between these two points. Without a doubt, the best known water is the River Moy with its principal lake, Lough Conn, forming a link at Pontoon to Lough Cullin. In addition, good runs of salmon and sea-trout are to be enjoyed at the Newport River and Lough Beltra system and at the Owenmore and Owenduff Rivers, together with the Burrishoole Fishery. Lough Cull, off the Mulraney to Achill road and Loughaun, set in picturesque Achill Island, may just surprise the dedicated angler, not only with the delightful setting but also the quality of the water.

Lough Beltra & the Newport

Lough Beltra and the Newport River can be found in south County Mayo, south west of Castlebar off the R311/R312. Lough Beltra is three miles long and one mile wide and is drained by the Newport river running into Clew Bay at Newport. Over seventeen miles long, with seventeen good holding pools, streams and glides, both the river and lough get a good run of spring salmon from the end of March (opening day is 20th March), grilse in June and sea-trout from mid-June. Unfortunately, there is no real brown trout fishing here.

Newport House in Newport (098) 41222 overlooks the river's estuary with the hotel gates facing you as you come into Newport from Castlebar. The house is set between Achill Island and the mountains of Mayo and the wild, unspoiled splendour of Erris and Connemara. The house owns the west side of the lough with five boats and five ghillies available for hire. The boats fish one side of an invisible line, although they can cross with permission, and generally the boats for hotel guests have priority. In addition, guests also have priority on an eight mile stretch of the river, which completes the Newport House fishery and there is a boat for use on Lough Furnace. Newport House can also arrange fishing on the Moy system should you wish to test those waters.

The east side of the Beltra is owned by Glenisland Co-op (094) 21302, where fishing costs around IR8 per day, plus IR10 for a boat for two people and IR6 for an outboard motor. Five boats are available for hire here and the salmon fishing is good, but due to lack of numbers, any sea-trout caught must be returned to the water. Late March, April and May tend to be the best fishing but this depends on the water level and weather conditions. An average of eighty to ninety salmon are caught on this side during the season, some up to 20lb in weight.

Lough Furnace & Lough Feeagh

Burrishoole Fishery is now owned and managed by the Salmon Research Agency of Ireland and comprises the tidal Lough Furnace and the freshwater Lough Feeagh. One of Ireland's few productive tidal loughs, Lough Furnace, rises and falls two feet each day. Both loughs are often referred to as spate loughs as they have a catchment area of approximately one hundred square miles and after heavy rain, the levels can rise very sharply. During hot, dry spells Furnace can become quite brackish and fish have to adjust to fluctuating salinity levels of between eight and twenty parts per thousand.

Furnace has two separate stocks of fish; a natural stock and a supplement from the agency's ocean ranched salmon. The season runs from 10th June to 30th September, with July being the best month when all the fish are fresh. However, September may give larger bags with the autumn run. Salmon are to be found at both the Salmon Leap and the Millrace, and also at Long Shore, Duffys Point and Fahys Bay. For sea-trout, try Black Stone and Blacksod Bay, although they are currently subject to a restrictive byelaw and any caught have to be returned. Furnace also has excellent mullet fishing—so don't be surprised if you land a mullet, or a bass for that matter!

Lying in a deep valley, Lough Feeagh, although best known for salmon, holds good stocks of sea-trout and brown trout and the agency records the number of fish passing up into the lough through the counter. Again, June and July are the best months for salmon, particularly around the mouth of the Black River and Glenamong River. The best water for sea-trout is the area towards the lower lough, around Schoolhouse Bay.

Furnace and Feeagh are set in the beautiful countryside of Nephin Beg, easily accessible from Newport. Permits are available from the Manager's Office at the Burrishoole Fishery (098) 41107 at Farran Laboratory, Furnace, Newport, some two miles outside Newport on the south shore. Bank fishing is not allowed and only five boats (with engines) are allowed on each lough. Fly only is the rule, with Green Peter, Daddy, Bibio, Black Pennell, Fiery Brown and Delphi recommended. The average weight for salmon from this water is around nine pounds and for sea-trout three quarters of a pound.

Bunarella Lough, managed and partially owned by the agency, is a good brown trout lough just ten miles north of Newport and enjoys a lovely tranquil setting. Trout are small, averaging about 8oz, but provide great fun on light tackle as they are quite free rising, especially during the summer hatch of sedges. In addition to the standard lough patterns, try Greenwells Spider and Glory and Connemara Black on the east and north shores.

The agency has recently opened up a new fishery at Ballinlough, two or three miles north of Westport on the N59. Generally speaking, this is the only lough run by the agency to allow bank fishing. It is very rich in limestone and well stocked with rainbows and browns, with 4oz fish growing to 4lb in two years. Visitors are advised to book well in advance for the whole fishery, especially for June, July and September and a ghillie is recommended. Permits are obtained from the office situated on the southern shore of Furnace, approximately two miles outside Newport. It's a signposted turning off to the right.

Carrowmore Lake

Situated twenty-eight miles west of Ballina and two miles north-west of Bangor Erris in County Mayo is Carrowmore Lake. Four miles long and approximately three miles wide it is primarily a brown trout fishery with occasional salmon and sea-trout. This is probably the last of the truly wild lakes as it has never been stocked. Owned by a syndicate in Dublin and controlled by Bangor Erris Angling Club, permits can be obtained from Seamus Henry at the post office in Bangor Erris (097) 83487 for around IR10 a day. There are twenty-five boats available and these are recommended, as bank fishing is not very productive. The post office is adjacent to the West End Bar—surely a recipe for disaster with regards to writing postcards! Mr Henry will also issue permits for the club's stretches on the River Owenmore and is happy to advise on both fishing and accommodation. Cloonamoyne Fishery (096) 31112, attached to the Enniscoe Hotel at Lough Conn, can also arrange fishing at Carrowmore. The Oweniny river flows into the Owenmore and then enters Carrowmore Lake before reaching the Atlantic at Blackrod Bay. On Carrowmore, the traditional fly patterns at Herritys and Derreens Islands on the north shore and the mouth of Glencullin River are the ones to use.

The Moy

The River Moy is one of the top salmon producing rivers in Ireland, flowing from the Ox Mountains to Killala Bay at Ballina. Its tributaries drain an area of some eight hundred square miles over its full sixty-three mile length and there are over thirty miles of double-bank fishing. Around eight thousand fish are taken from its waters every season, with stretches to suit fly fishing and spinning. The season starts on 1st February but it is more usual for serious fishing to start towards the end of the month. The main grilse run starts in May and peaks in June with an unbelievable number of fish in the river. Angling on the Moy is reasonably priced and available in spring and summer through to the autumn. Sea-trout can be taken from boats in the seven mile long estuary from Ballina to Killala Bay. The Moy Fishery Office (096) 21332 at Ridge Pool Road, Ballina controls some of the best beats on the river, including the famous Ridge Pool, where sixteen fish were taken in two days in June 1991. Prices range from IR8 to IR60 for two rods, boat hire and a ghillie in high season for the Ridge Pool. Advance booking is essential. The Ballina Angling Centre (096) 21850 at Dillon Terrace, Ballina is run by Michael Swartz who claims to be able to organise everything. Certainly permits, tuition, ghillies and general information are available here pertaining to the fishery which stretches out on both banks, from the Weir to the confluence with the Corroy river

The Downhill Hotel (096) 21033, Ballina is set in beautiful landscaped gardens overlooking the River Brosna, a tributary of the Moy. Mount Falcon Castle Fishery, between the Corroy and Foxford, controls seven and a half miles of double-bank fishing with good fly and spinning stretches. The Mount Falcon (096) 21172 is four miles from Ballina on the Foxford Road, set in one hundred acres of beautiful parkland. The Alpine Hotel (096) 36144 overlooks Killala Bay some fifteen miles away, where guests have priority over one mile of left bank fishing, just upstream from the junction of the Rivers Yellow and Moy.

The Armstrong Family are one of the few Irish families that own a piece of the Moy. The cost to fish here is IR10 per day or IR50 and you are advised to book in advance for this one and a half mile stretch. The Armstrongs (094) 56580 live almost on the river, down a track off the Ballina Foxford Salmon Anglers control both banks immediately to the south of Foxford and anglers should contact Jack Wallace (094) 56238 at Swinford Road, Foxford. Cloongee Fishery permits can be purchased from Michael Ruane (094) 56634 in Cloongee for fishing on both banks where Lough Cullin enters the Moy. The East Mayo Anglers' Association control the Moy from around Cloongee House by the Ballylahan Bridge, to beyond the point where the Gweestion river joins the Moy. Permits cost IR12 per day and are available from Mrs Wills at Ballylahan Bridge (094) 56221 and Bolands Lounge, Bridge Street, Swinford (094) 51149. In addition, a short stretch downstream of Foxford Bridge offers free fishing.

Lough Conn

A few miles west of the Moy is the infamous Lough Conn. At around 13,000 acres, this beautiful lake provides the fisherman with an excellent challenge in stunning surroundings. Nephin, rising to almost two and a half thousand feet, dominates the western horizon. A limestone water of about nine miles in length and two to four miles in width, it has vast areas of relatively shallow water that sustain a huge population of wild trout. During fly hatches, trouting is excellent and with the many attractive bays and islands, Conn remains a firm favourite with all fishermen. The angling season begins in March with traditional wet fly fishing over shallow water. Brownies average just over the pound mark but three pounders are not uncommon. The chronomids hatch throughout the first half of the season but the fun really begins when the mayfly starts to hatch in mid-May. The latter is extensive and lasts until the end of June with the lesser hatch extending until mid-August. Sedges hatch towards the end of the season and so do not forget your sedge patterns at this time of year. Salmon are also present in fair numbers and are mainly taken by trolling from the end of March to July. Historically, the best areas have been at the northern end—try Masebrook, Cornakillew and Castlehill Bay. Access is not difficult and all your needs can be organised through the Pontoon Bridge Hotel, Foxford, (094) 56120. There are several people who have boats to hire and it is recommended that, even if you do not wish a boatman to accompany you, a guide of some sort would make a difference to the size of your bag. At the very least, on a blank day, you can exchange jokes! Michael Schwartz in the Angling Centre, Ballina (open 7.00am to midnight) (096) 21850 can also help you here. On the northern shore Enniscoe House (096) 31112 stands alone amongst its gardens and parkland. Just off the N59 Crossmolina to Ballina road, this lovely Georgian house is the place to stay for all that is splendid. Barry Segrave is the fishery manager and can organise an impressive fishing package.

Lough Cullin

Lough Cullin is connected to the southern tip of Lough Conn at Pontoon. This 2000 acre lake holds a good stock of brown trout up to about 4lb and also has a good run of salmon. In fact, all the fish must pass through Cullin to get to Lough Conn and its feeder rivers. The narrow inlet that joins the two lakes is a favourite haunt of the salmon fisherman. Salmon are often caught by anglers fly fishing for trout. So, if it is trout you are after, use a slightly heavier leader than normal. In addition to the contacts for Lough Conn, you might prefer to speak to Healy's Hotel, Pontoon (094) 56443.

Lough Arrow

Lough Arrow is drained by the river of the same name. Only fifteen miles in length, the River Arrow is not widely fished. Access is awkward, with many overhanging trees and after June ends, the weed growth becomes too thick to cast a fly. There are, however, large trout in this river but they are not often seen as they feed deep down. Guests of Coopershill, Riverstown, County Sligo (071) 65108 are welcome to fish it but the O'Haras would prefer to organise fishing for you on Lough Arrow. This fine Irish water is one of the best mayfly fisheries in the country and is situated close to the border of County Sligo and Roscommon. At just over 3000 acres this rich limestone lough is small by comparison to some but brownies are here in good numbers and fish to 6lb and 7lb are caught on the fly every year. There are significant hatches of duckfly, olives, murroughs and even Green Peter. The season runs from March to September and all fishing is free. Before you start, though, ring or pop into the N.W. Fisheries Board Information Centre (079) 66033 in Ballinafad, beside the cemetery, for a fishing report and advice. First thing in the morning is the best time to catch a fishery officer; or contact Tim McGrath at the Rock View Hotel (079) 66073.

Fermanagh's loughs and rivers, tree-lined glens and islands, stately mansions and ruined castles form the perfect accompaniment to the spectacular fishing to be found in Loughs Erne and Melvin. Here, in the south west corner, are two of the best trout loughs in the land. The Upper and Lower Lough Erne is over fifty miles long with the medieval town of Enniskillen dividing the lough; and Lough Melvin, straddling Fermanagh's border with the Republic.

Lough Melvin

Approximately five thousand acres, eight miles long by nearly two miles wide, Lough Melvin is unique. It is scientifically accepted that there are four genetically distinct trout in this lough—brown, ferox, gillaroo and sonaghan. The latter rare salmonid displays the normal attributes of sea-trout—powerful tails and hard fighters—although much darker in colouring than sea-trout. They only grow to about 1½lb and are typically mid-water feeders of daphnia and emerging insects. The gillaroo is very similar to a brown trout but with more spots and a yellow belly. They feed a lot on the bottom in shallow water but do come up for the dry fly in the evening. Ferox are usually caught by trolling the deeper sections of the lake and char are caught at even greater depths. Brownies are best caught fishing a team; with a dark pattern on the point, a traditional wet fly, such an Invicta, on the dropper and a local favourite, like a Gosling or Dabbler, on the bob. These latter two are based on patterns from two hundred years of fly-tying experience passed down through the years. Local fly-tyers still tie in the traditional way—hooks held in the hand without help from a vice!

One word of caution, Lough Melvin is scenic but can sometimes cut up rough and dangerous as it is very exposed to the prevailing westerlies. A good man to speak to for local advice is Terence Bradley (072) 54029, whose house, Eden Point, is situated on the east shore, the first house on the left as you leave Rossinver on the R282. Gillaroo Angles (0232) 862419, based in Newtownabbey, are also able to organise fishing forays throughout this area and the man to contact here is John Todd.

The Drowse

The River Drowse drains Lough Melvin and provides some spectacular sport when the salmon are running in the spring. Thomas Gallagher (072) 41208 owns the fishing rights on this short six mile river. There are fifty two named pools that yielded eight hundred fish in the first seven months of 1991. March produced over one hundred and fifty fish alone, with half caught on the fly. A tip here—use size 8 to 10 doubles for spring salmon, which have an average weight of 10lb, and size 10 to 12 for the grilse, which average 5lb. Mr Gallagher charges a very reasonable IR7 per day or IR30 per week, operating from the Kinlough end, and also hires boats for the lough. February to July is best for salmon here.

Lower Lough Erne

Picturesque Lower Lough Erne is a huge expanse of water (37,000 acres), twenty six miles long, running north west from Enniskillen to Rosscar viaduct, where the River Erne enters the ocean at Ballyshannon. The whole Erne system provides superb brown trout fishing in clean unpolluted waters containing plenty of fish. Trout up to 20lb in weight are caught every season, usually on the troll in spring, whilst duckfly fishing begins in earnest in April. The numerous islands, rocky outlets and secluded coves and bays make for an idyllic setting for the fisherman to enjoy whilst pursuing his sport. Near Enniskillen, try St Catherine's and Rabbit Island where mayfly sport is particularly good for the trout, when fish of 6lb can be taken. Trout fishing naturally tends to die away in late June and early July but returns with a vengeance in August with the arrival of the daddy-longlegs and sedges and you may even pick up a salmon, which are now returning in larger numbers. The season generally runs from 1st March to 30th September, with some minor extensions, and details of permits and State licences can be obtained from John Richardson (0365) 322608, 9 East Bridge Street, Enniskillen, who also has holiday cottages to let on Lusty Island.

For those anglers keen to try their luck with the salmon, the stretch from Rosscor viaduct to Belleek has been good in August and September in recent years and Michael McGrath (0365) 658181 at Carlton Cottages, Belleek is an excellent source of local knowledge. The scenic Ballinamallard and Colebrooke, which are feeder rivers for the lough, get a run of large brown trout during August and September which provide great sport. Permits are also available from the following sources: Bailey D. Blainey Service Station (03656) 634, Dickie and Sons (0365) 322165, Erne Marine (036582) 267, Home, Field and Stream (0365) 323481, Lochside Cruisers (0365) 324368 and Manor House Marine (03656) 28100.

The Foyle System

Managed by The Foyle Fisheries Commission, the Foyle System is unique in that it extends into Donegal in the Republic, as well as Derry and Tyrone. It was once the best salmon fishery in Western Europe but the ravages of UDN and overfishing, both legally and illegally, took their toll, although there are signs that things are improving. Consisting of Lough Foyle and the Rivers Finn, Strule, Derg, Mourne, Glenelly, Owenkilliew, Carnowen and Drumragh, the Foyle System has some superb fishing in this area on private, semi-private and association waters. Mr Ronnie Kerrigan at the Commission (0504) 42100 is very helpful and will give you advice on all areas to fish.

Classic fly fishing is available on the Mourne which like the Tay and Spey, fishes best in low to medium water. Good spring fishing can often be found on the Finn, but it is usually mid June before there is any consistency. Most of the other rivers are of a spatey nature and therefore require a good deal of rain. This is not usually a problem as Ulster's lush countryside testifies! Patrick Bonner (06487) 65920 is a very helpful water bailiff who fishes all over Northern Ireland and he can be contacted after 11.00am. (He is out fishing until midnight!)

The Rivers Roe and Faughan are part of the Foyle System and often yield first class salmon and sea-trout, with stretches on the Roe controlled by Roe Anglers' Association and Dungiven Anglers' Association. Sea-trout of up to 4lb are not uncommon and grilse between 4lb and 10lb are regularly caught here. Salmon from these waters tend to weigh around 8lb to 10lb.

For further information on fishing in Northern Ireland contact the Department of Agriculture which is responsible for the public waters and can give advice on angling permits, stocking and other matters. They can be contacted at The Department Of Agriculture, Fisheries Division, Hut 5, Castle Grounds, Stormont, Belfast. Telephone (0232) 63939. Licences are available from either the Fisheries Board or the Foyle Fisheries Commission.

Lough Neagh

Lough Neagh is the biggest lake in the British Isles and its main rivers are the Upper Bann and Blackwater to the south and Moyola to the west, and the Maine and its tributaries to the north. The system drains a vast area of central Ulster. The Lower Bann drains the lough to the north, through Lough Beg to the Atlantic near Coleraine.

All these rivers enjoy a reasonable run of salmon from July to October and produce an indigenous population of brown trout from a quarter to one and a quarter pounds. Dollaghan, a big lough trout, sometimes over ten pounds, can be taken during the autumn. Similar to sea-trout in colour and size, they are best caught at dusk but, unfortunately, do not put up the entertaining resistance of the sea-trout.

The Blackwater

The River Blackwater is the largest of the rivers but, according to the locals, is virtually unfishable due to the Department of Agriculture's arterial drainage scheme. The last seven or eight miles of the upper part of the river in the Benburb area has some reasonable trout fishing and a few salmon. Permits are available from Hamiltons (06487) 63682. Around Blackwatertown there is a one and a half mile stretch of right bank fishing with good trout fishing here run by the Department of Agriculture. Permits should be purchased from Cahoon, 2 Irish Street, Dungannon (0867) 22754.

The Upper Bann

The Upper Bann rises in the Mourne Mountains and meanders and tumbles through the delightful County Down countryside to Lough Neagh. Between Banbridge and Hilltown, the Department has two ten-mile stretches of water. Brown trout and some late season salmon are taken from the banks between March and October.

The Ballinderry

The Ballinderry river is about thirty miles long and flows east to enter the lough near Ardhoe Cross. About two thirds of its length yields good brown trout and some dolaghan. Permits are obtainable from Cookstown Angling Club.

The Moyola, the Maine & the Lower Bann

From the Sperrin Mountains in South Derry, the Moyola river twists and winds its way to the north west corner of the lough, yielding some brown trout and a few salmon in the latter part of the season. This is private land and anglers must seek the landowner's permission to fish these waters. Principally a brown trout river, with some big lough dolaghan, the Maine flows south from Glarryford Bogs. Several angling clubs and the Department of Agriculture own stretches on the river. Cullybackey has two and a half miles of the best trout waters, with day tickets obtained from local newsagents in Cullybackey. In recent years there have been some very good runs of salmon in the Maine and its tributaries, the Braid and Glenwhiry, providing the angler with excellent sport. The Lower Bann, which is the largest river in the British Isles in terms of water volume, is a slow running river which drains Lough Neagh. The water is owned by Bann Systems but most of the river can be fished without day permits although there are several private stretches fished by syndicates on Monday to Thursday and only available to day visitors at weekends. Although expensive, up to £160 per day, the salmon fishing can be fantastic below the weirs and lockgates, where fast-running waters can produce many salmon. Portna and Culiff rock are good stretches. Possibly the best, however, is Camroe where the number of fish taken is quite phenomenal, although this is a restricted stretch. There are several small rivers feeding into the Lower Bann which can yield some good salmon in their own right. From Coleraine to the river mouth there is some very good sea-trout fishing, especially from boats. Contact Bann Systems Ltd at Coleraine (02657) 31215.

The Bush

Wholly owned by Bann Systems Ltd., the thirty mile River Bush flows from the Tievebulliagh, through Bushmills village and distillery—one of the oldest in the world—to the Atlantic near the Giant's Causeway. The owner of Bann Systems, Sir Patrick McNaughton, sells day tickets on two miles of the river at the mouth where the fishing is mainly restricted to salmon, although there are some trout to be had. The remainder of the river is leased by the internationally-renowned Research Station of the Department of Agriculture, who allow fishing only on the strict understanding that anglers co-operate with the research project's progress by returning day tickets with details of the catch and whenever possible, submitting salmon for examination. It is particularly important to recover fin-clipped fish (those from which the adipose fin has been removed) as these individuals may contain minute tags which can only be detected using specialised equipment at the hatchery. All fish will be returned to anglers immediately and a reward is currently payable for each salmon submitted. Anyone catching a fin-clipped fish outside office hours or at the weekend is asked to retain the fish's head and report the catch on a returned day ticket or by telephone at their earliest convenience.

Angling on the river has been deliberately divided up so as to give the best sport to as many people as possible and to cater for varying desires, but the river is of a flashy nature and does not remain in top class order for extended periods. When in form, however, it can be excellent. At present the season lasts from 1st March until 30th September. Advance booking is essential for these waters and contact should be made with the Department. Ask for form ARB1 and bear in mind that applications are dealt with on a first come first served basis. Rods for spring and September go in a day as it is reputed to be bursting with salmon. If you can track down Sean Fleming (02657) 32422 at the Tackle Shop in Bushmills, he will be happy to advise you on all waters in the area. Permits are also available from Barry Jones (02657) 31435 at the Hatchery Office in Bushmills.

The following index lists the major lochs, rivers, lakes and stillwaters emphasised in *Fishing Forays*—a number of smaller tributaries or waters located near to these are not included in the index, but should of course be considered when planning a fishing foray.

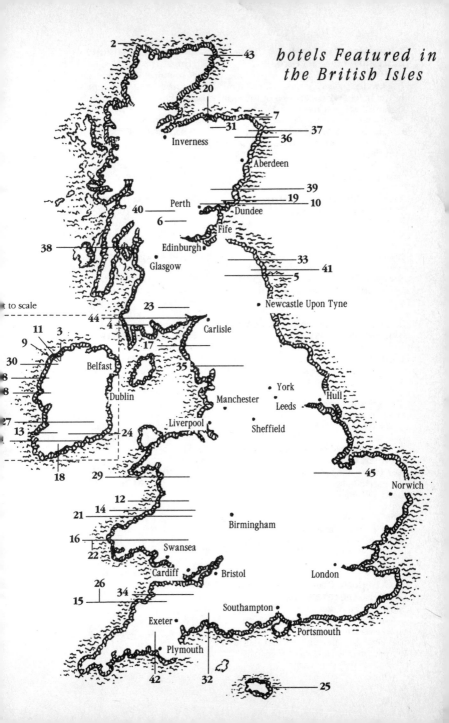

hotels Featured in
the British Isles

1. Blackwater Lodge Hotel, Upper Ballyduff, Co Waterford.
Tel: (010 353) 58 60235
Blackwater Lodge is a cosy, relaxed family run hotel overlooking one of the most beautiful salmon rivers in Europe, the Munster Blackwater. The quality of the fishing is excellent but for non-anglers the area also offers a variety of other pursuits. The atmosphere here is unique and guests are assured of a relaxing and hassle free holiday.

2. Cape Wrath Hotel, Durness, Sutherland. Tel: (0971) 511212
The Cape Wrath Hotel stands on a peninsular of the beautiful Kyle of Durness. The hotel prides itself on the high standard of cuisine and there is a wine cellar to complement the food. For the fisherman the area offers excellent fishing and there are other activities to interest those who do not fish.

3. Coopershill, Riverstown, Co Sligo, Tel: (010 353 71) 65108
This elegant Georgian manor house has been in the same family since 1774 and commands 500 acres. One of Ireland's finest limestone lakes, Lough Arrow, is 5 miles away. The river from the lake flows through the property and contains large brown trout which are a challenge to the fly fisherman.

4. Corsemalzie House Hotel, Newton Stewart, Wigtownshire.
Tel: (0988 886) 254
This secluded country mansion set in the heart of Wigtownshire allows guests to relax away from the rigours of city life. The hotel has exclusive salmon and trout fishing rights on four and a half miles of the River Bladnoch and five miles on the River Tarff. Fishing can also be organised in the Mazie Burn.

5. Cringletie House Hotel, Peebles, Borders. Tel: (07213) 233
This turreted Baronial style mansion commands 28 acres of beautiful gardens and woodland. Inside is an impressive panelled lounge with carved oak and marble fireplace and painted ceilings.

6. Culcreuch Castle, Fintry, Stirlingshire. Tel: (036 086) 228
This beautiful castle has been lovingly converted by its present owners the Haslam family into a comfortable, friendly country house hotel. The eight individually furnished bedrooms are all en suite and have full modern facilities. The Loch Lomond, Stirling and Trossachs area offers the visitor a wide and varied range of country activities including fishing and birdwatching.

7. Delnashaugh Inn, Ballindalloch, Banffshire. Tel: (0807) 500255
The Delnashaugh Inn enjoys a beautiful setting in the heart of the Highlands. The hotel provides nine bedrooms all en suite and all with every modern comfort. The bar stocks local malts as the area is home to the Whisky Trail. Extensive use is made of local produce in creating the varied menus provided in the restaurant.

8. Delphi Estate, Leenane, Co Galway. Tel: (010 353 95) 42213
Delphi Lodge is one of the finest sporting lodges in Ireland. With fine antique furniture, beautiful decor, roaring fires and excellent food and wines, the Lodge is elegant yet totally informal and relaxing. The Delphi Fishery is the perfect haven for the discerning salmon and sea-trout angler and the Estate has attracted generations of anglers from all over the world.

9. Downhill Hotel, Ballina, Co Mayo. Tel: (010 353 96) 21033
Adjacent to the famous salmon fishing river - the Moy, the Downhill Hotel is in an excellent position to organise your fishing holiday. The hotel offers fine cuisine and personal, friendly service. The grounds are beautiful and there are extensive leisure facilities. Whether there for the fishing or not guests will enjoy a peaceful holiday.

10. Dunkeld House Hotel, Dunkeld, Perthshire. Tel: (0350) 727771

The Dunkeld House Hotel has an enviable position on the banks of the River Tay and owns two miles of salmon fishing water. A warm welcome is afforded to experienced and novice anglers alike. Experienced ghillies are on hand to give help and advice. Definitely a fisherman's paradise.

11. Enniscoe House, Ballina, Co Mayo. Tel: (010 353 96) 31112

This splendid Irish Georgian house rests in 300 acres of woodland which include a lake with isles. The hotel has a long fishing tradition and is the ideal base for the keen fisherman, situated on the shores of Lough Conn, renowned for its wild brown trout and spring salmon fishing.

12. Glanhyd-y-Psgod Farm, Pencader, Dyfed. Tel: (055935) 253

Set in beautiful woodland surroundings in the unspoilt countryside of the Teifl Valley this is an ideal place for a fishing holiday or even just a relaxing break away from it all. The four attractive and tastefully furnished store cottages are self catering and fitted to a very high standard.

13. Glencar Hotel, Glencar, Co Kerry. Tel: (010 353 66) 60102

For two hundred year's the Glencar Hotel has been providing its own brand of warmth and hospitality. Standing near the banks of the River Caragh it is perfect for the salmon angler. Not only this but the countryside around invites hill walking and other outdoor pursuits. The hotel meets the requirements of the most discerning guests with superb cuisine and all modern comforts.

14. Gliffaes Country House Hotel, Crickhowell, Powys. Tel: (0874) 730371

Dating from 1885, this distinctive hotel is set in 29 acres of gardens with private fishing and offering stunning views of the surrounding National Park and River Usk. The hotel is elegantly furnished although the atmosphere is distinctly informal. Many visitors stay at the hotel because of the excellent fishing in the area. However there is plenty to occupy those who do not wish to participate.

15. Great Tree Hotel, Chagford, Devon. Tel: (0647) 432491

An hotel in quiet secluded surroundings on the edge of Dartmoor with 25 miles of single bank Salmon, Sea Trout and Trout fishing on the River Teign. Tickets for Upper Teign Fishing Association waters from hotel. Reservoir fishing available nearby. Excellent REFFIS instructor with added access to River Exe fishing.

16. Griffin Inn, Brecon, Powys. Tel: (0874) 754241

Dating back to the 15th century, The Griffin Inn is believed to be one of the oldest sporting inns in Wales. That tradition is continued today. The inn can offer 20 miles of salmon fishing on the Wye and there are residential courses on offer. The Griffin has an outstanding reputation for serving fine food prepared from local produce.

17. Hornby Hall, Penrith, Cumbria. Tel: (0768) 89114

This 17th century farmhouse has been refurbished and furnished with antiques in keeping with the period of the red sandstone building. Meals are taken in the sandstone flagged main hall. The hotel has two miles of fishing on the Eamont and there are many other country pursuits available.

18. Innishannon House Hotel, Innishannon, Co Cork. Tel: (010 353 21) 775121

The Innishannon House Hotel has a reputation for being "the most romantic hotel in Ireland" and it effortlessly lives up to this. There is salmon and sea-trout fishing from the hotel lawns on both banks of the River Brandon, or on the quarter mile stretch of the Brinny River where the hotel holds exclusive rights.

19 Kinnaird, Dunkeld, Perthshire.
Tel: (0796) 482440
A spectacular country mansion at the heart of the Kinnaird Estate makes home for a splendid hotel which will not fail to impress. Delightfully refurbished and marvellously stylish. Kinnaird owns 25 miles of high quality fishing on the Tay and employs two full time ghillies.

20. Knockomie Hotel, Forres, Morayshire.
Tel: (0709) 673146
This rare Scottish example of the Arts and Crafts house stands amid 25 acres of grounds and parts of the house date back 150 years. There is exciting and varied sport to be had on the River Findhorn and trout fishing is available on Loch of Blairs and Lochindorb.

21. Lake Country House, Llangammarch Wells, Powys.
Tel: (05912) 202
Complete with open fireplaces and antiques, this riverside hotel is set in 50 acres of beautiful lawns, woods, fascinating walks and a private lake where guests may fish for trout. The hotel offers spacious and luxurious accommodation, and has a splendid restaurant which has won several commendations.

22. Llangoed Hall, Llyswen, Brecon, Powys. Tel: (0874) 754525
A splendid house which was the first major commission of architect Sir Clough Williams-Ellis. Sir Bernard Ashley has bestowed similar love in its restoration and the bedrooms are simply marvellous. Food is also outstanding. Extensive gardens complete a delightful picture. Guests may fish for salmon and trout on the Upper Wye and River Irfon.

23. Lockerbie Manor Country Hotel, Lockerbie, Dumfries and Galloway
Tel: (05762) 2610
This luxurious country house hotel stands in 78 acres of park and woodland. The period furniture, Adam fireplaces and wood panelled dining room combine to create an atmosphere of history and hospitality. For the fisherman, the rivers Annan, Milk, Cree, Blanock and Penkiln all beckon.

24. Longueville House, Mallow, Co Cork.Tel: (010 353 22) 47156
Resting in a 500 acre cattle and sheep farm this substantial Georgian hotel has a very relaxed and informal atmosphere, with a pretty collection of antiques to decorate the interior. Longueville offers three miles of game fishing on the famous Blackwater.

25. Longueville Manor, St Saviour, Jersey. Tel: (0534) 25501
The 13th centry Manor stands in 15 acres at the foot of its own private wooded valley and is one of the most prestigious small hotels in Europe. Exquisitely furnished with fine antiques and fabrics, the the manor is a haven of tranquillity in which to enjoy fine food and wine.

26. Mill End Hotel, Sandy Park, Chagford, Devon.
Tel: (0647) 432282
A delightful old water mill converted to hotel use in the twenties has been owned and managed by the Craddock family for twenty years. It has an idyllic setting on the banks of the Teign with some excellent fishing and marvellous walks leading down the Teign gorge and to nearby Drogo castle.

27. Mount Juliet, Thomastown, County Kilkenny.
Tel: (010 353 56) 24455
1500 acres of unspoiled parkland in the south east of Ireland with a history that goes back to the 15th century. One of Ireland's premier hotel and sporting estates. The experienced angler can fish both the River Nare and King's River for salmon and trout while instruction for novices is also on hand.

28. Newport House, Newport, Co Mayo. Tel:(010 353 98) 41222
This is a superb ivy clad, bow fronted Georgian Mansion encircled by mountains, lakes and streams. Renowned as an angling centre it holds private salmon and sea-trout fishing rights to 8 miles of

the Newport River. The hotel is famed for its hospitality and there is a rare feeling here of continuity and maturity.

29. Pale Hall, Llanderfel, Gwynedd. Tel: (06783) 285

An imposing 19th century mansion with delightful oak panelling and galleried staircase. A bath used by none other than Queen Victoria is an unexpected and unusual treasure. There are many added extras to make a stay both luxurious and memorable.

30. Pontoon Bridge Hotel, Co Mayo, Eire. Tel: (010 353 94) 56120

Set between Lake Conn and Lake Cullin the hotel was built towards the end of the 19th century yet has all the amenities that the modern guest expects The hotel houses both its own School of Fly Fishing and School of Landscape Painting.

31. Seafield Lodge, Grantown-on-Spey, Moray. Tel: (0479) 2152

Open to visitors since 1881, the "Lodge" has now been restored to its former glory with the facilities and personal service expected of a first class hotel. It is the home of Britain's longest running angling courses under the personal supervision of renowned Chief Instructor Arthur Oglesby.

32. Shrubbery Hotel, Ilminster, Somerset. Tel:(0460)52108

Modern facilities and a reputation for high standards of cuisine are two factors to be considered when selecting any hotel and the Shrubbery does not disappoint on either score. With an atmosphere at once both 'relaxing and vital' this former Victorian gentleman's residence is perfect for the modern traveller and fisherman.

33. Sunlaws House Hotel, Kelso, Roxburghshire. Tel: (0573) 5331

Owned by the Duke of Roxburgh and resting in 200 acres of beautiful gardens beside the Teviot, this hotel boasts a fine library bar with open log fire and leather bound tomes. The 22 bedrooms have all been furnished with care and include every modern comfort. Salmon and trout fishing are available at the hotel.

34. Tarr Steps Hotel, Hawkridge, Nr Dulverton, Somerset. Tel: (064) 385293

The Tarr Steps Hotel is a fisherman's paradise with three miles (both banks) of trout and salmon fishing on the River Barle. Beginners courses can be arranged with a Grade 1 Game Angling instructor. Away from the sport guests can relax in an atmosphere of quiet luxury, enjoy excellent food and the attractions of a well stocked bar.

35. The Black Swan, Kirkby Stephen, Cumbria. Tel: (05396) 23204

This is a charming country hotel built at the turn of the century. There are 16 bedrooms, all tastefully furnished and 3 are suitable for the disabled. The Kitchen makes extensive use of local produce and has an excellent reputation. Excellent fishing is available with rods on a private stretch of the Bela and Eden.

36. The Castle Hotel, Huntly, Aberdeenshire. Tel: (0466) 792696

This magnificent hotel stands in its own grounds above the ruins of Huntly Castle on the banks of the River Deveron. A family run hotel, there is comfortable accommodation and good food. The Castle Beat is the hotel's own double-banked salmon and sea trout fishing which offers a variety of attractive pools which are a delight to fish.

37. The Dowans Hotel, Aberlour, Banffshire. Tel: (0340) 871488

Overlooking the Spey in beautiful countryside the Dowans Hotel has recently been refurbished. Meal times are flexible to suit the needs of sportsmen and the hotel is happy to arrange fishing, shooting or stalking by prior arrangement.

38. The Glendaruel Hotel, Clachan of Glendaruel, Argyll. Tel: (039682) 274

The Glendaruel Hotel is a small, friendly, family run hotel offering the best in Scottish hospitality and delicious home cooking. The hotel offers private salmon and trout fishing on the Ruel which flows behind the hotel and arrangements can also be made to fish other waters. For a break from fishing, the area provides a wealth of open air activities.

39. The Lands of Loyal Hotel, Alyth, Perthshire. Tel(08283)3151.

An impressive Victorian mansion overlooking the Vale of Strathmore and set in ten acres of tiered and rambling gardens. Fundamentally a sportsman's hotel, the Lands of Loyal offers early breakfasts and flexible dining arrangements. Quality packed lunches are offered courteously.

40. The Roman Camp, Callander, Perthshire. Tel: (0877) 30003

Standing on the banks of the River Tieth amongst twenty acres of secluded gardens, the house was originally built as a hunting lodge for the Dukes of Perth in 1625. Guests may fish for wild brown trout or salmon on the hotel's private beat of the river and the hotel can also arrange fishing on the many lochs surrounding Callander.

41. Tillmouth Park Hotel, Cornhill-on-Tweed, Northumberland. Tel: (0890) 882255

A traditional country house hotel set in lovely grounds with good fresh food, friendly service and five miles of fishing on the River Tweed for you to have the experience of a life time. The hotel offers a unique Tweed package for salmon and sea trout and a service to cover all angling requirements.

42. Two Bridges Hotel, Dartmoor, Devon. Tel: (082289) 581

From this beautiful hotel in the middle of Dartmoor there is excellent fishing available on the West Dart which flows through the hotel's 60 acres of grounds. Modern first clas facilities and service combined with superb cuisine make for a memorable sporting break in splendid countryside.

43. Ulbster Arms Hotel, Halkirk, Caithness. Tel: (084783) 206

The Ulbster Arms is the centre for fishing the River Thurso, one of Scotland's finest salmon rivers. But as well as fishing, many other outdoor pursuits can be undertaken using the hotel as a base. Birdwatching, photography, rambling, painting and geology, to name but a few can all provide the visitor with the relaxation or stimulus that is desired.

44. Warmanbie Hotel, Annan, Dumfries & Galloway Tel: (0461) 204015

A Georgian country house hotel and restaurant set in 40 acres of secluded woodland grounds overlooking the River Annan. Fishing for brown trout, sea trout and salmon is free on the hotel's private stretch of the river. The hotel also has access to fishing on the River Eden and the River Nith.

45. Whipper-In Hotel, Oakham, Leicestershire. Tel: (0572) 756971

This is an intriguing antique furnished, 17th century inn. The atmosphere is appealing, the restaurant proudly serves good British food and the service is excellent. If fishing is your pleasure, Rutland Water offers the largest freshwater fishing in Europe and is located one and a half miles from the hotel.

PRINTED AND BOUND BY
GROUPE HÉRISSEY (FRANCE)